GRIND HOUSE

DOORS OPEN AT MIDNIGHT

DOUBLE FEATURE

COMING SOON

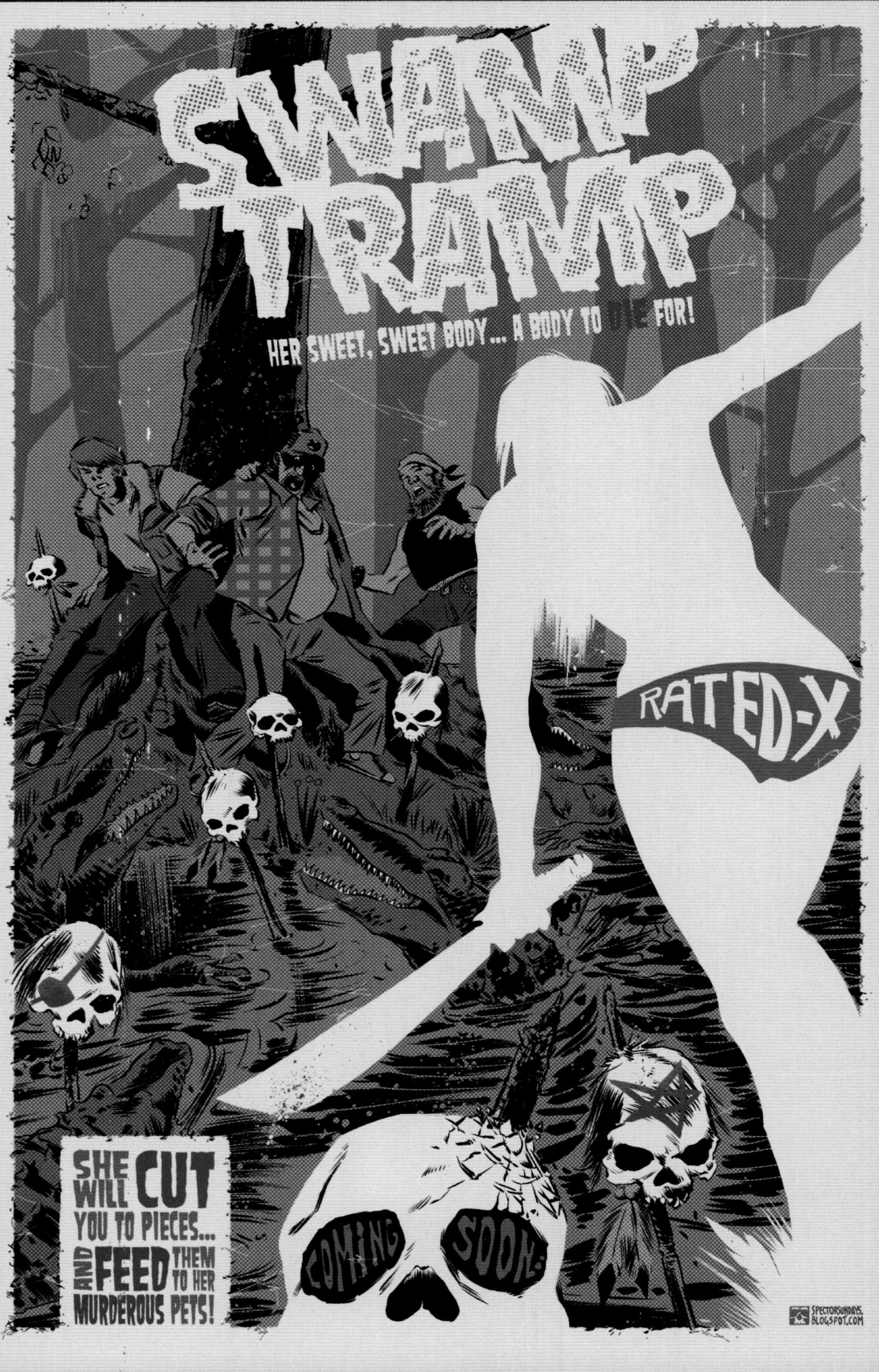
SWAMP TRAMP
HER SWEET, SWEET BODY... A BODY TO DIE FOR!
RATED-X
SHE WILL CUT YOU TO PIECES... AND FEED THEM TO HER MURDEROUS PETS!
COMING SOON.
SPECTORSUNDAYS. BLOGSPOT.COM

LUCA PIZZARI

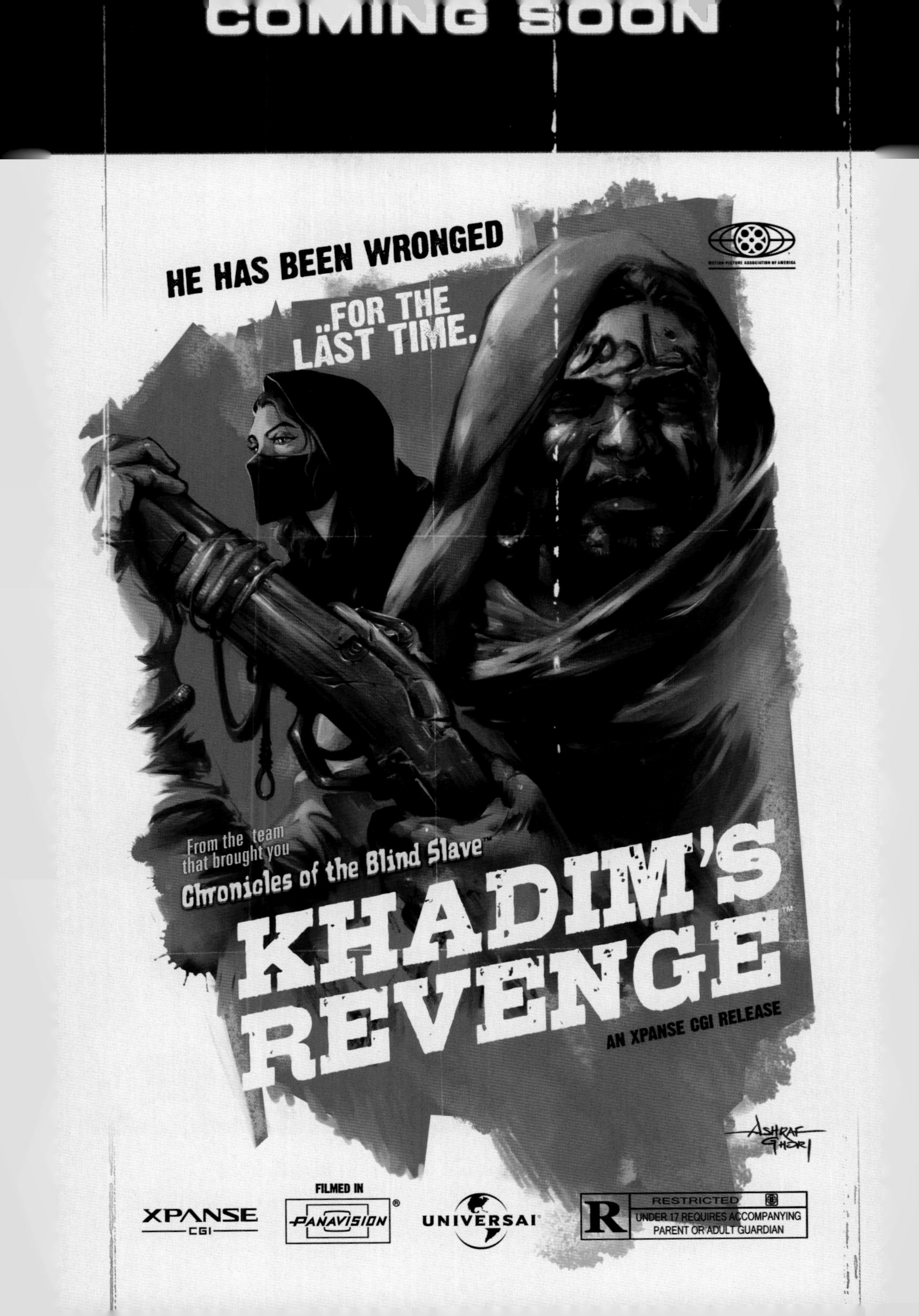
COMING SOON
HE HAS BEEN WRONGED
..FOR THE LAST TIME.
From the team that brought you
Chronicles of the Blind Slave™
KHADIM'S REVENGE™
AN XPANSE CGI RELEASE
ASHRAF GHORI
FILMED IN
XPANSE CGI
PANAVISION®
UNIVERSAI
R
RESTRICTED
UNDER 17 REQUIRES ACCOMPANYING PARENT OR ADULT GUARDIAN

FEATURE PRESENTATION

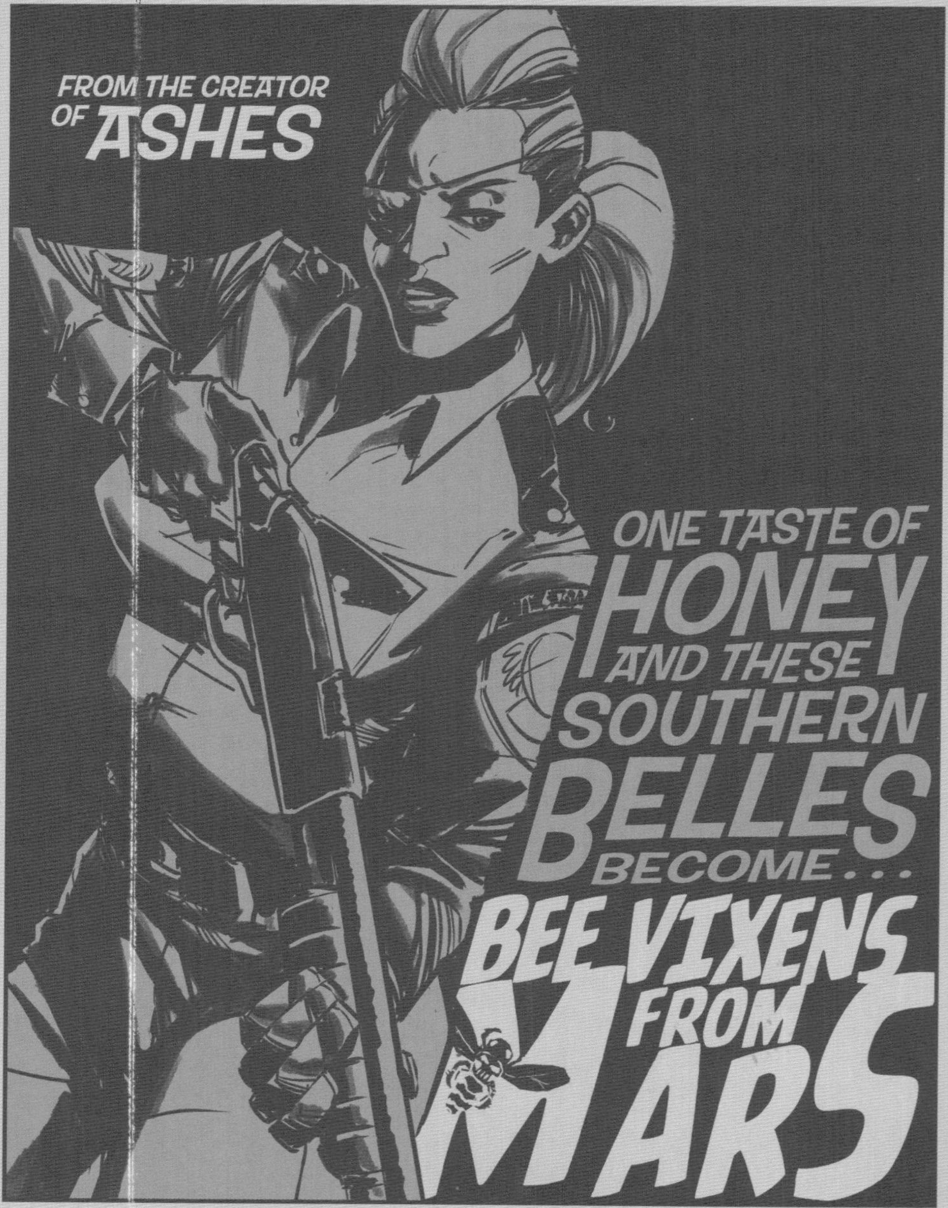
FROM THE CREATOR OF ASHES
ONE TASTE OF HONEY AND THESE SOUTHERN BELLES BECOME...
BEE VIXENS FROM MARS

DARK HORSE COMICS PRESENTS AN ALEX DE CAMPI PRODUCTION "BEE VIXENS FROM MARS"

BEE VIXENS LUSTY LADIES CONFOUNDED SHERIFF CONVENIENCE STORE OWNERS AND THE ONE-EYED DEPUTY

FILM EDITOR BRENDAN WRIGHT A.C.E. ASSISTANT EDITOR IAN TUCKER PRODUCTION DESIGNER JIMMY PRESLER CGI ARTIST RYAN JORGENSEN DIRECTOR OF PHOTOGRAPHY NOLAN WOODARD A.S.C.

PRODUCED BY MIKE RICHARDSON SCREENPLAY BY ALEX DE CAMPI DIRECTED BY CHRIS PETERSON

10•02•13

BEE VIXENS FROM MARS ™

SCRIPT AND LETTERS
ALEX DE CAMPI

ART AND TITLE PAGE
CHRIS PETERSON

COLORS
NOLAN WOODARD

COVER
DAN PANOSIAN

DARK HORSE BOOKS

EDITOR
BRENDAN WRIGHT

ASSISTANT EDITOR
IAN TUCKER

DESIGN
JIMMY PRESLER

DIGITAL PRODUCTION
RYAN JORGENSEN

PUBLISHER
MIKE RICHARDSON

PUBLISHED BY DARK HORSE BOOKS, A DIVISION OF DARK HORSE COMICS, INC.
10956 SE MAIN STREET MILWAUKIE, OR 97222 DARKHORSE.COM

TO FIND A COMICS SHOP IN YOUR AREA, CALL THE COMIC SHOP LOCATOR SERVICE TOLL-FREE AT (888) 266-4226.

INTERNATIONAL LICENSING: (503) 905-2377

FIRST EDITION: JULY 2014

LIBRARY OF CONGRESS CATALOGING-IN-PUBLICATION DATA

DE CAMPI, ALEX.
GRINDHOUSE, DOORS OPEN AT MIDNIGHT DOUBLE FEATURE : BEE VIXENS FROM MARS/PRISON SHIP ANTARES / SCRIPT AND LETTERS, ALEX DE CAMPI ; BEE VIXENS FROM MARS ART, CHRIS PETERSON ; PRISON SHIP ANTARES ART, SIMON FRASER ; COVERS, DAN PANOSIAN, FRANCESCO FRANCAVILLA. -- FIRST EDITION.
PAGES CM. -- (GRINDHOUSE, DOORS OPEN AT MIDNIGHT ; VOLUME 1)
SUMMARY: "INSPIRED BY THE GRIMY MIDNIGHT MOVIES OF THE 1970S, ALEX DE CAMPI AND HER COLLABORATORS CREATE OVER-THE-TOP TALES OF ALIEN BEES INVADING A SOUTHERN TOWN AND SPACE-FARING CONVICTS PLOTTING A PRISON BREAK"-- PROVIDED BY PUBLISHER.
ISBN 978-1-61655-377-7 (PAPERBACK)
1. GRAPHIC NOVELS. I. PETERSON, CHRIS, 1976- ILLUSTRATOR. II. FRASER, SIMON, 1969- ILLUSTRATOR. III. PANOSIAN, DAN, ILLUSTRATOR. IV. FRANCAVILLA, FRANCESCO, ILLUSTRATOR. V. TITLE. VI. TITLE: BEE VIXENS FROM MARS. VII. TITLE: PRISON SHIP ANTARES.
PN6737.D4G75 2014
741.5'973--DC23
2014013915

1 3 5 7 9 10 8 6 4 2
PRINTED IN CHINA

THIS VOLUME COLLECTS ISSUES #1—#4 OF THE DARK HORSE COMIC-BOOK SERIES *GRINDHOUSE: DOORS OPEN AT MIDNIGHT.*

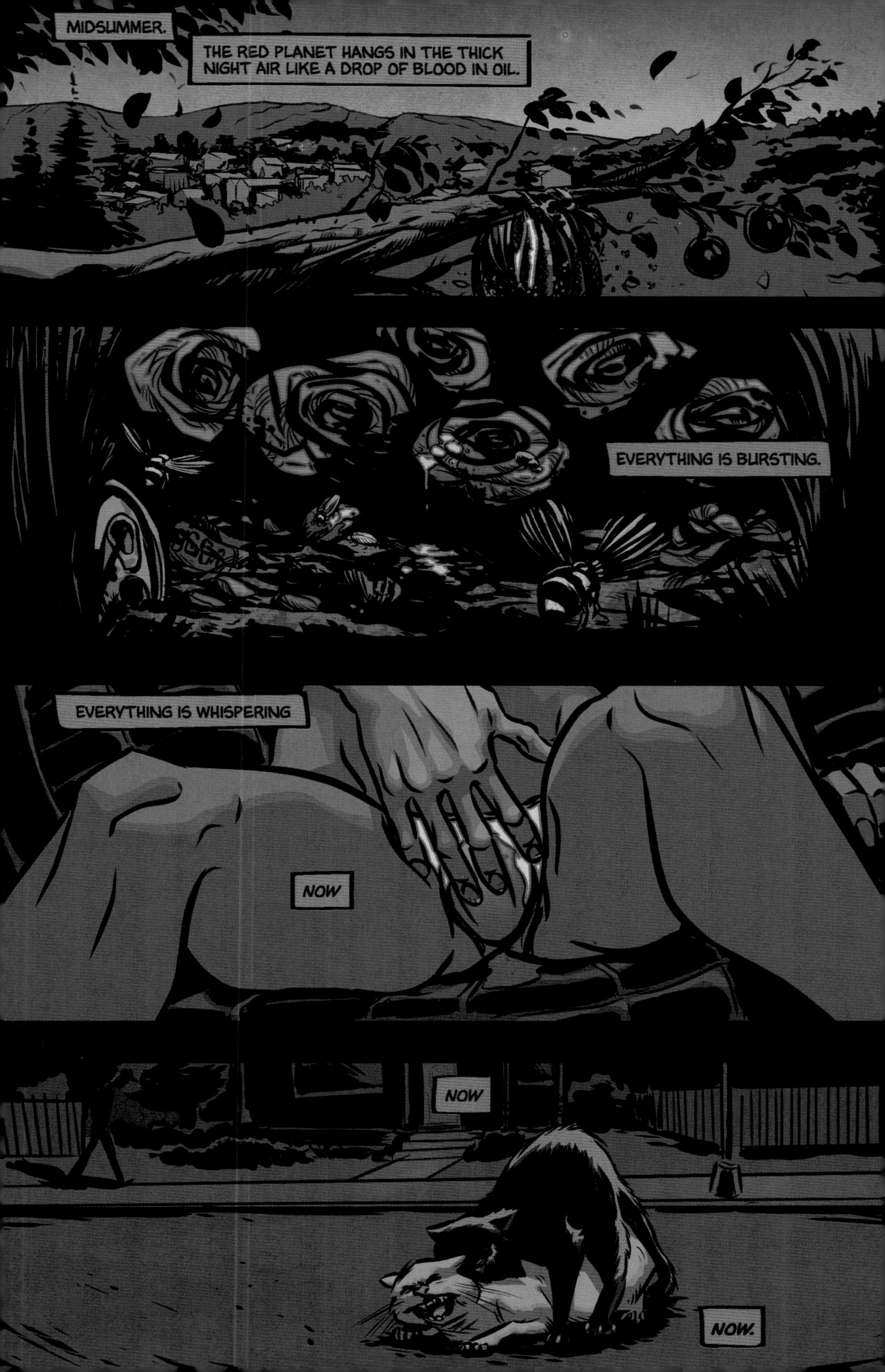
MIDSUMMER.
THE RED PLANET HANGS IN THE THICK NIGHT AIR LIKE A DROP OF BLOOD IN OIL.
EVERYTHING IS BURSTING.
EVERYTHING IS WHISPERING
NOW
NOW
NOW.

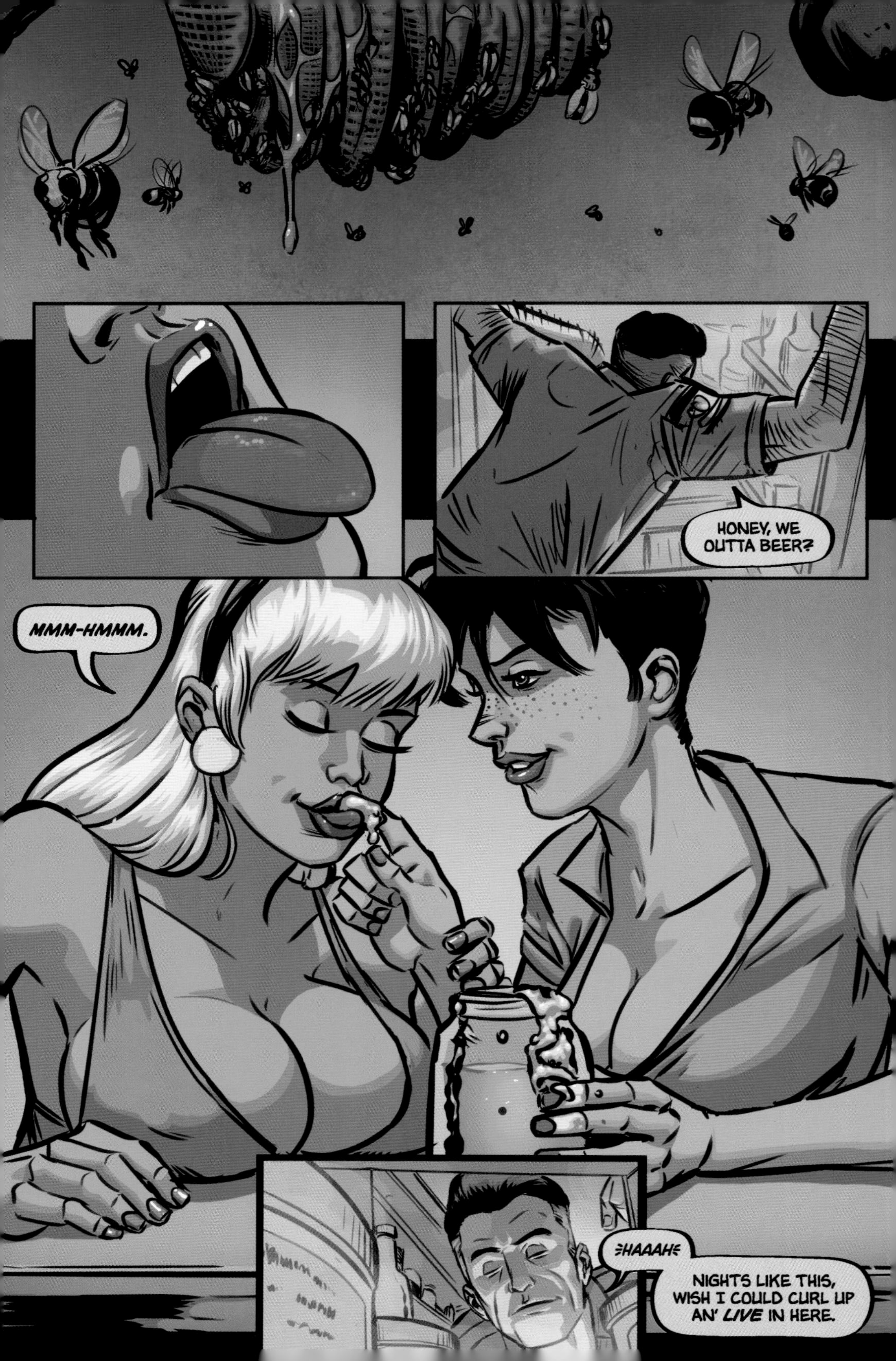
HONEY, WE OUTTA BEER?
MMM-HMMM.
HAAAH
NIGHTS LIKE THIS, WISH I COULD CURL UP AN' LIVE IN HERE.

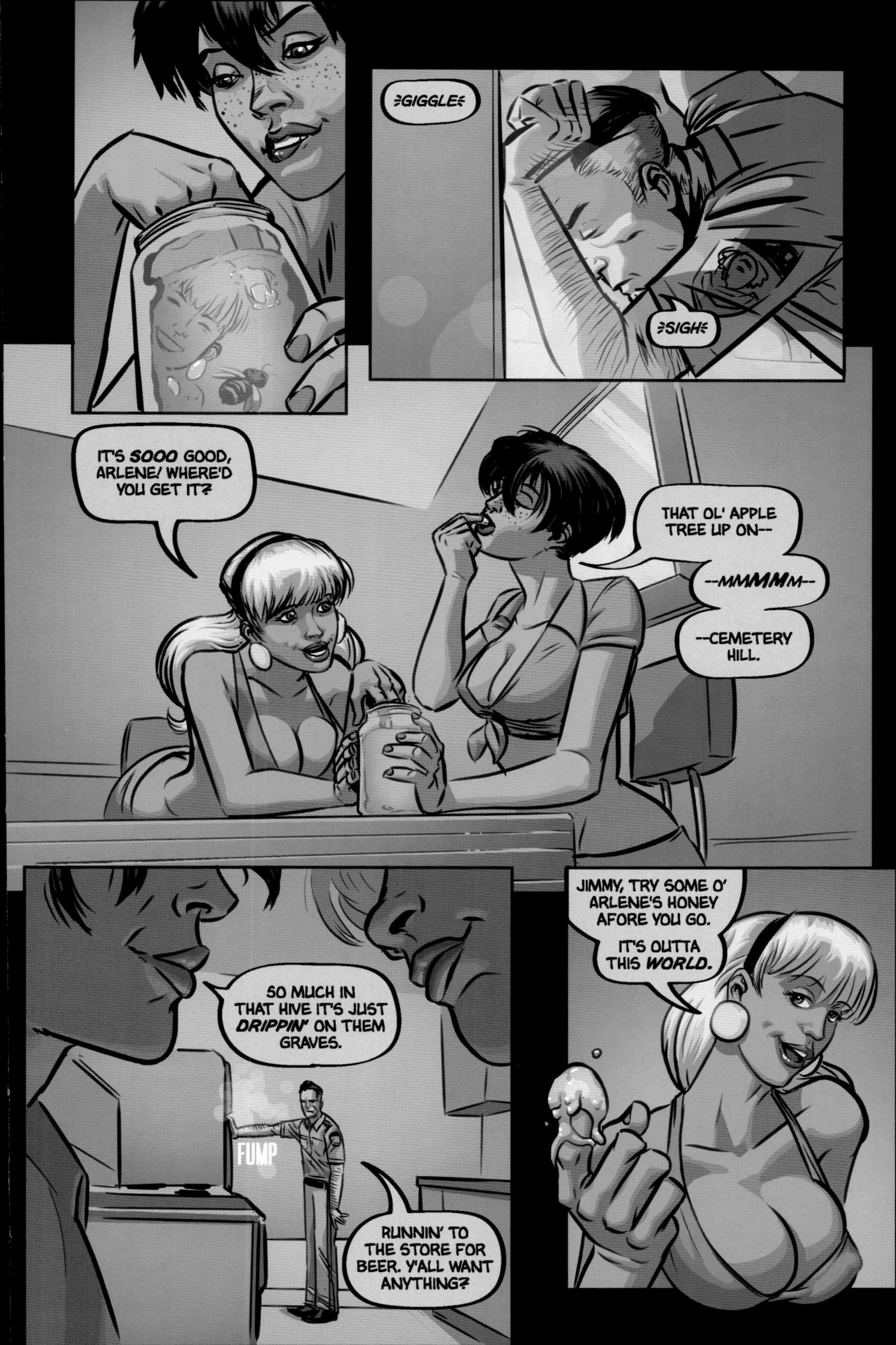

GIGGLE
SIGH
IT'S SOOO GOOD, ARLENE! WHERE'D YOU GET IT?
THAT OL' APPLE TREE UP ON--
--MMMMM--
--CEMETERY HILL.
SO MUCH IN THAT HIVE IT'S JUST DRIPPIN' ON THEM GRAVES.
FUMP
RUNNIN' TO THE STORE FOR BEER. Y'ALL WANT ANYTHING?
JIMMY, TRY SOME O' ARLENE'S HONEY AFORE YOU GO.
IT'S OUTTA THIS WORLD.

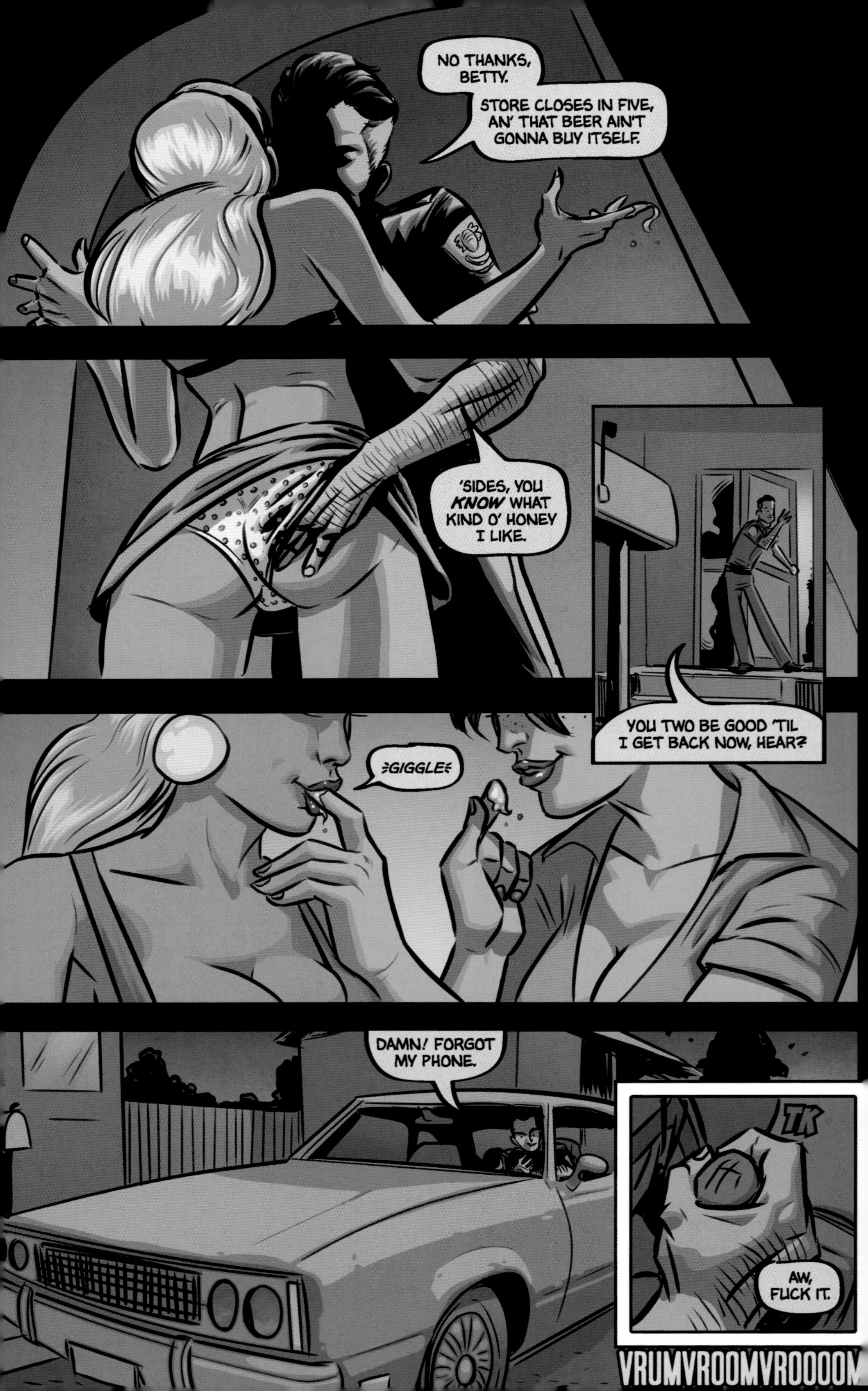
NO THANKS, BETTY.
STORE CLOSES IN FIVE, AN' THAT BEER AIN'T GONNA BUY ITSELF.
'SIDES, YOU *KNOW* WHAT KIND O' HONEY I LIKE.
YOU TWO BE GOOD 'TIL I GET BACK NOW, HEAR?
GIGGLE
DAMN! FORGOT MY PHONE.
TK
AW, FUCK IT.
VRUMVROOMVROOOOM

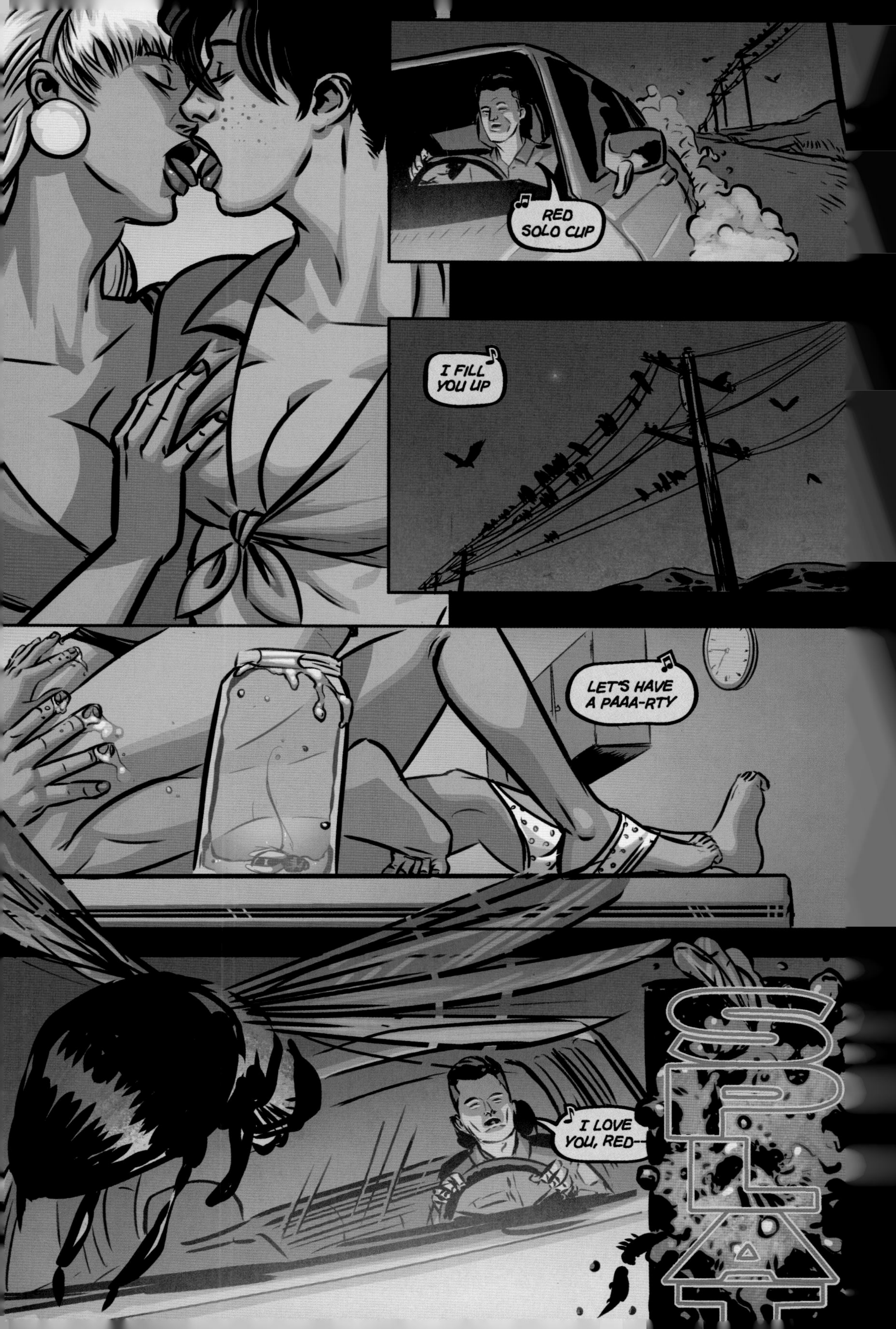
RED SOLO CUP
I FILL YOU UP
LET'S HAVE A PAAA-RTY
I LOVE YOU, RED--

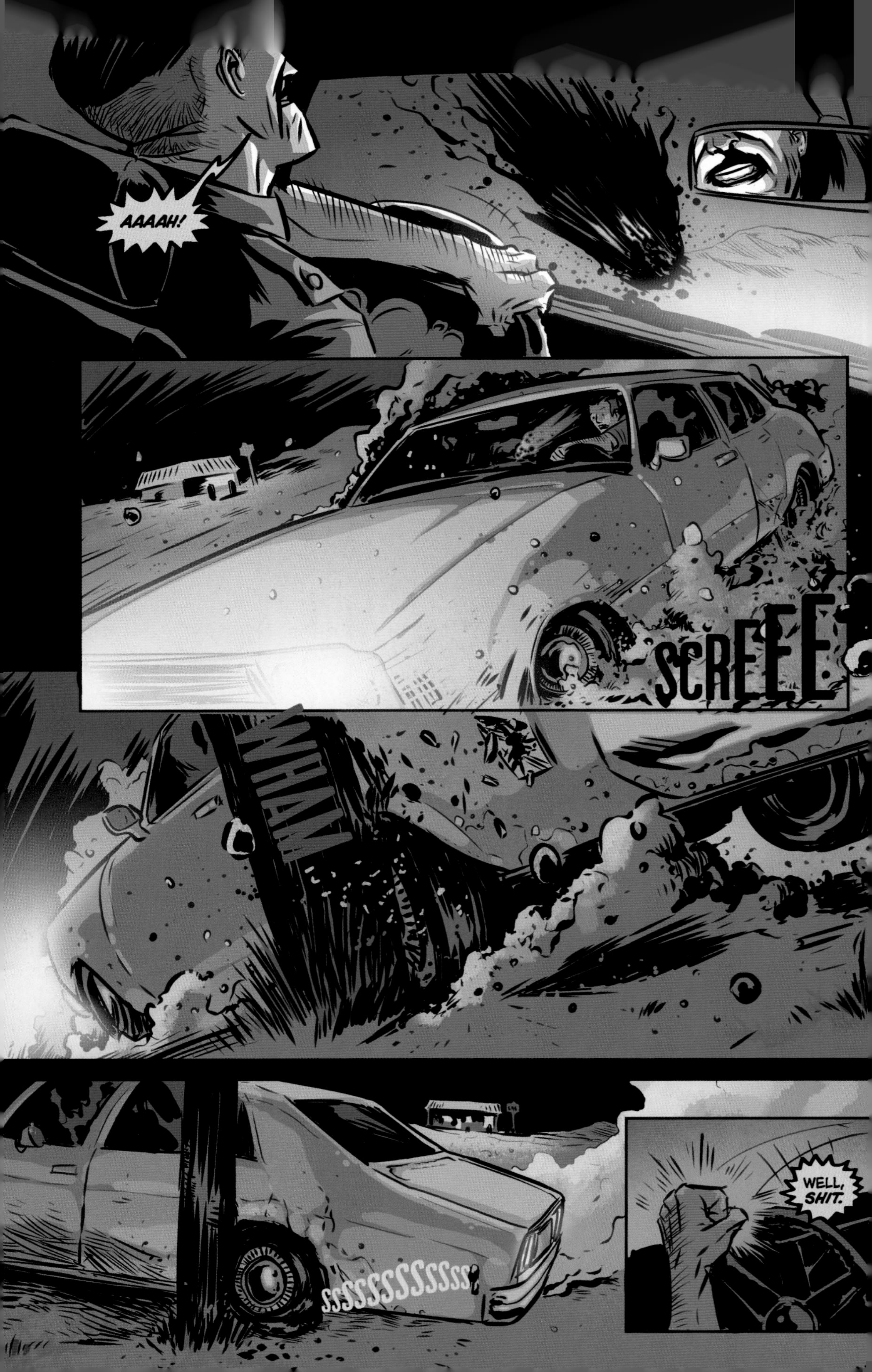
AAAAH!
SCREEE
WHAM
SSSSSSSSSSSS
WELL, SHIT.

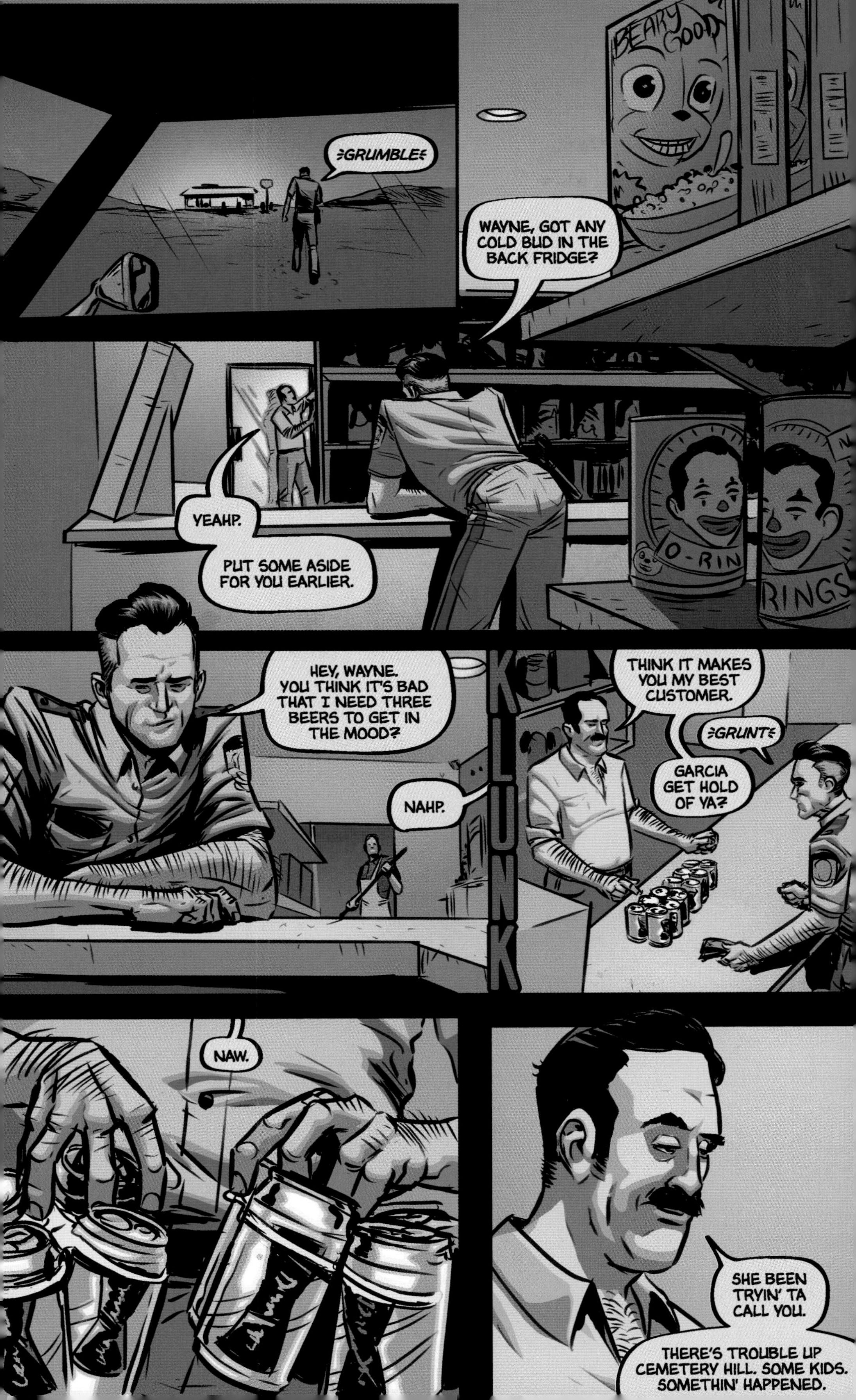
GRUMBLE
BEARY GOOD
WAYNE, GOT ANY COLD BUD IN THE BACK FRIDGE?
YEAHP.
PUT SOME ASIDE FOR YOU EARLIER.
O-RIN
RINGS
HEY, WAYNE. YOU THINK IT'S BAD THAT I NEED THREE BEERS TO GET IN THE MOOD?
NAHP.
KLUNK
THINK IT MAKES YOU MY BEST CUSTOMER.
GRUNT
GARCIA GET HOLD OF YA?
NAW.
SHE BEEN TRYIN' TA CALL YOU.
THERE'S TROUBLE UP CEMETERY HILL. SOME KIDS. SOMETHIN' HAPPENED.

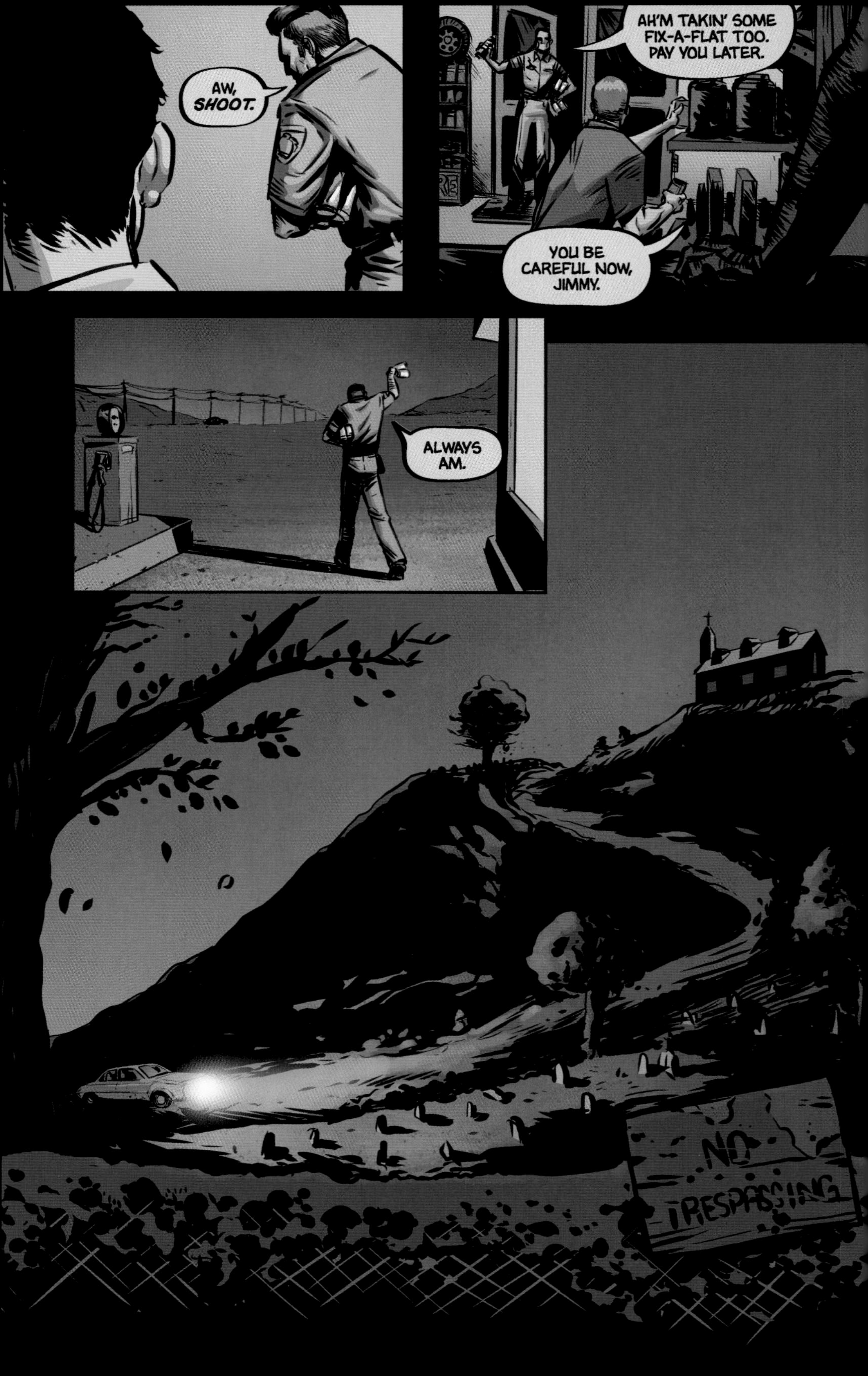
AW, SHOOT.
AH'M TAKIN' SOME FIX-A-FLAT TOO. PAY YOU LATER.
YOU BE CAREFUL NOW, JIMMY.
ALWAYS AM.
NO TRESPASSING

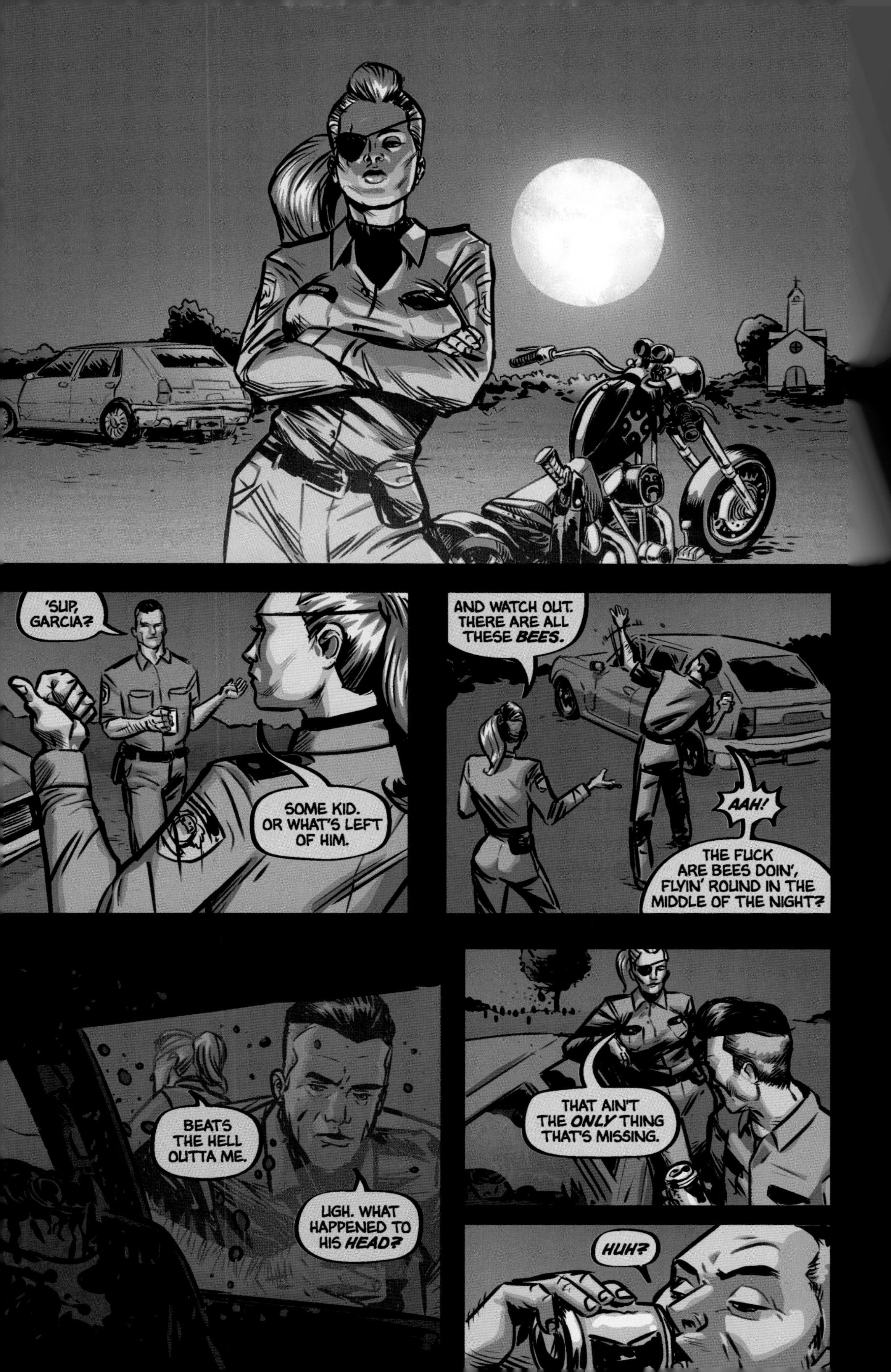

'SUP, GARCIA?
SOME KID. OR WHAT'S LEFT OF HIM.
AND WATCH OUT. THERE ARE ALL THESE *BEES*.
AAH!
THE FUCK ARE BEES DOIN', FLYIN' ROUND IN THE MIDDLE OF THE NIGHT?
BEATS THE HELL OUTTA ME.
UGH. WHAT HAPPENED TO HIS *HEAD*?
THAT AIN'T THE *ONLY* THING THAT'S MISSING.
HUH?

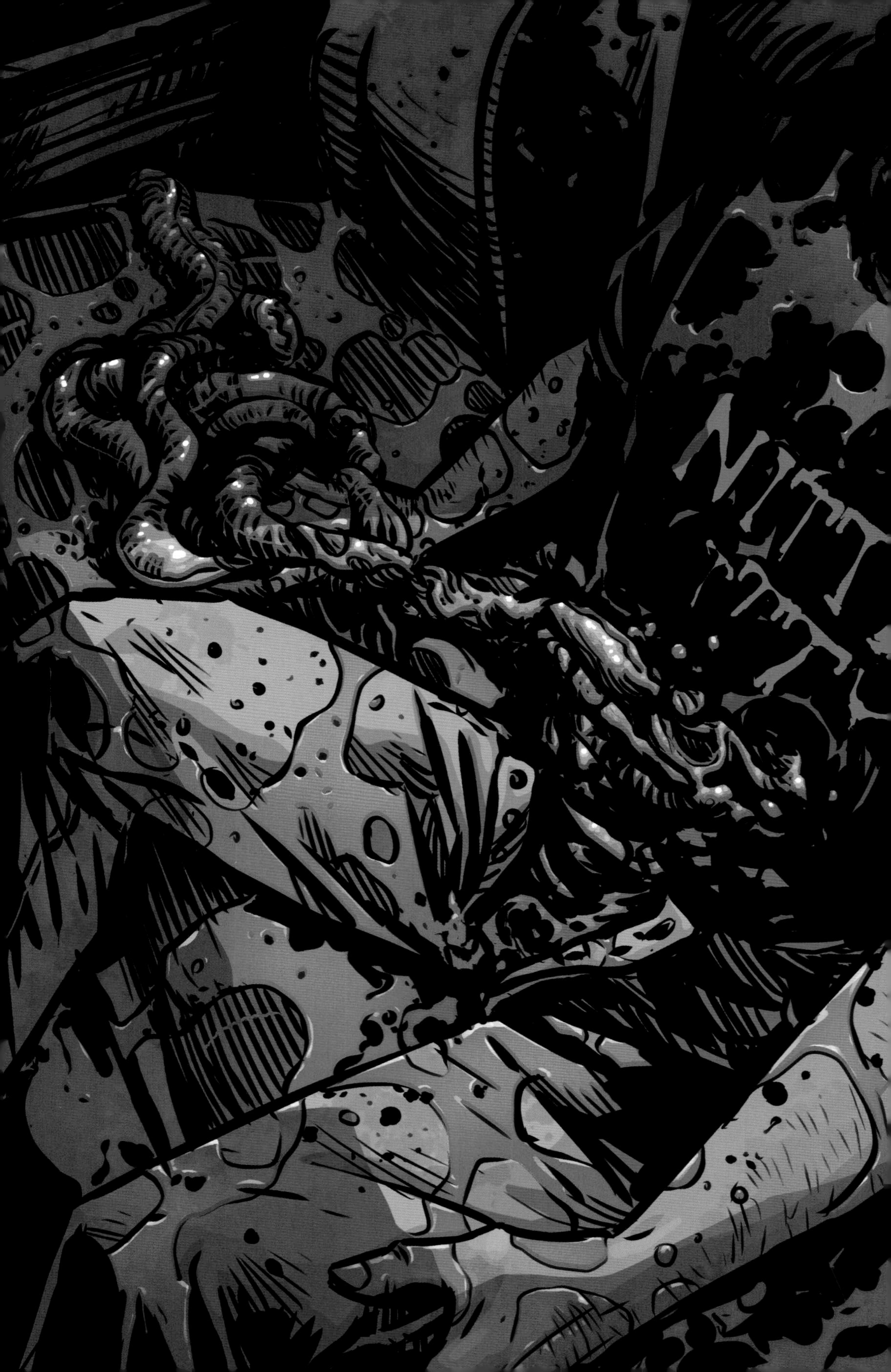

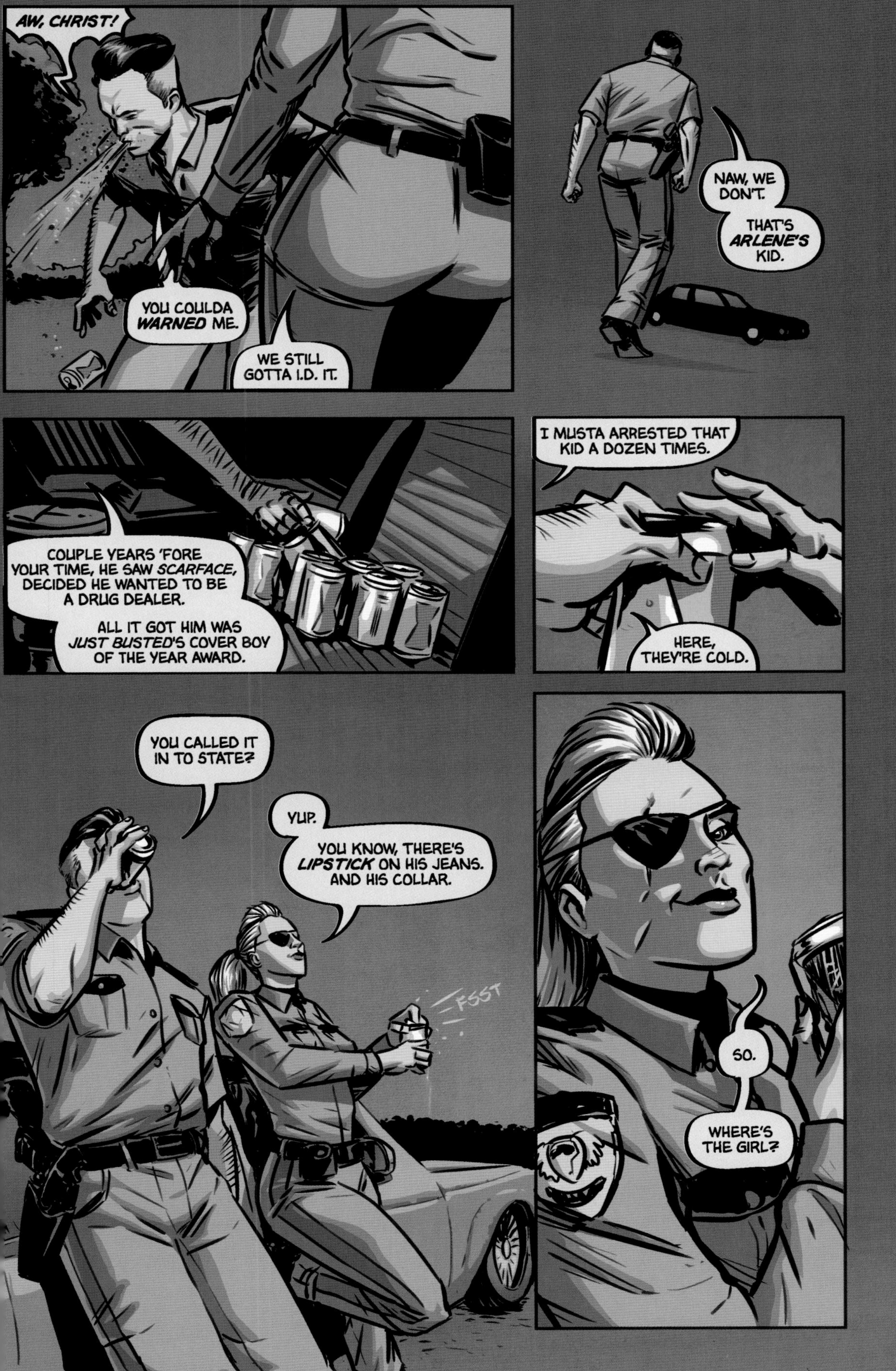
AW, CHRIST!
YOU COULDA WARNED ME.
WE STILL GOTTA I.D. IT.
NAW, WE DON'T.
THAT'S ARLENE'S KID.
COUPLE YEARS 'FORE YOUR TIME, HE SAW SCARFACE, DECIDED HE WANTED TO BE A DRUG DEALER.
ALL IT GOT HIM WAS JUST BUSTED'S COVER BOY OF THE YEAR AWARD.
I MUSTA ARRESTED THAT KID A DOZEN TIMES.
HERE, THEY'RE COLD.
YOU CALLED IT IN TO STATE?
YUP.
YOU KNOW, THERE'S LIPSTICK ON HIS JEANS. AND HIS COLLAR.
FSST
SO.
WHERE'S THE GIRL?

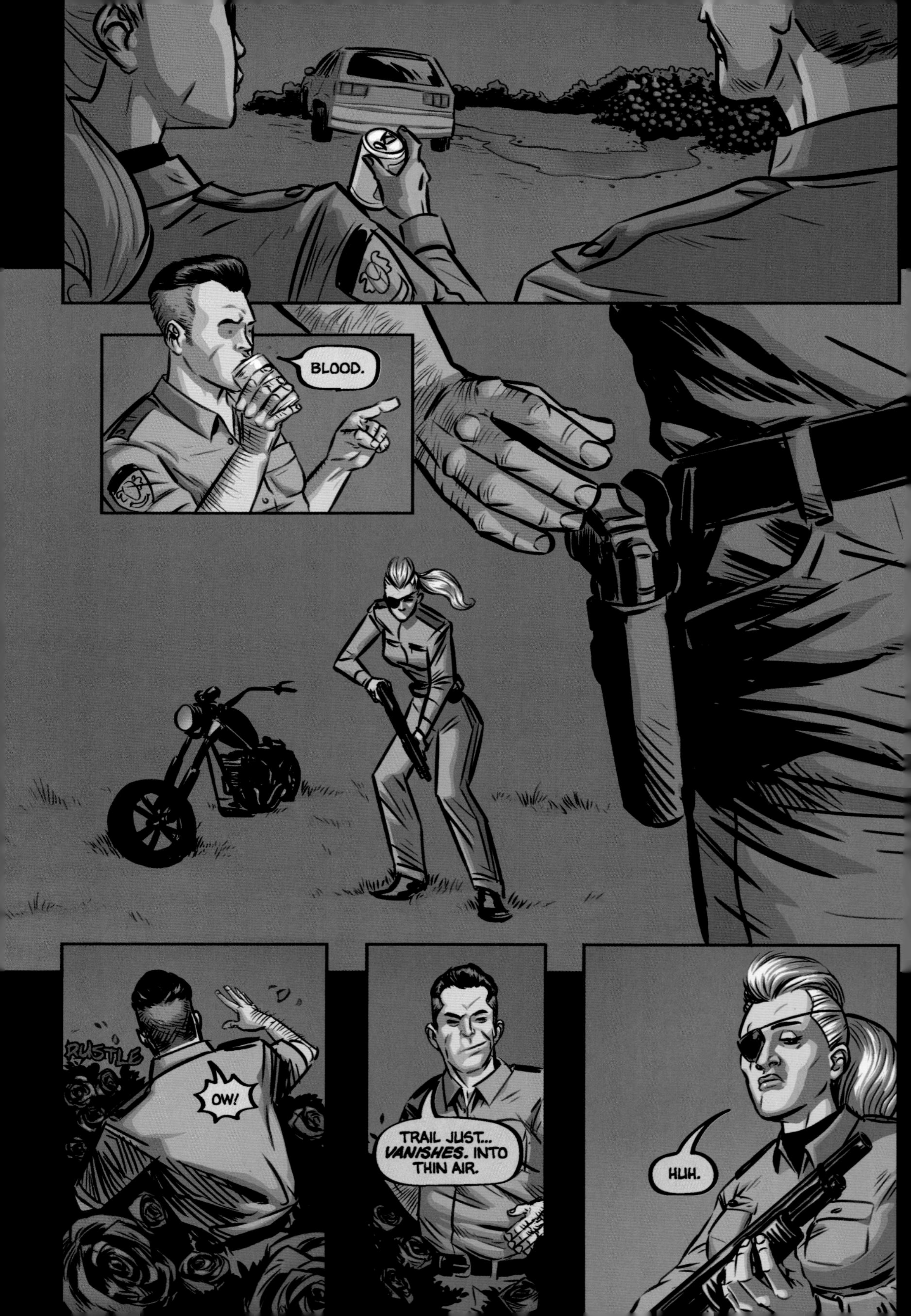
BLOOD.
RUSTLE
OW!
TRAIL JUST... VANISHES. INTO THIN AIR.
HUH.

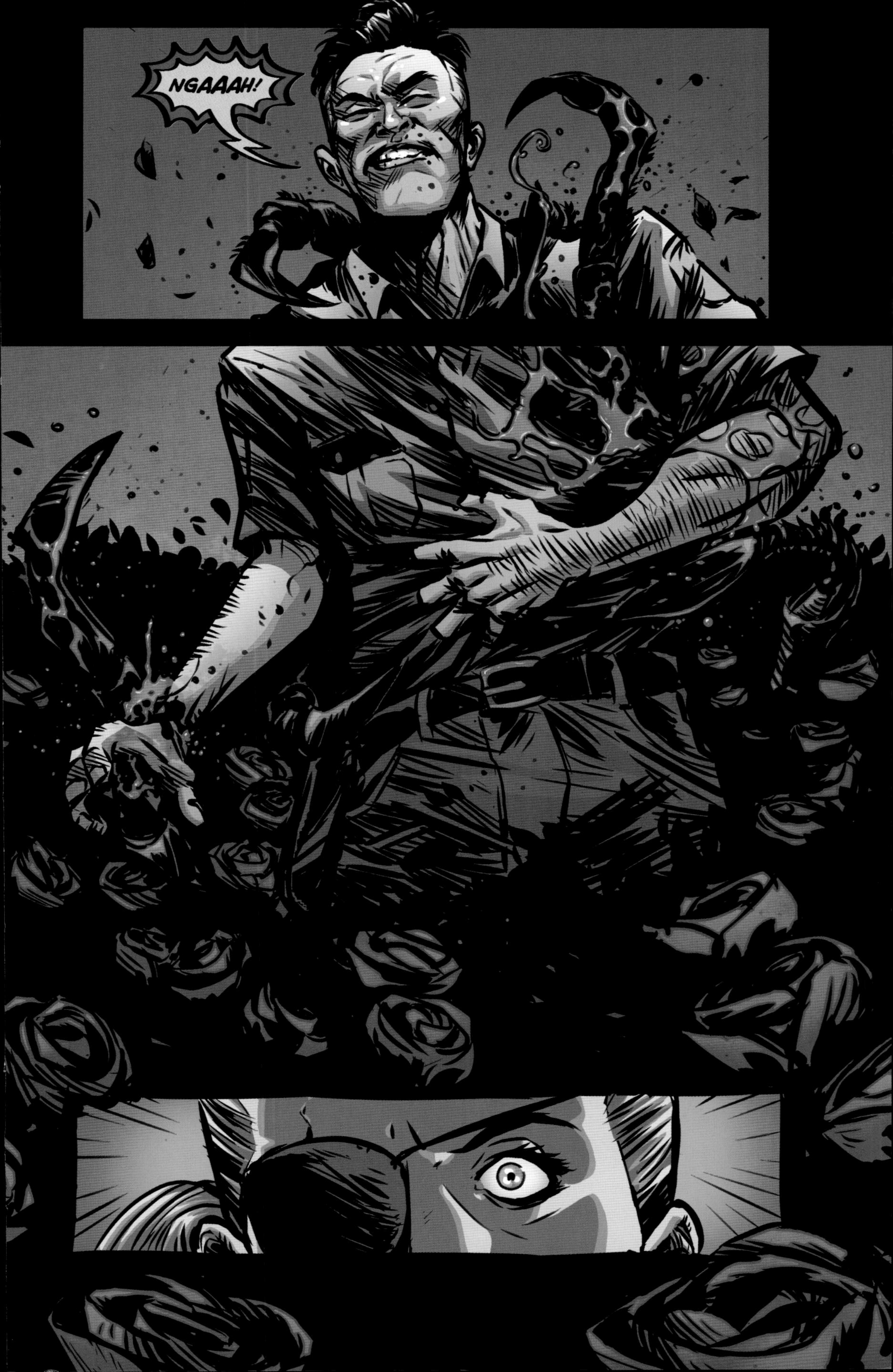
NGAAAH!

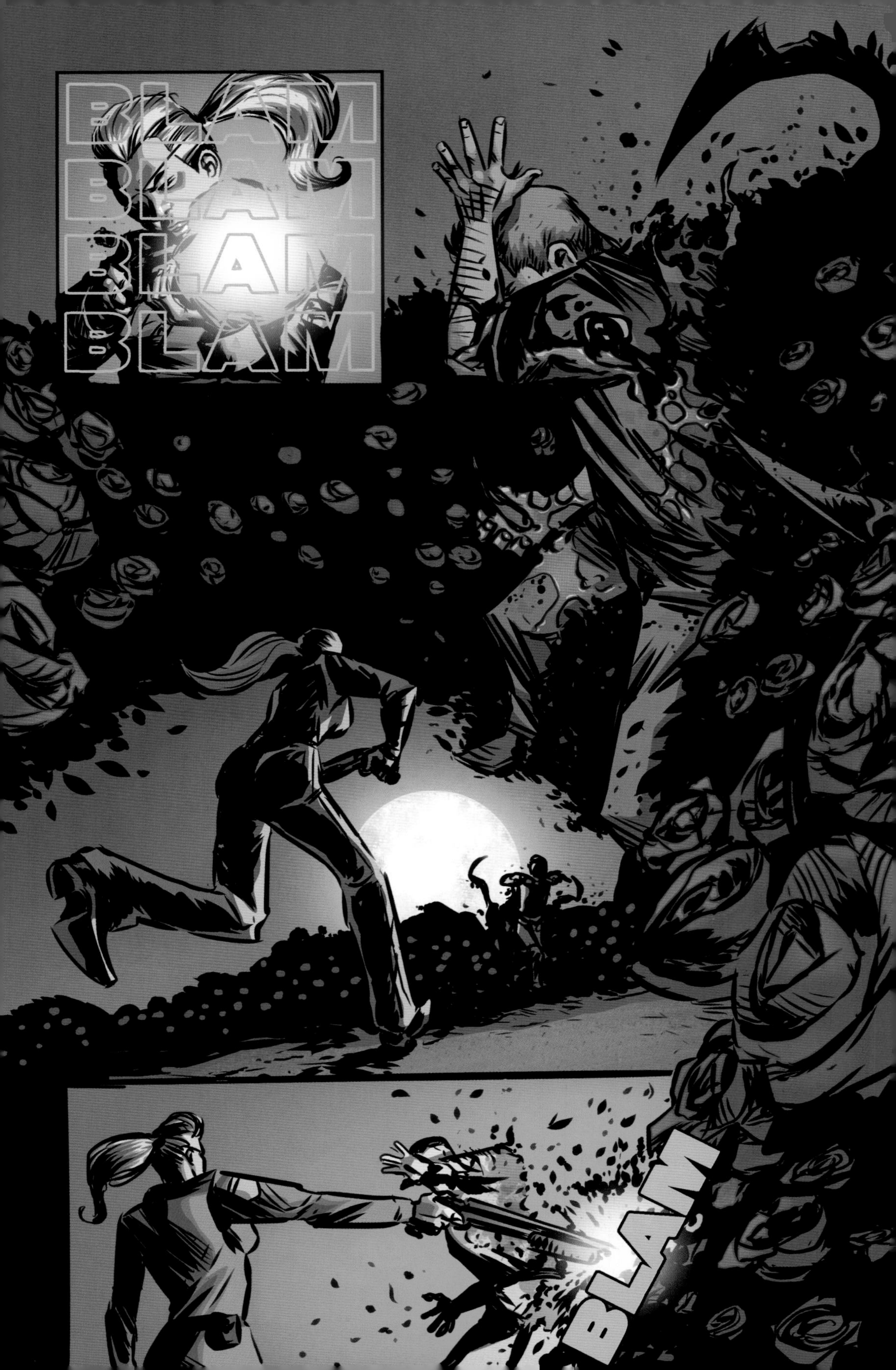
BLAM
BLAM
BLAM
BLAM
BLAM

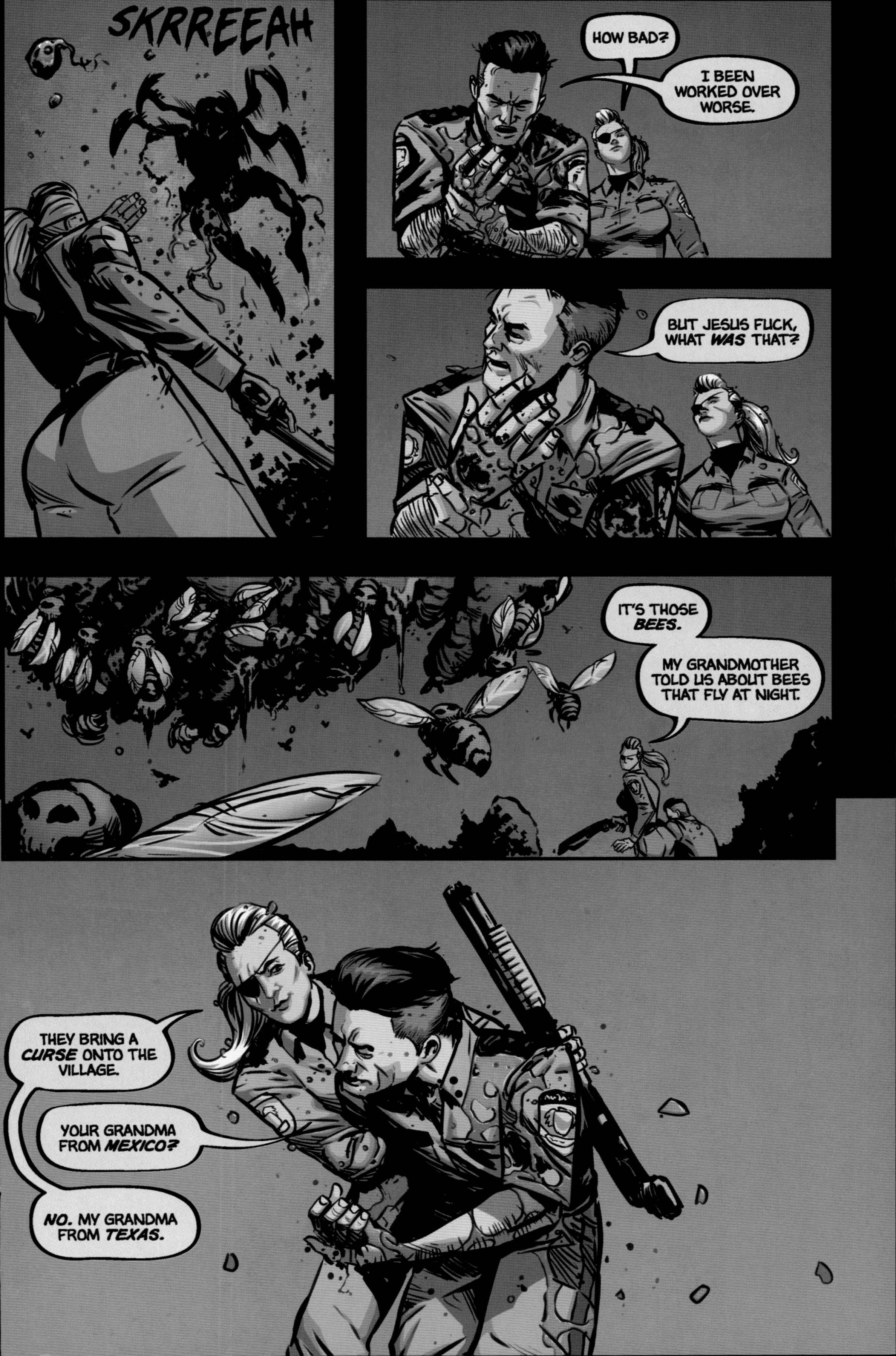
SKRREEAH
HOW BAD?
I BEEN WORKED OVER WORSE.
BUT JESUS FUCK, WHAT *WAS* THAT?
IT'S THOSE *BEES.*
MY GRANDMOTHER TOLD US ABOUT BEES THAT FLY AT NIGHT.
THEY BRING A *CURSE* ONTO THE VILLAGE.
YOUR GRANDMA FROM *MEXICO?*
NO. MY GRANDMA FROM *TEXAS.*

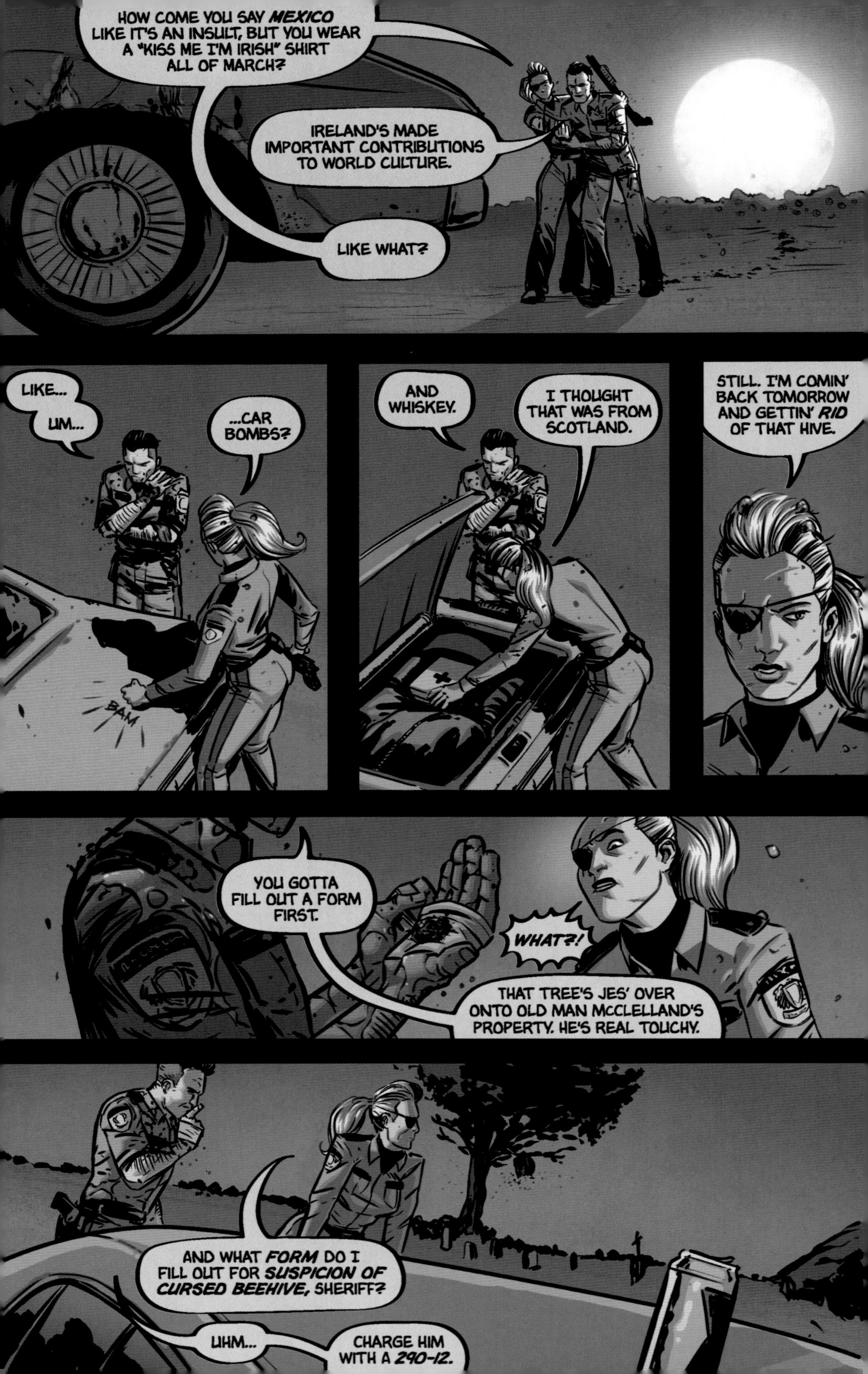
HOW COME YOU SAY *MEXICO* LIKE IT'S AN INSULT, BUT YOU WEAR A "KISS ME I'M IRISH" SHIRT ALL OF MARCH?
IRELAND'S MADE IMPORTANT CONTRIBUTIONS TO WORLD CULTURE.
LIKE WHAT?
LIKE...
UM...
...CAR BOMBS?
BAM
AND WHISKEY.
I THOUGHT THAT WAS FROM SCOTLAND.
STILL. I'M COMIN' BACK TOMORROW AND GETTIN' *RID* OF THAT HIVE.
YOU GOTTA FILL OUT A FORM FIRST.
WHAT?!
THAT TREE'S JES' OVER ONTO OLD MAN McCLELLAND'S PROPERTY. HE'S REAL TOUCHY.
AND WHAT *FORM* DO I FILL OUT FOR *SUSPICION OF CURSED BEEHIVE,* SHERIFF?
UHM...
CHARGE HIM WITH A *290-12.*

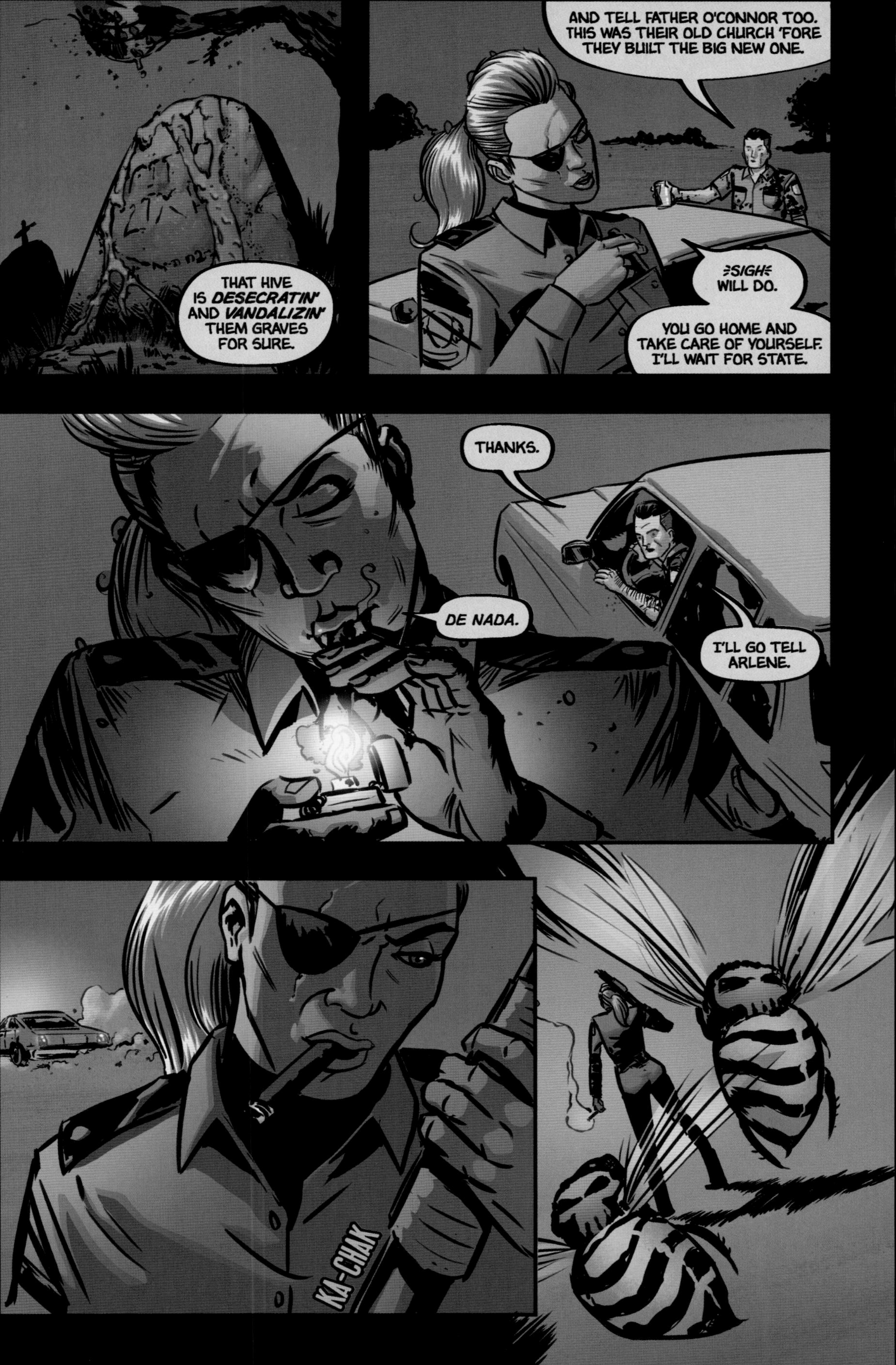
THAT HIVE IS DESECRATIN' AND VANDALIZIN' THEM GRAVES FOR SURE.
AND TELL FATHER O'CONNOR TOO. THIS WAS THEIR OLD CHURCH 'FORE THEY BUILT THE BIG NEW ONE.
SIGH WILL DO.
YOU GO HOME AND TAKE CARE OF YOURSELF. I'LL WAIT FOR STATE.
THANKS.
DE NADA.
I'LL GO TELL ARLENE.
KA-CHAK

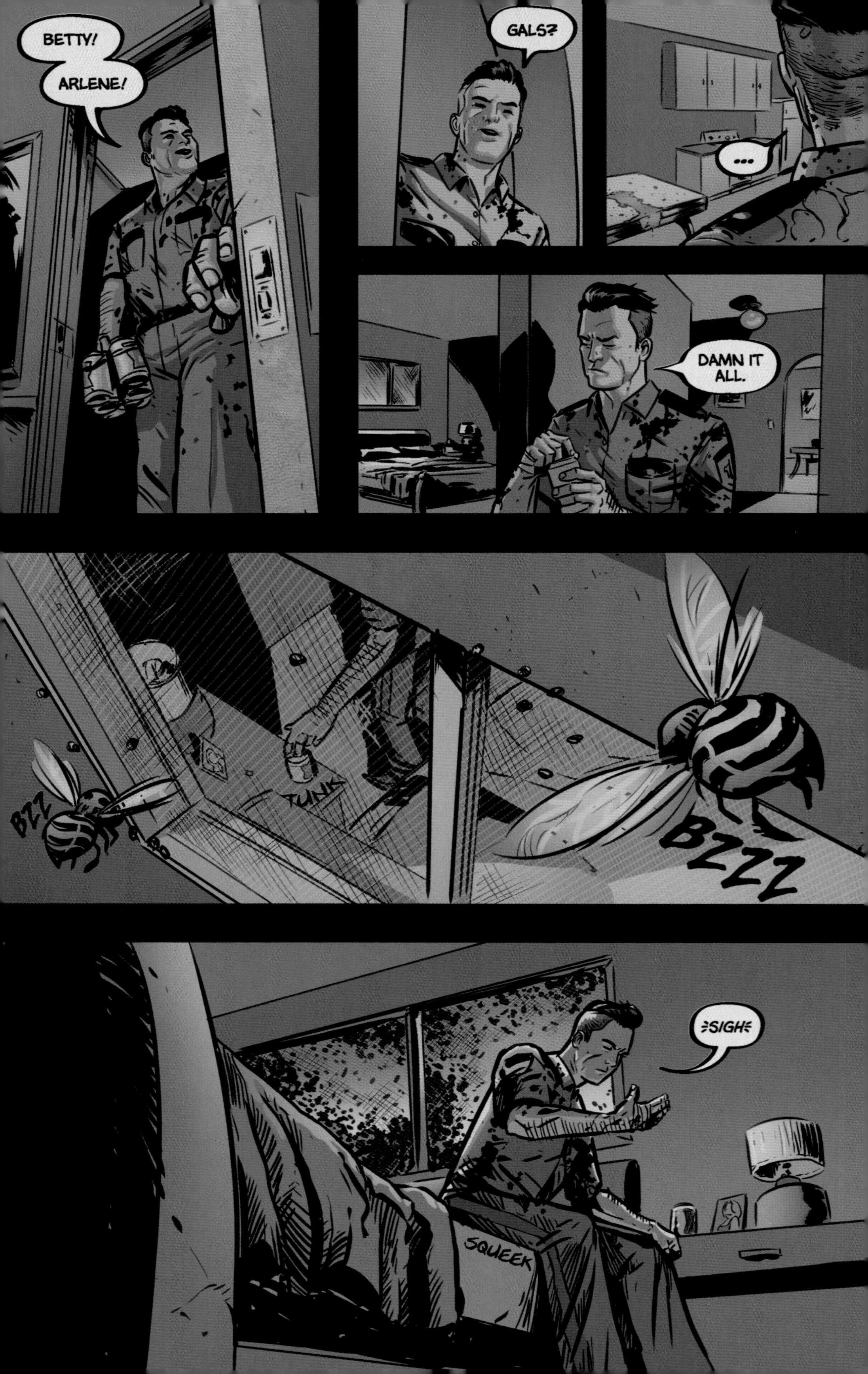
BETTY!
ARLENE!
GALS?
...
DAMN IT ALL.
TUNK
BZZ
BZZZ
SIGH
SQUEEK

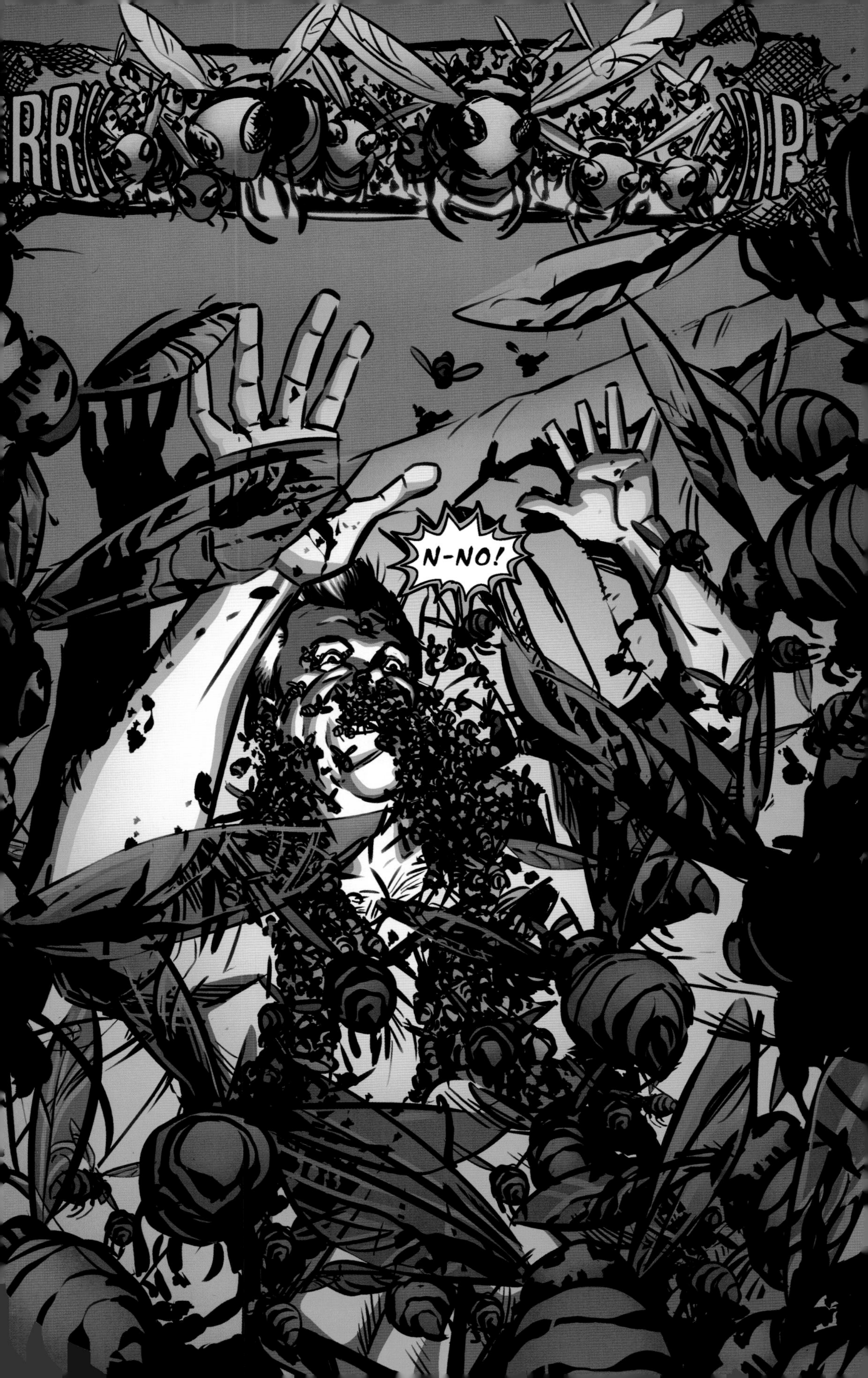
N-NO!

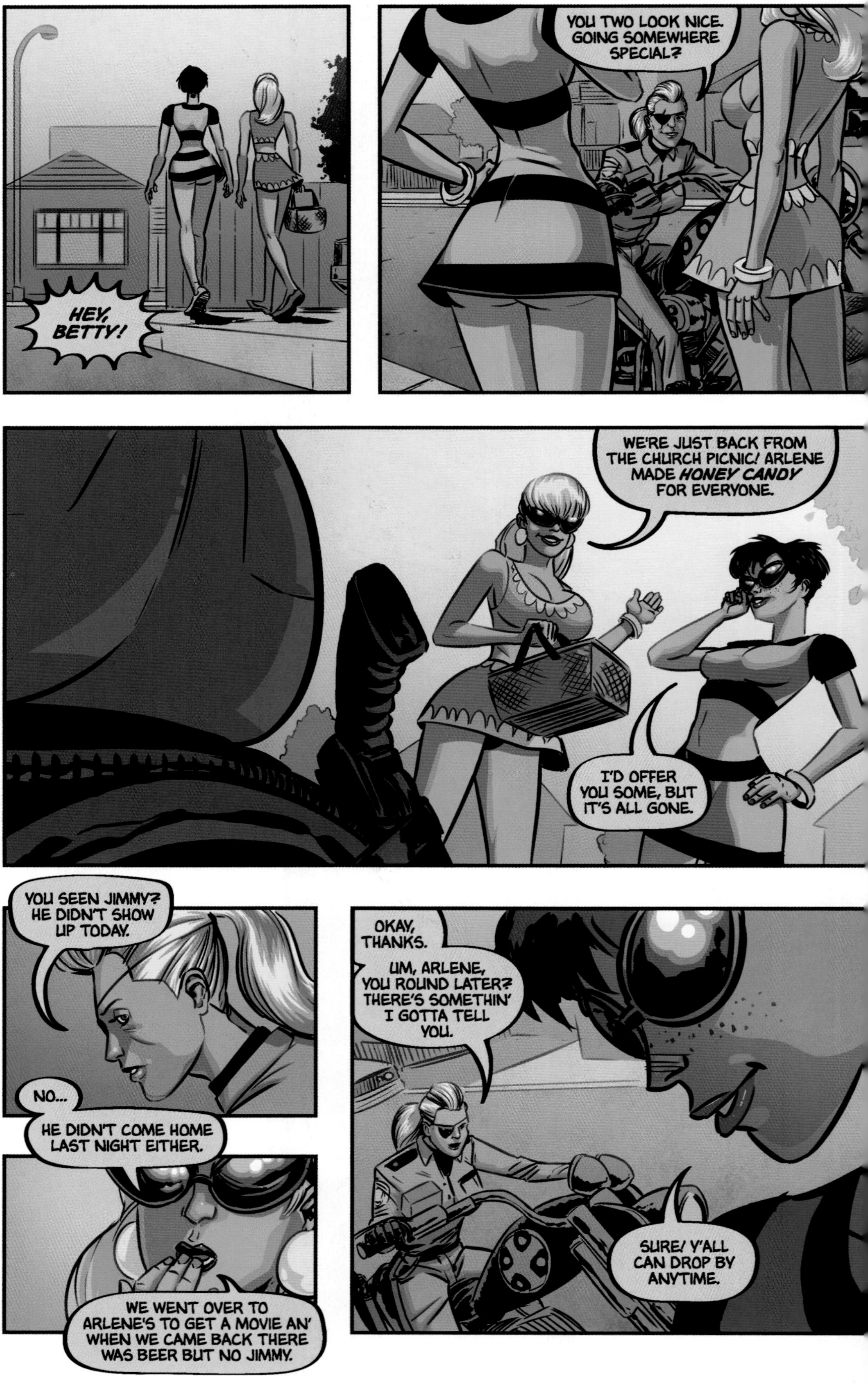
HEY, BETTY!
YOU TWO LOOK NICE. GOING SOMEWHERE SPECIAL?
WE'RE JUST BACK FROM THE CHURCH PICNIC! ARLENE MADE *HONEY CANDY* FOR EVERYONE.
I'D OFFER YOU SOME, BUT IT'S ALL GONE.
YOU SEEN JIMMY? HE DIDN'T SHOW UP TODAY.
NO...
HE DIDN'T COME HOME LAST NIGHT EITHER.
WE WENT OVER TO ARLENE'S TO GET A MOVIE AN' WHEN WE CAME BACK THERE WAS BEER BUT NO JIMMY.
OKAY, THANKS.
UM, ARLENE, YOU ROUND LATER? THERE'S SOMETHIN' I GOTTA TELL YOU.
SURE! Y'ALL CAN DROP BY ANYTIME.

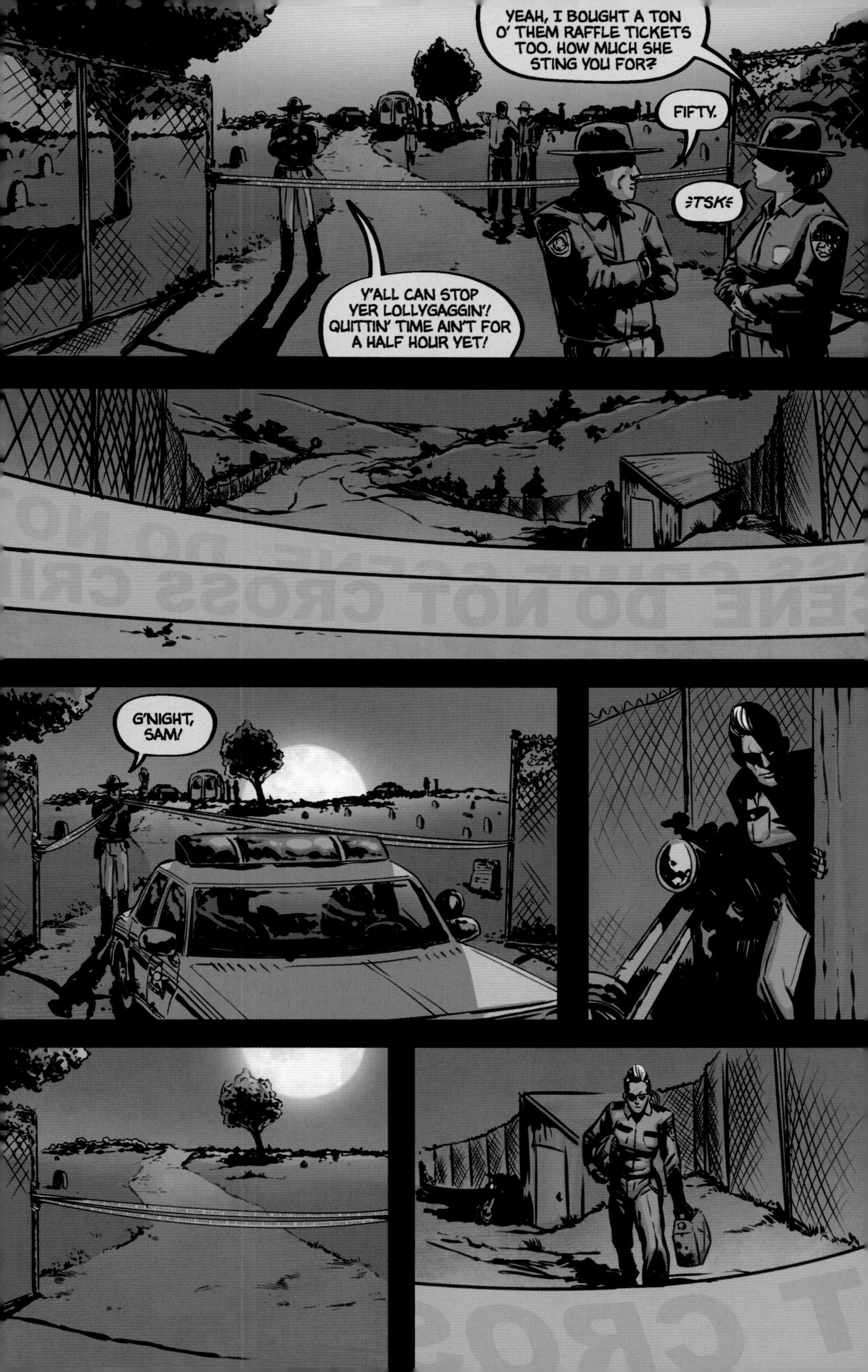
YEAH, I BOUGHT A TON O' THEM RAFFLE TICKETS TOO. HOW MUCH SHE STING YOU FOR?
FIFTY.
TSK
Y'ALL CAN STOP YER LOLLYGAGGIN'! QUITTIN' TIME AIN'T FOR A HALF HOUR YET!
G'NIGHT, SAM!

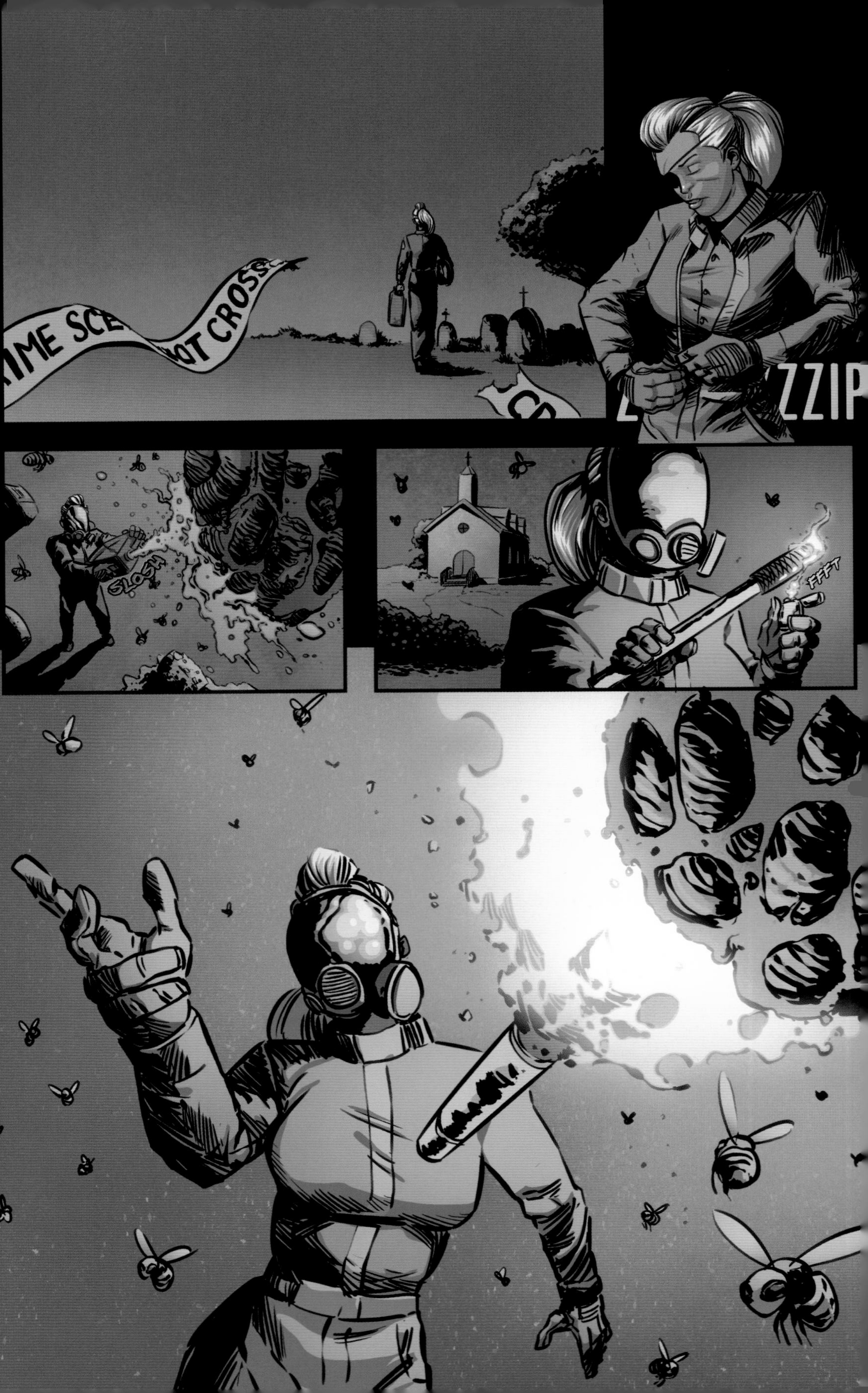
IME SCE
OT CROSS
ZZIP
SLOSH
FFFT

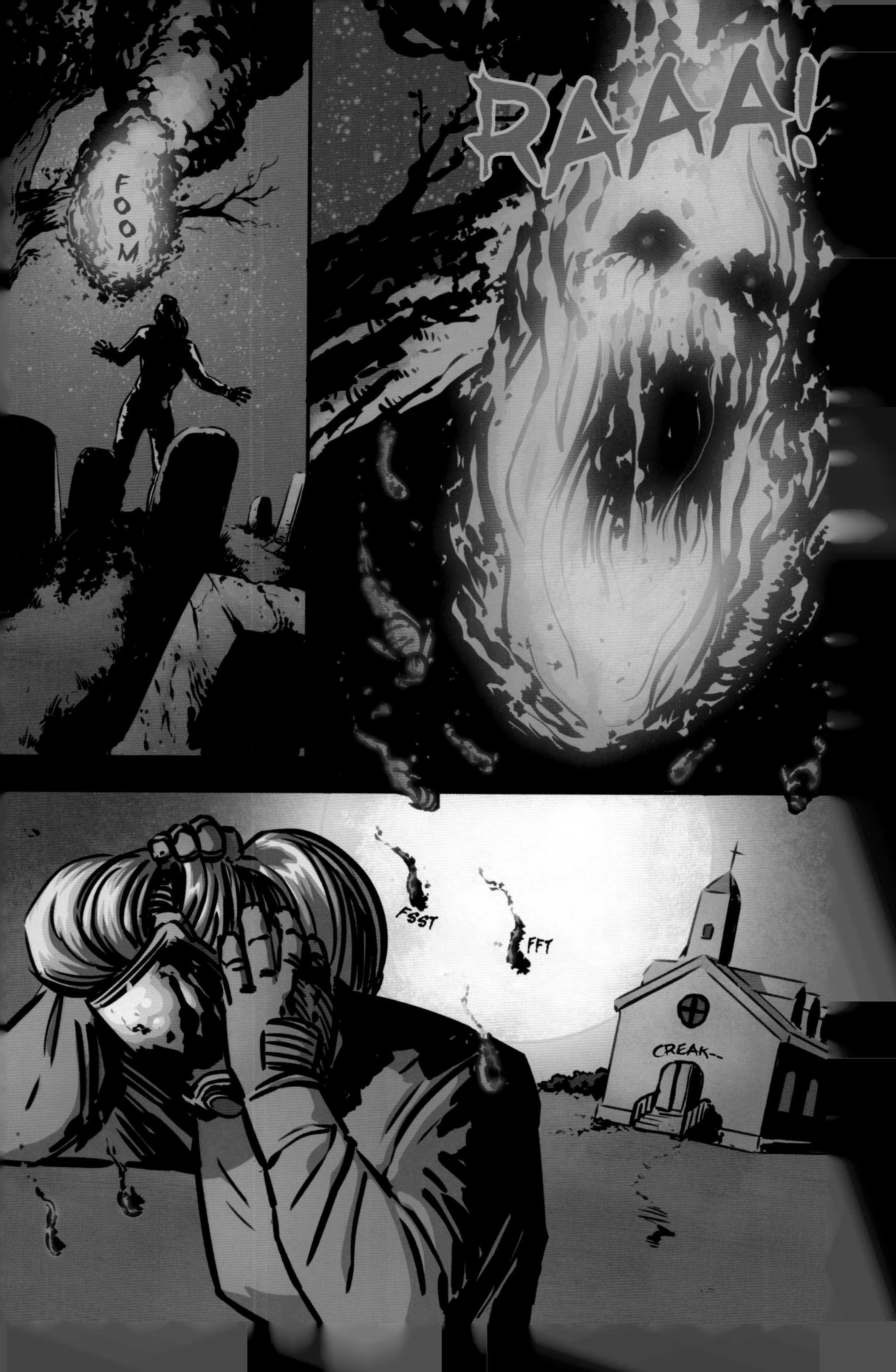
FOOM
RAAA!
FSST
FFT
CREAK--

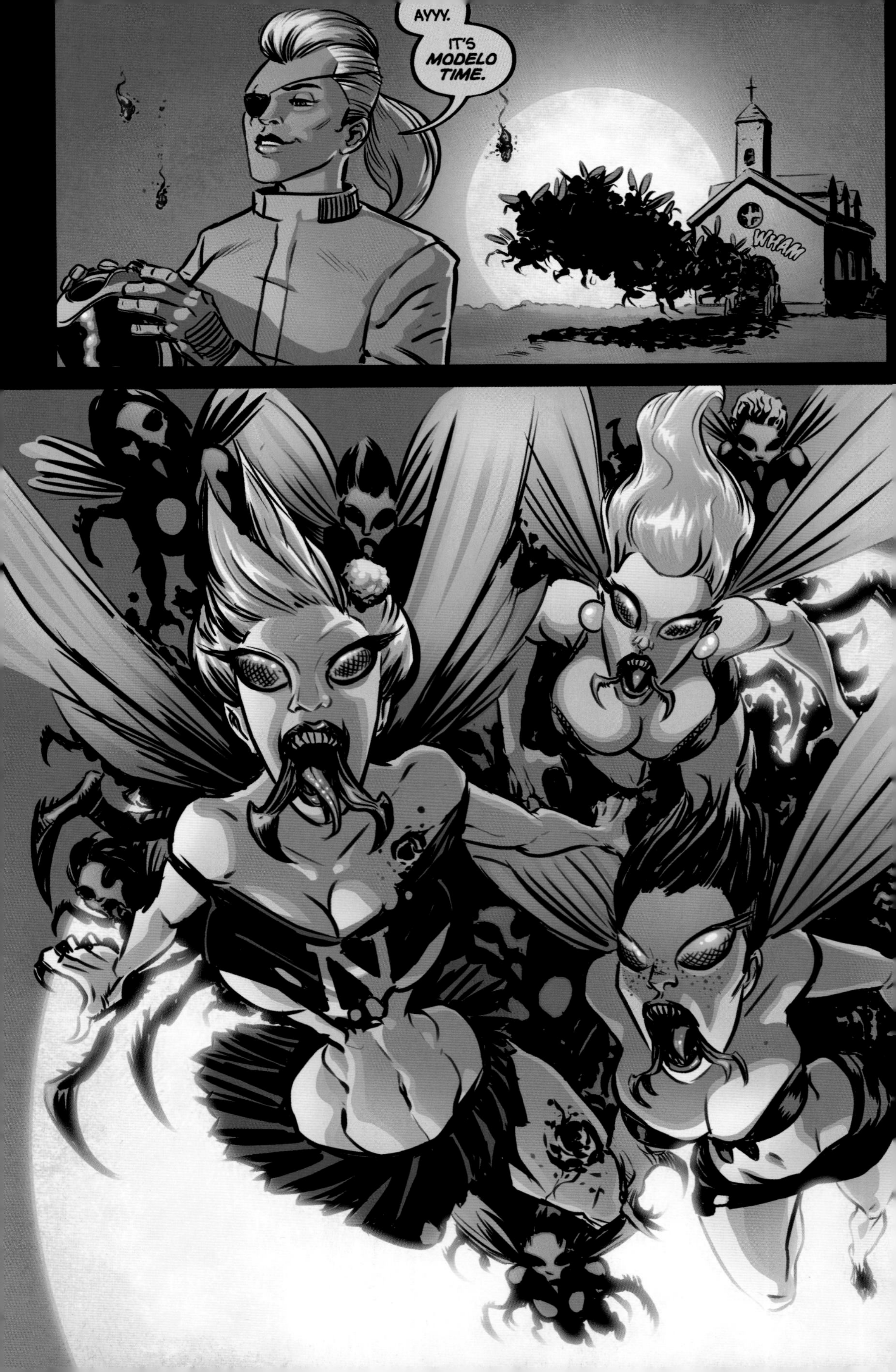
AYYY.
IT'S MODELO TIME.
WHAM

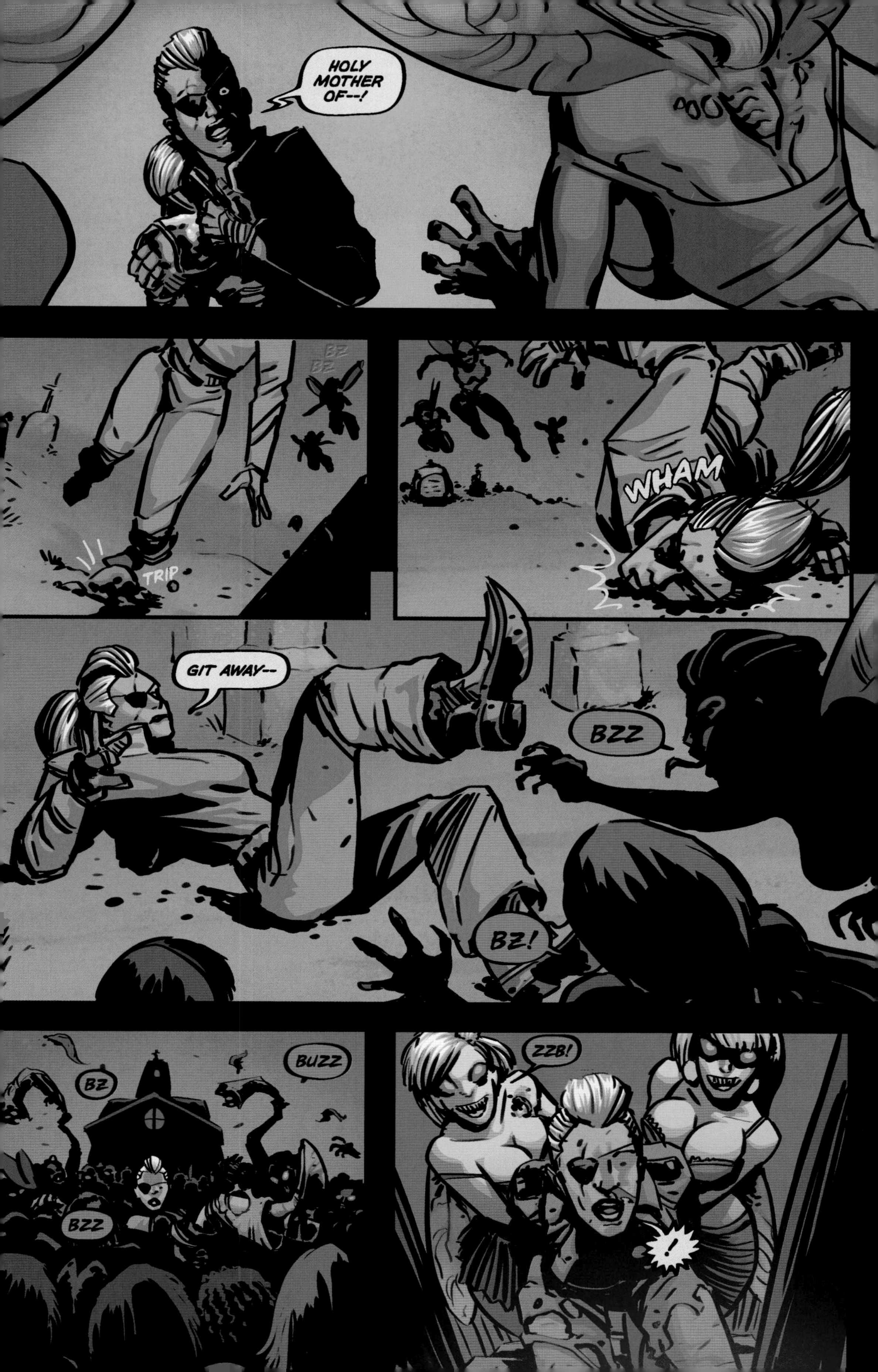
HOLY MOTHER OF--!
BZ BZ
TRIP
WHAM
GIT AWAY--
BZZ
BZ!
BZ
BUZZ
BZZ
ZZB!
!

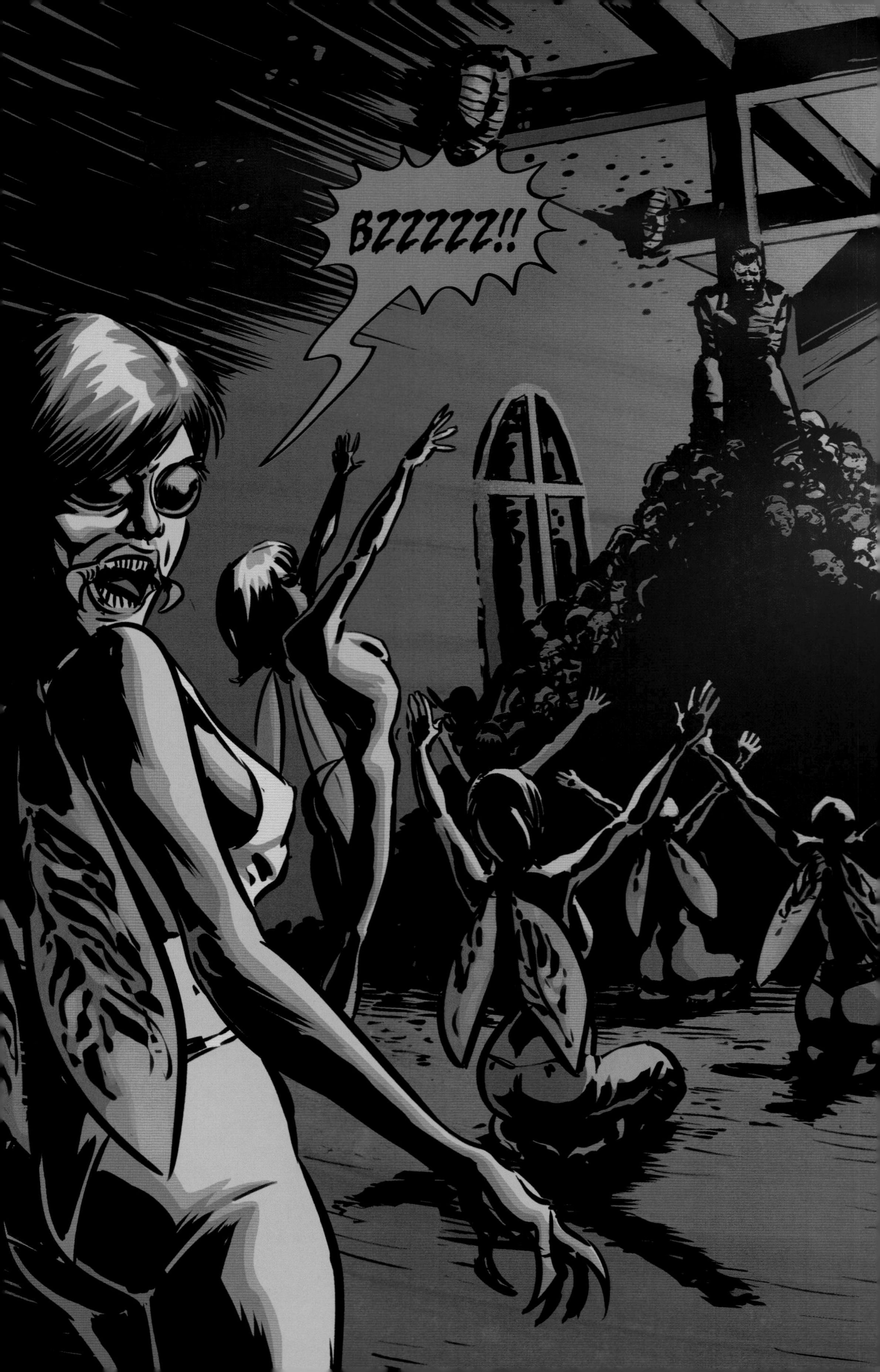
BZZZZZ!!

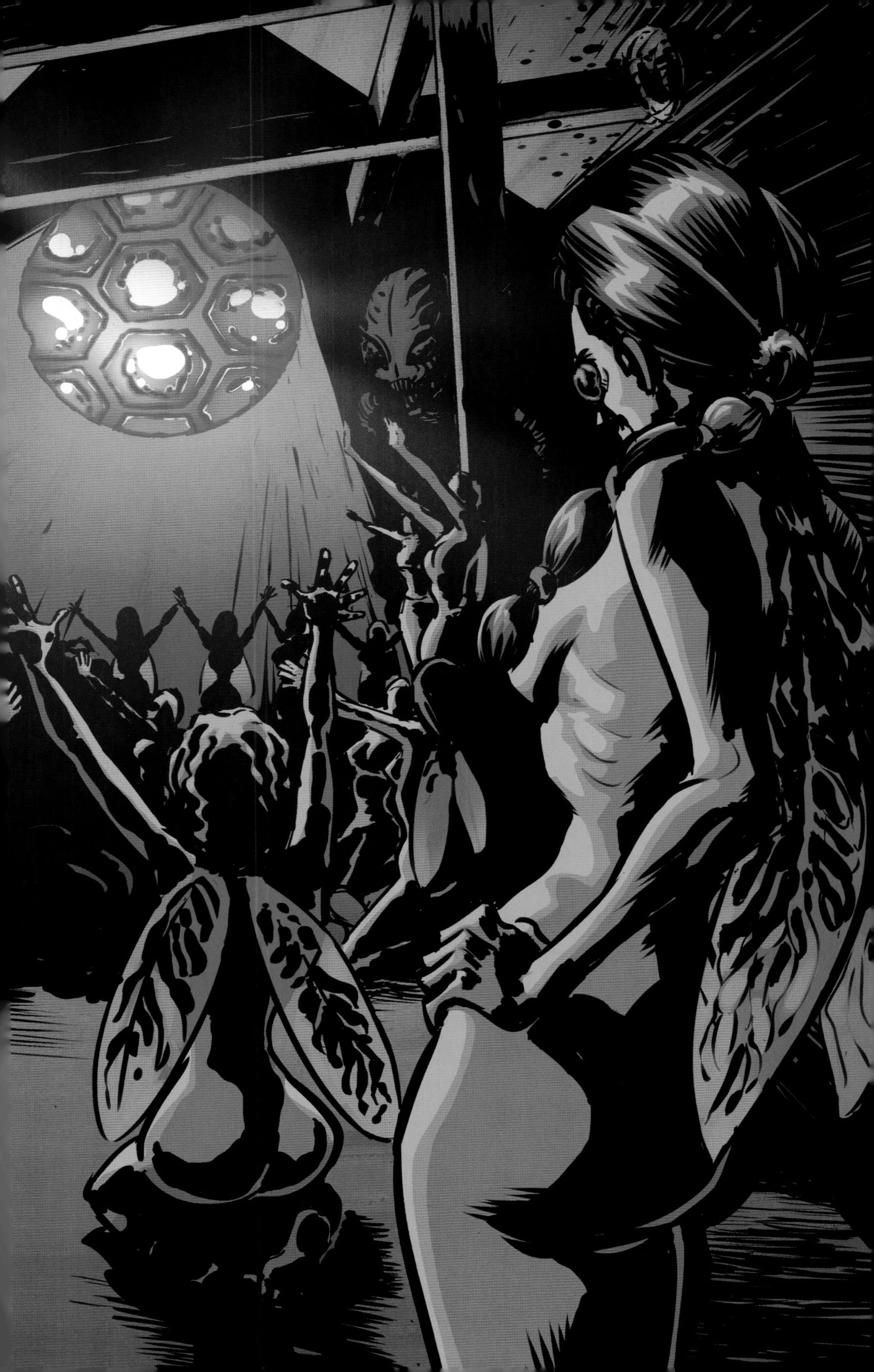

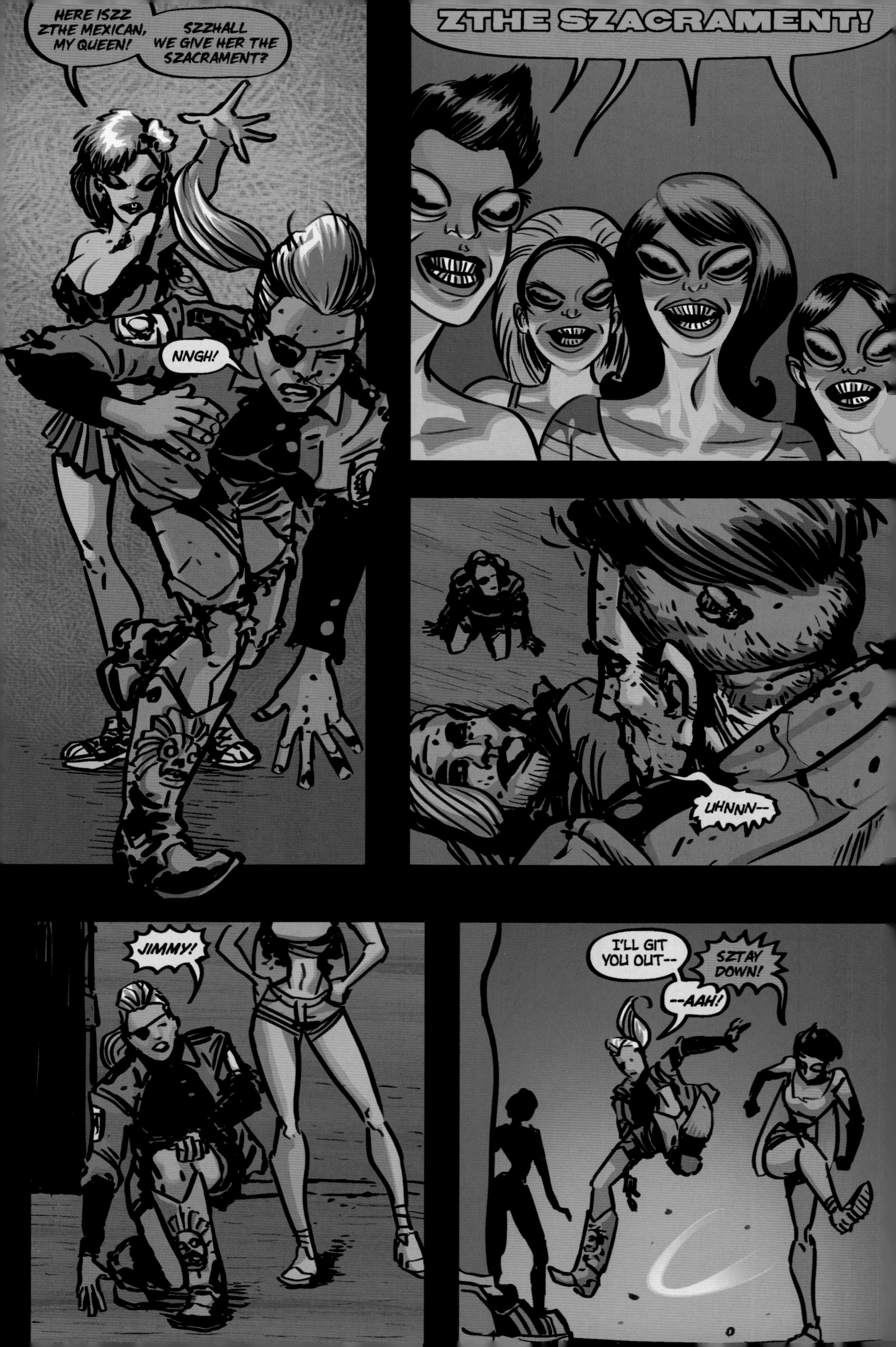
HERE ISZZ ZTHE MEXICAN, MY QUEEN!
SZZHALL WE GIVE HER THE SZACRAMENT?
NNGH!
ZTHE SZACRAMENT!
UHNNN--
JIMMY!
I'LL GIT YOU OUT--
SZTAY DOWN!
--AAH!

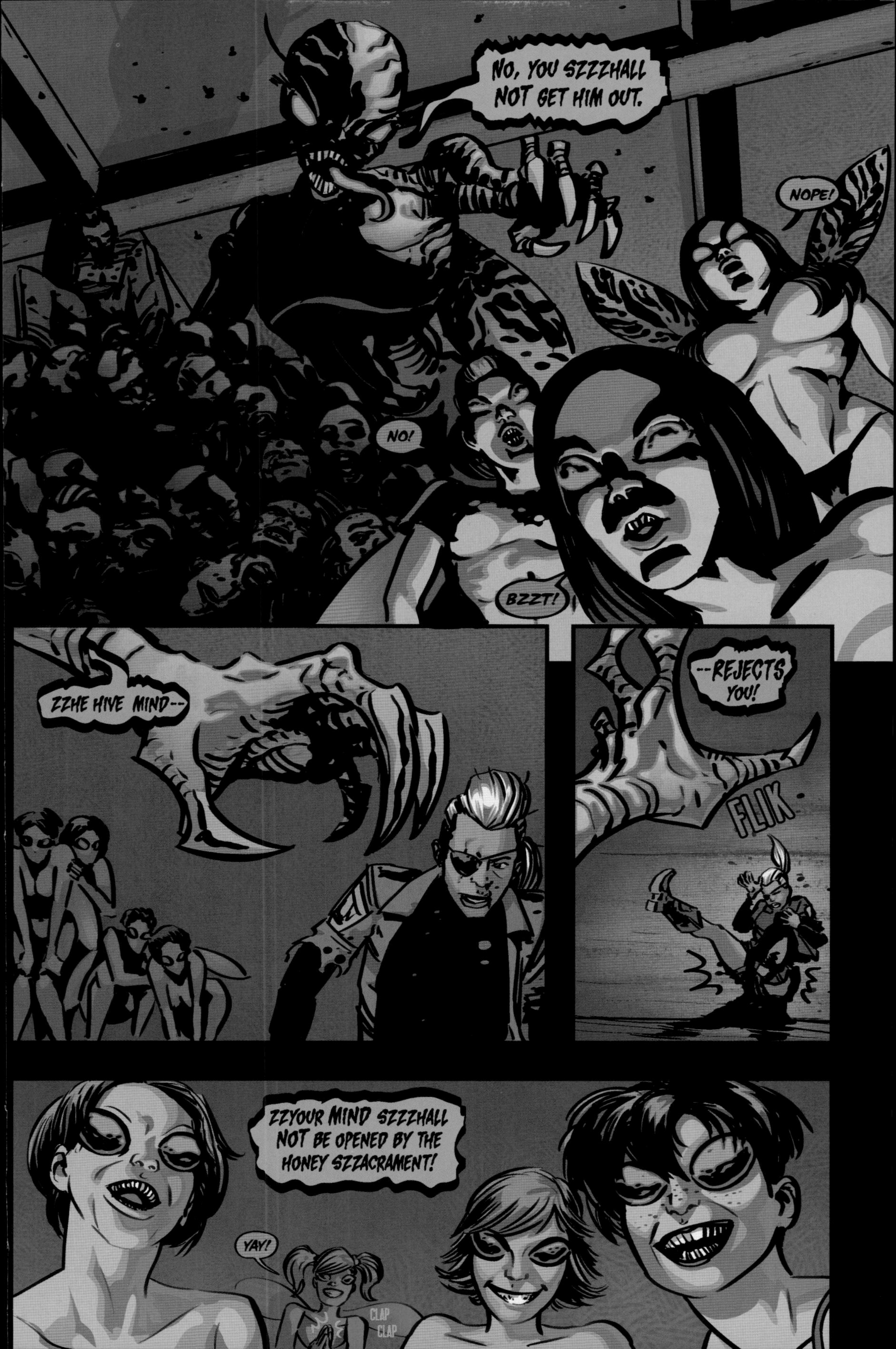
NO, YOU SZZZHALL NOT GET HIM OUT.
NOPE!
NO!
BZZT!
ZZHE HIVE MIND--
--REJECTS YOU!
FLIK
ZZYOUR MIND SZZZHALL NOT BE OPENED BY THE HONEY SZZACRAMENT!
YAY!
CLAP
CLAP

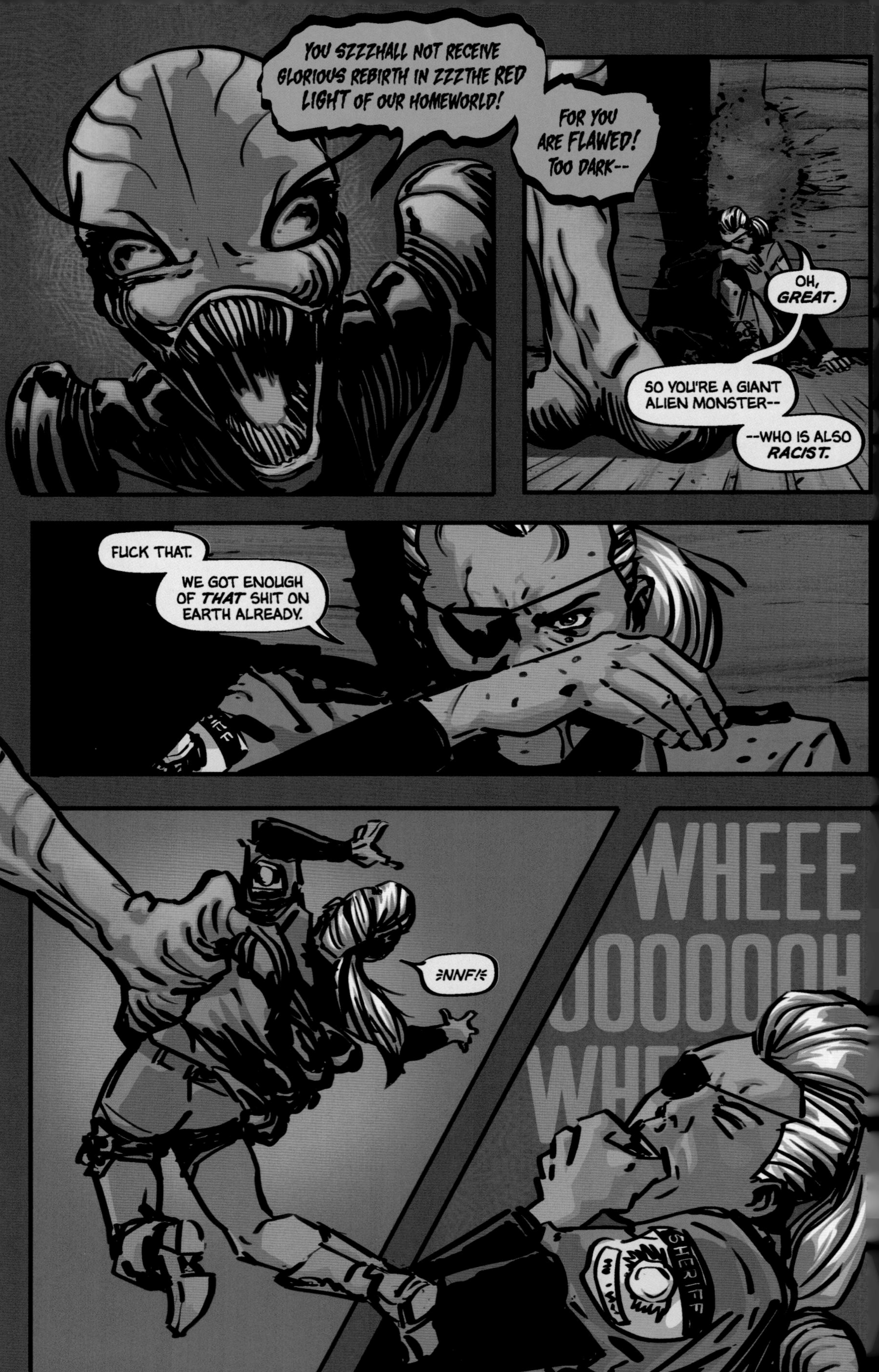
YOU SZZZHALL NOT RECEIVE GLORIOUS REBIRTH IN ZZZTHE RED LIGHT OF OUR HOMEWORLD!
FOR YOU ARE FLAWED! TOO DARK--
OH, GREAT.
SO YOU'RE A GIANT ALIEN MONSTER--
--WHO IS ALSO RACIST.
FUCK THAT.
WE GOT ENOUGH OF THAT SHIT ON EARTH ALREADY.
NNF!
WHEEE OOOOOOH
SHERIFF

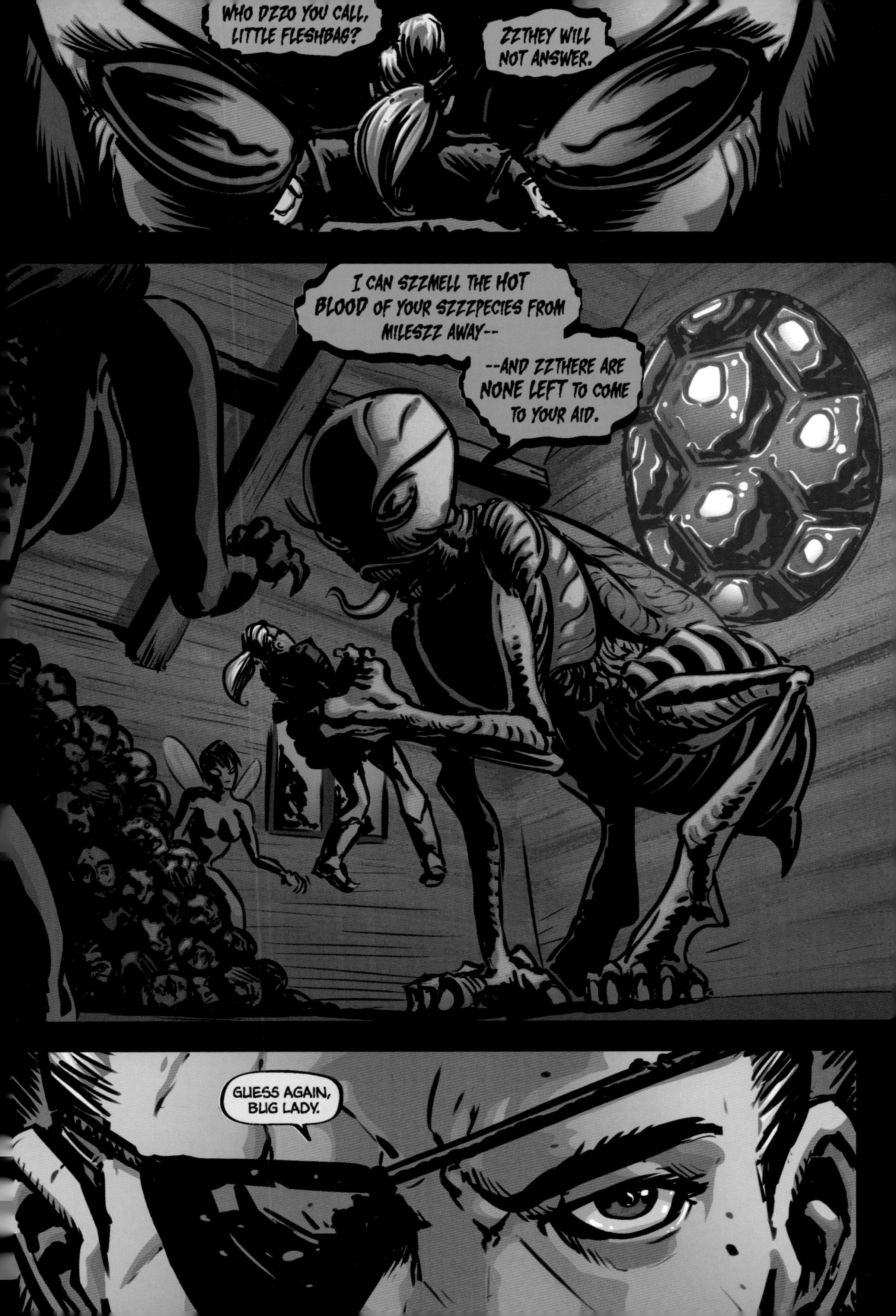
WHO DZZO YOU CALL, LITTLE FLESHBAG?
ZZTHEY WILL NOT ANSWER.
I CAN SZZMELL THE HOT BLOOD OF YOUR SZZZPECIES FROM MILESZZ AWAY--
--AND ZZTHERE ARE NONE LEFT TO COME TO YOUR AID.
GUESS AGAIN, BUG LADY.

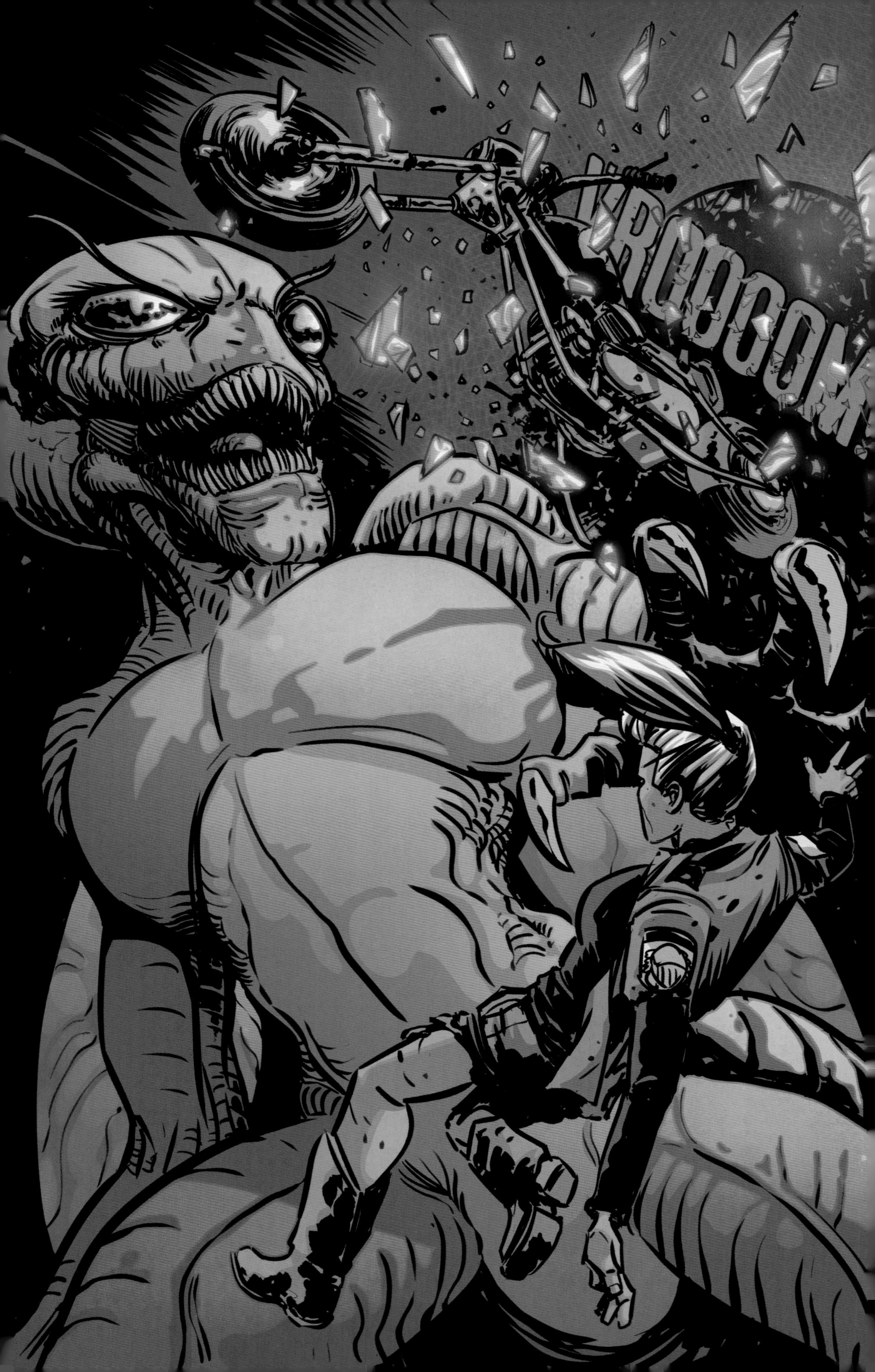
VROOOOM

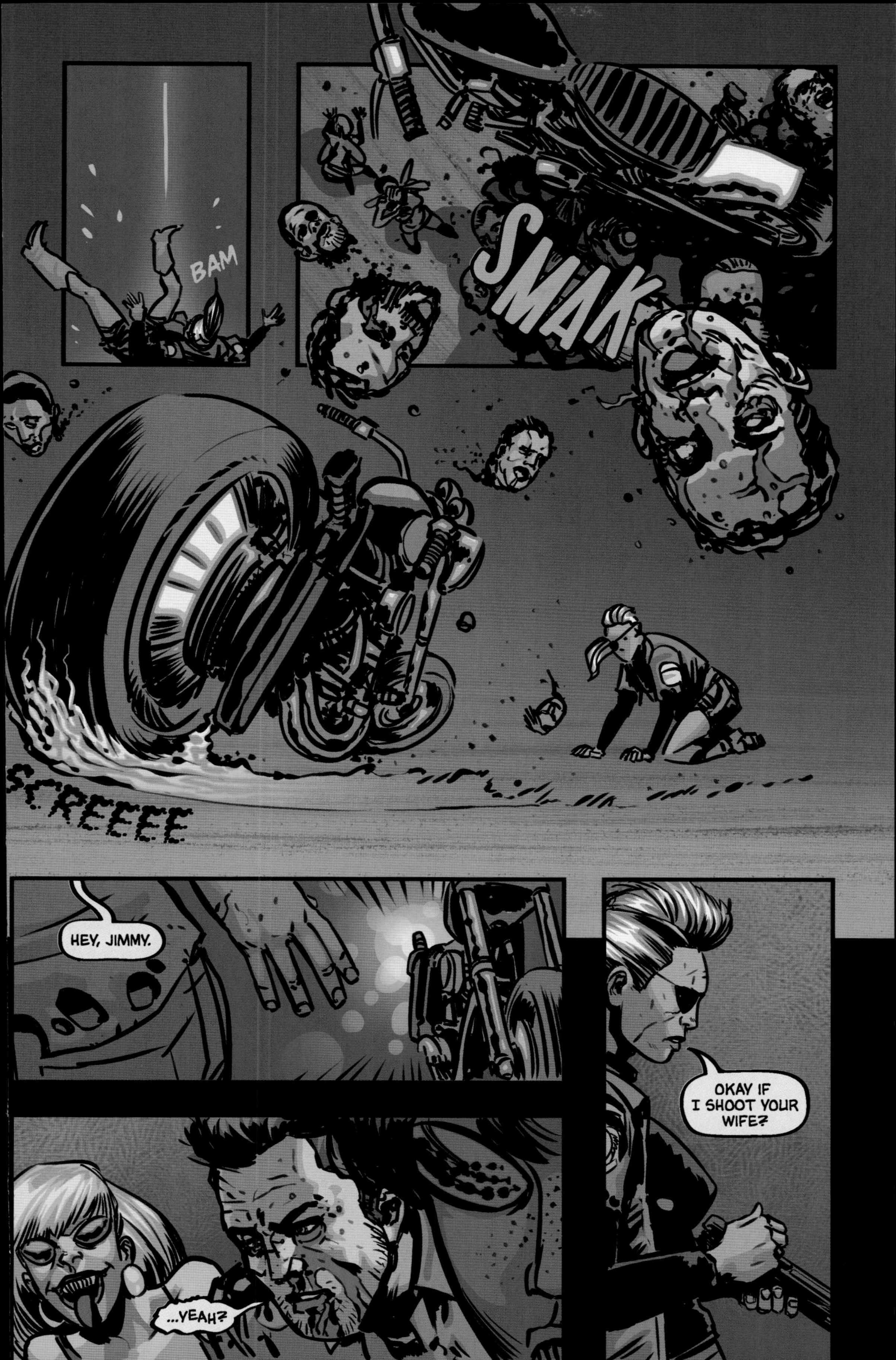
BAM
SMAK
SCREEEE
HEY, JIMMY.
OKAY IF I SHOOT YOUR WIFE?
...YEAH?

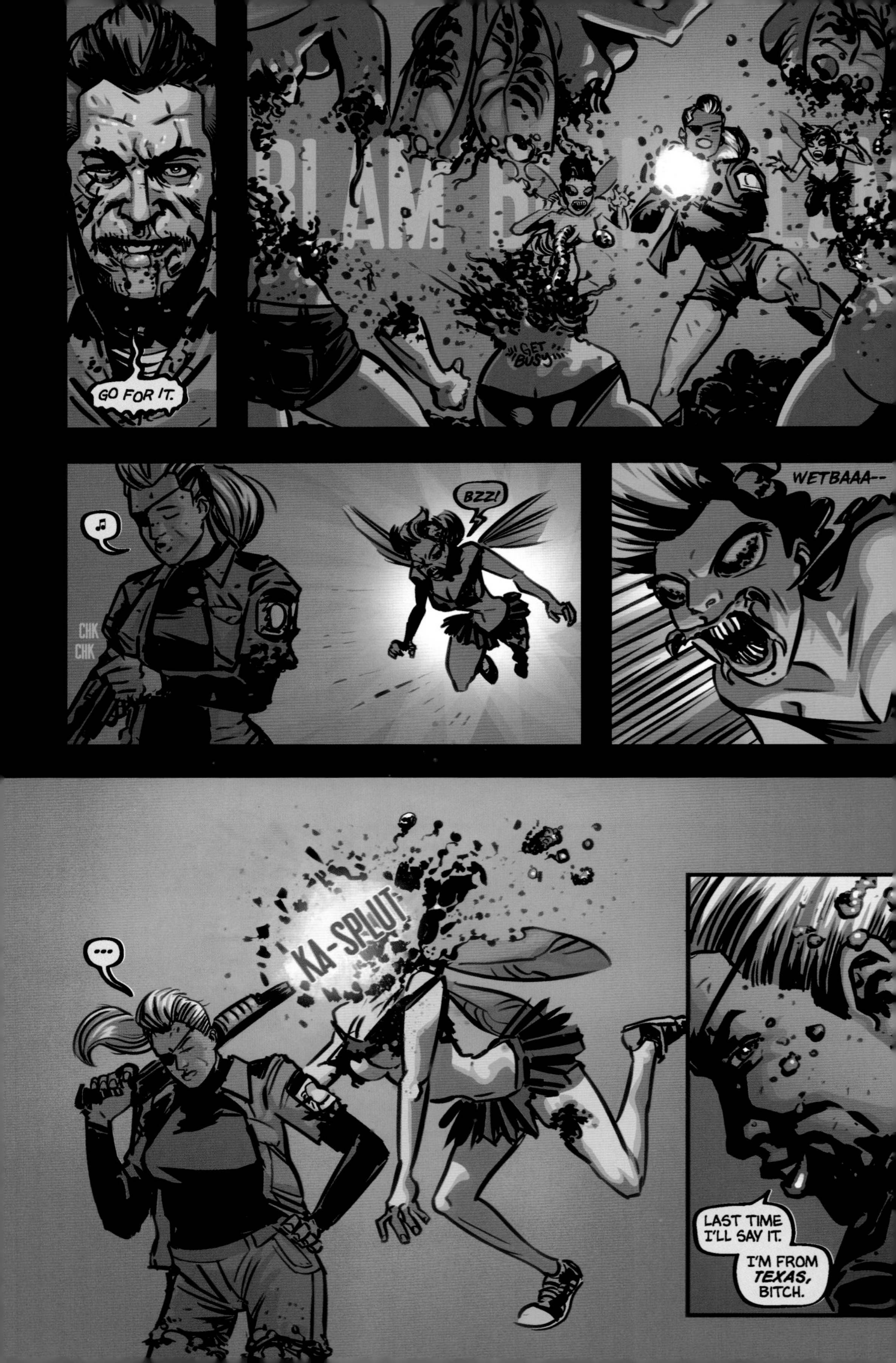
GO FOR IT.
BLAM BLAM BLAM
GET BUSY
♪
CHK CHK
BZZ!
WETBAAA--
...
KA-SPLUT!
LAST TIME I'LL SAY IT.
I'M FROM *TEXAS,* BITCH.

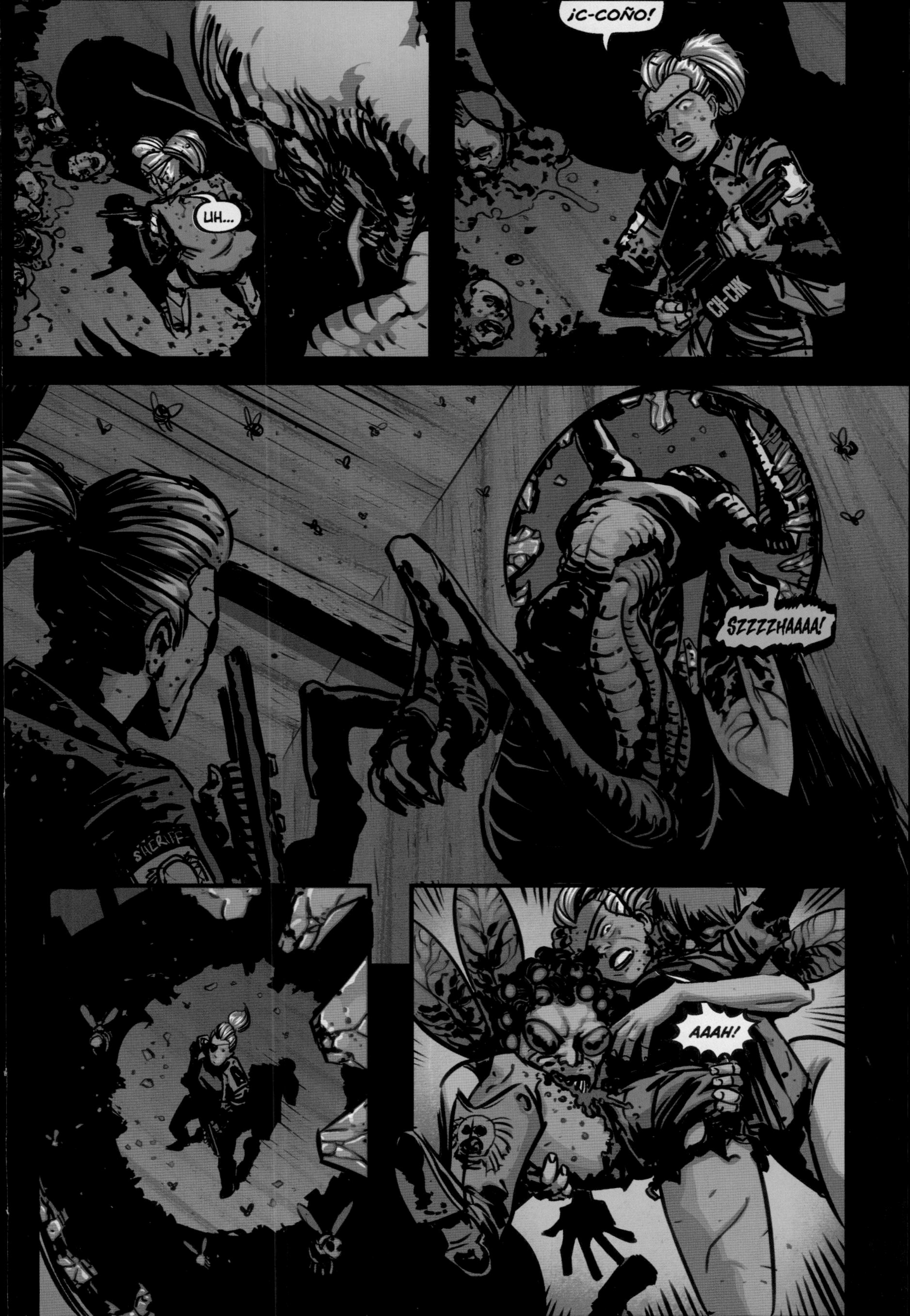
UH...
¡C-COÑO!
CH-CHK
SZZZZHAAAA!
SHERIFF
AAAH!

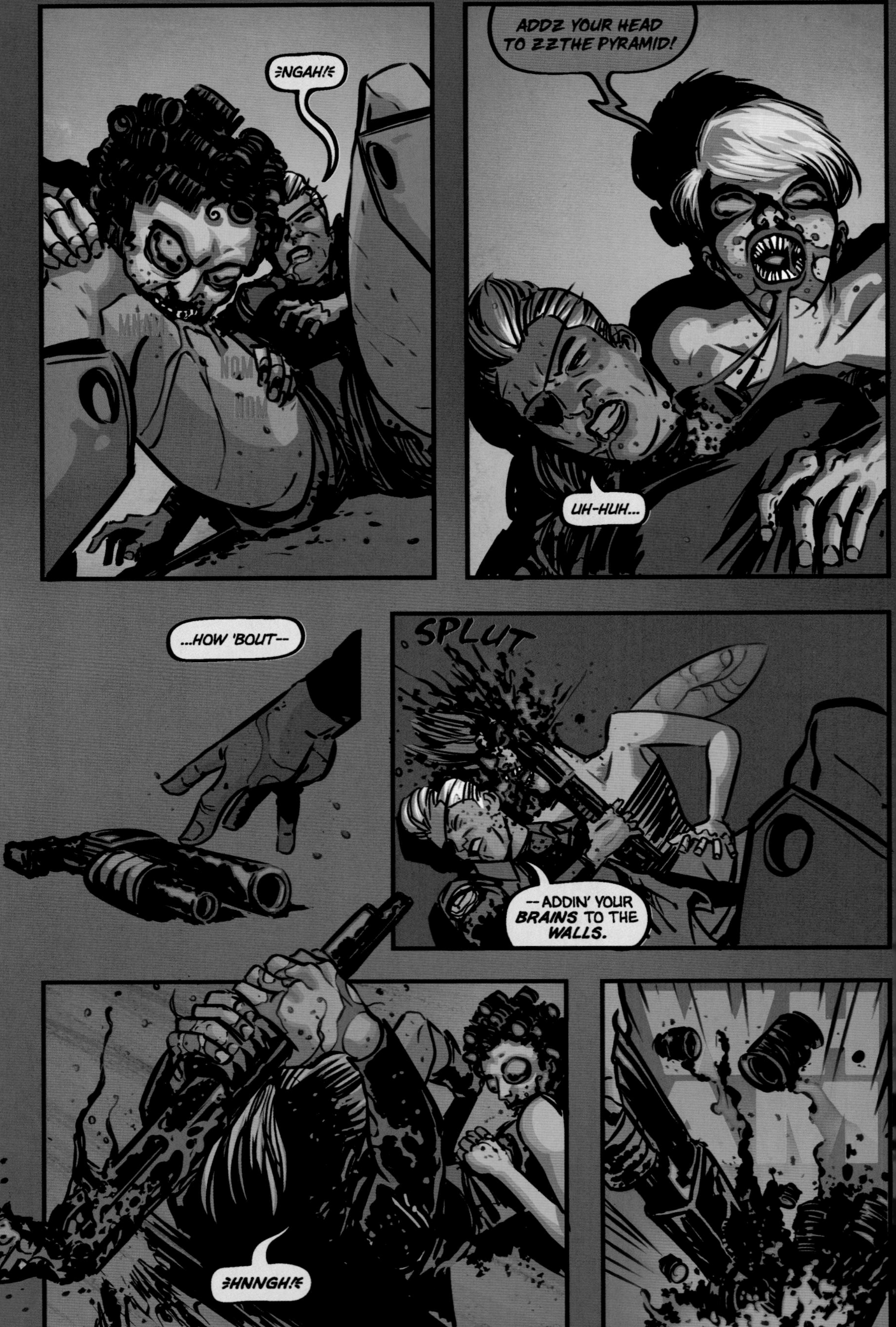
NGAH!
MNAM
NOM
NOM
ADDZ YOUR HEAD TO ZZTHE PYRAMID!
UH-HUH...
...HOW 'BOUT--
SPLUT
--ADDIN' YOUR BRAINS TO THE WALLS.
HNNGH!

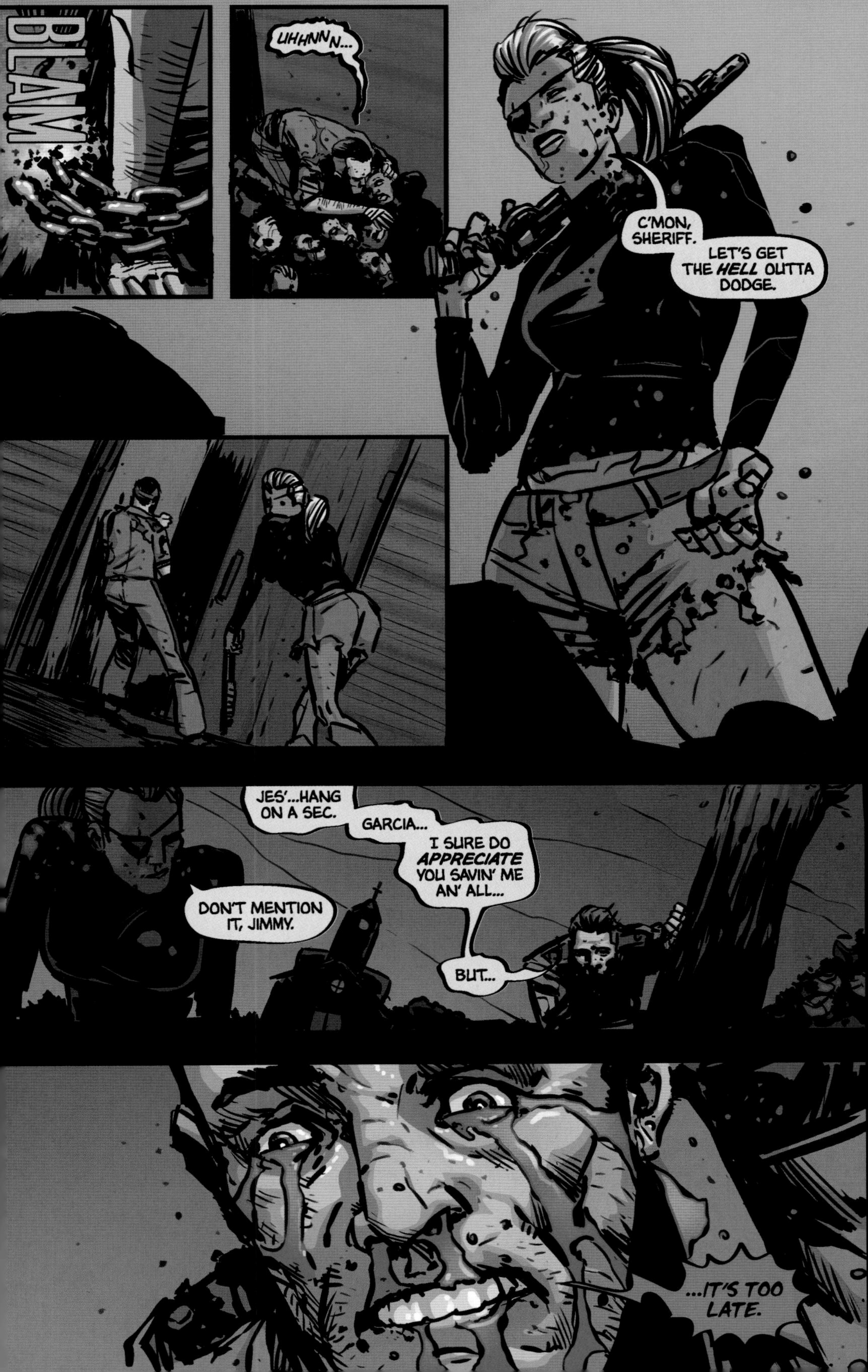
BLAM
UHHNNN...
C'MON, SHERIFF.
LET'S GET THE *HELL* OUTTA DODGE.
JES'...HANG ON A SEC.
GARCIA...
I SURE DO *APPRECIATE* YOU SAVIN' ME AN' ALL...
DON'T MENTION IT, JIMMY.
BUT...
...IT'S TOO LATE.

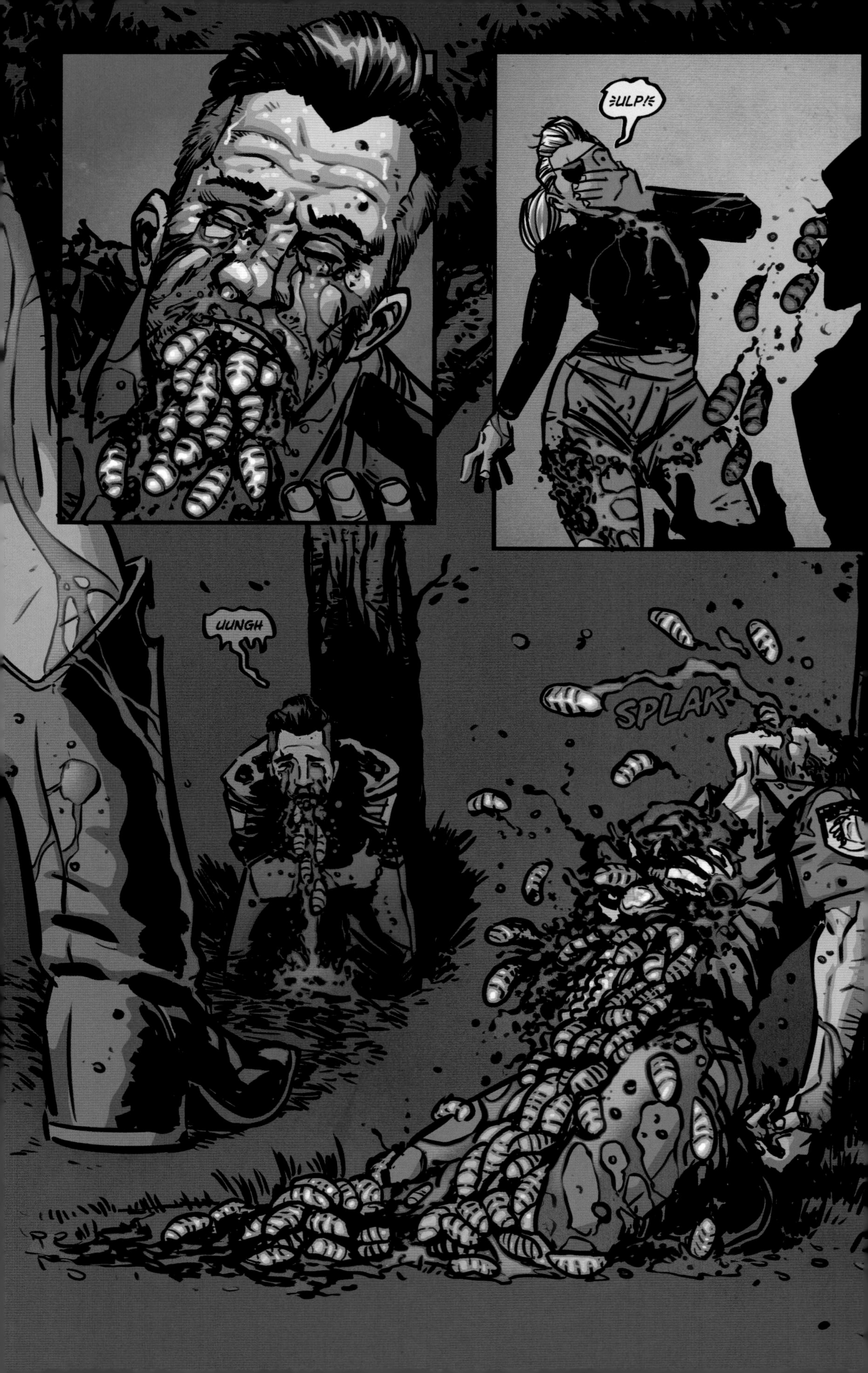
ULP!
UUNGH
SPLAK

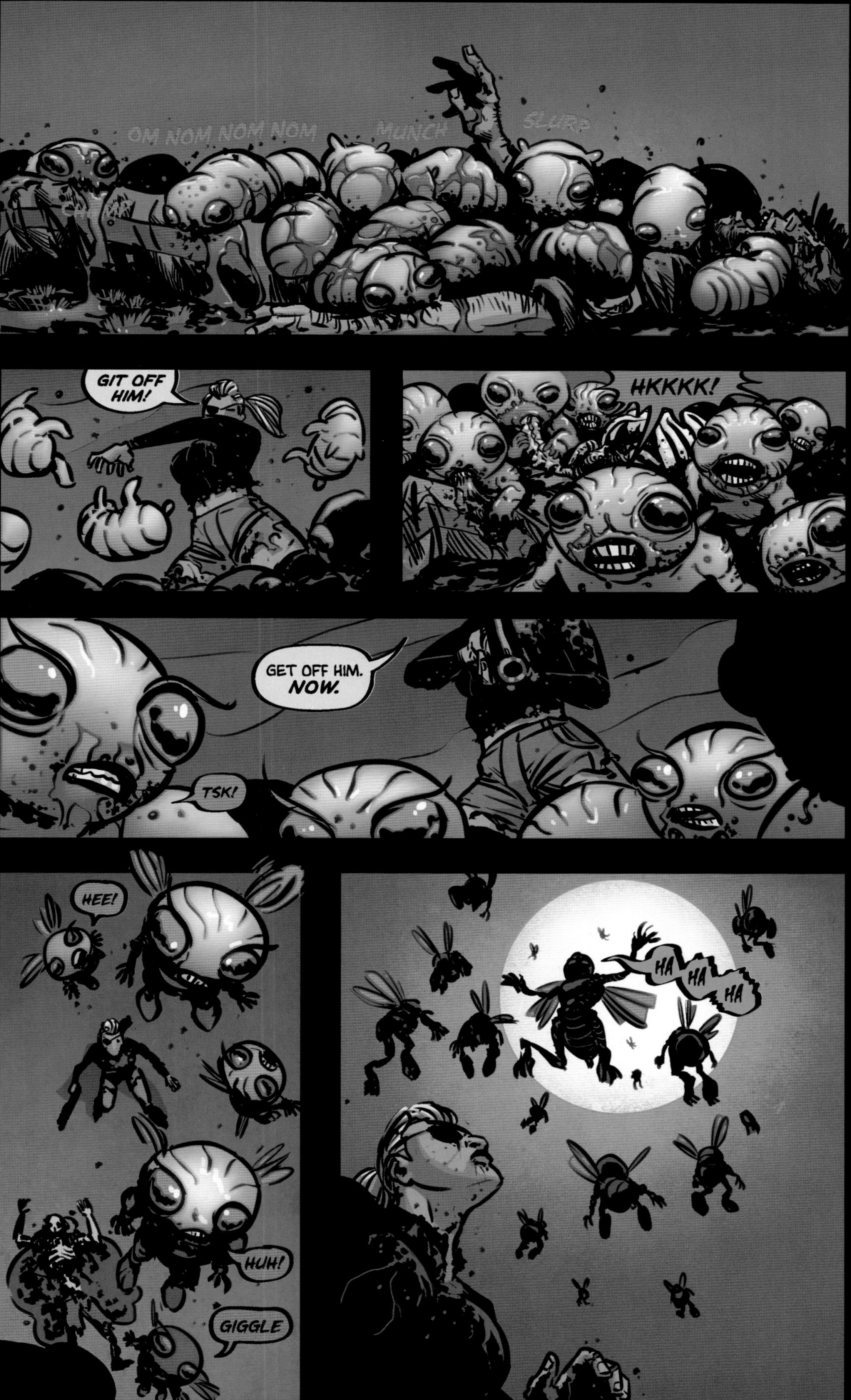
OM NOM NOM NOM
MUNCH
SLURP
GIT OFF HIM!
HKKKK!
GET OFF HIM. NOW.
TSK!
HEE!
HUH!
GIGGLE
HA
HA
HA

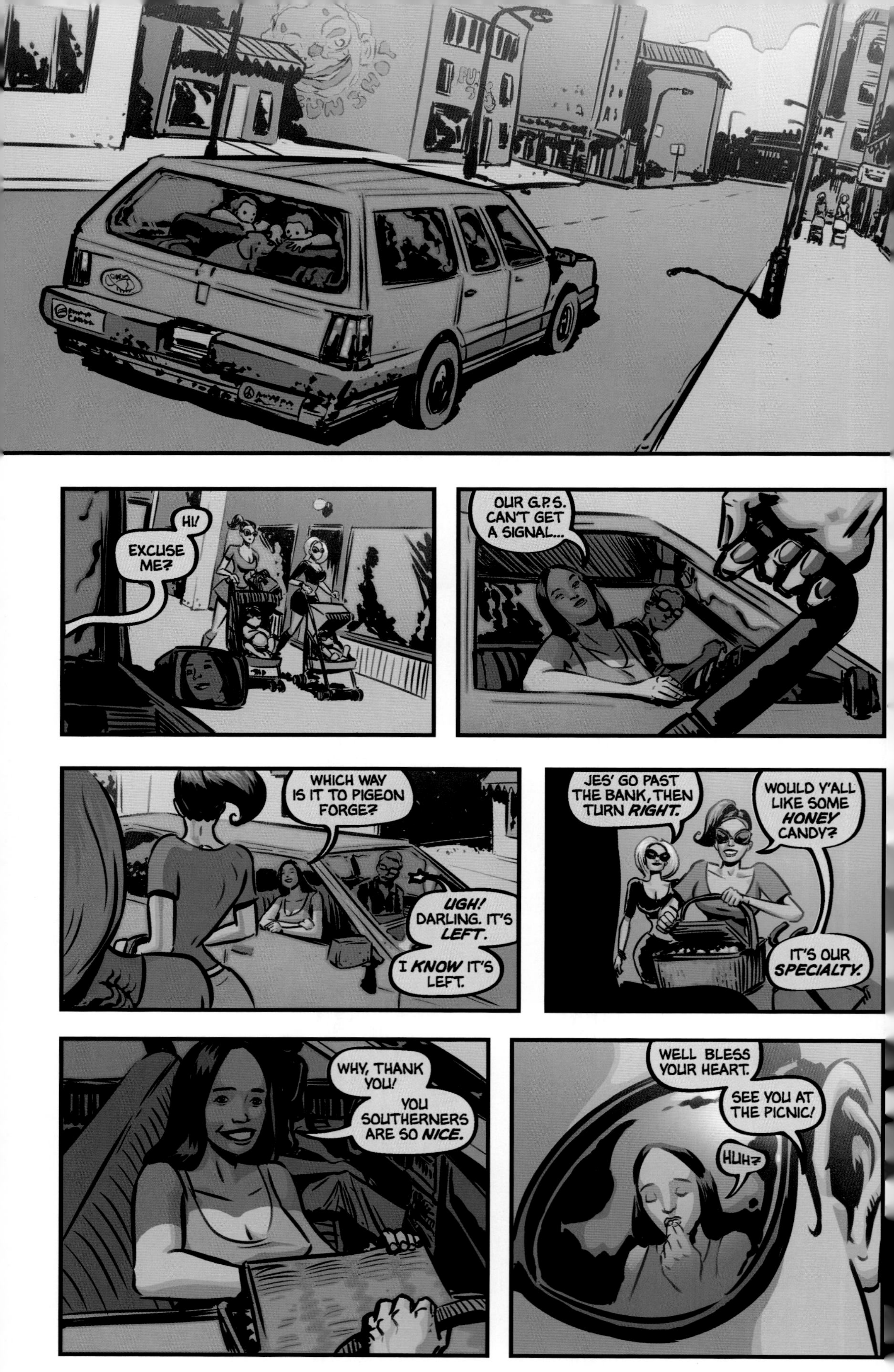
HI!
EXCUSE ME?
OUR G.P.S. CAN'T GET A SIGNAL...
WHICH WAY IS IT TO PIGEON FORGE?
UGH! DARLING. IT'S LEFT.
I KNOW IT'S LEFT.
JES' GO PAST THE BANK, THEN TURN RIGHT.
WOULD Y'ALL LIKE SOME HONEY CANDY?
IT'S OUR SPECIALTY.
WHY, THANK YOU!
YOU SOUTHERNERS ARE SO NICE.
WELL BLESS YOUR HEART.
SEE YOU AT THE PICNIC!
HUH?

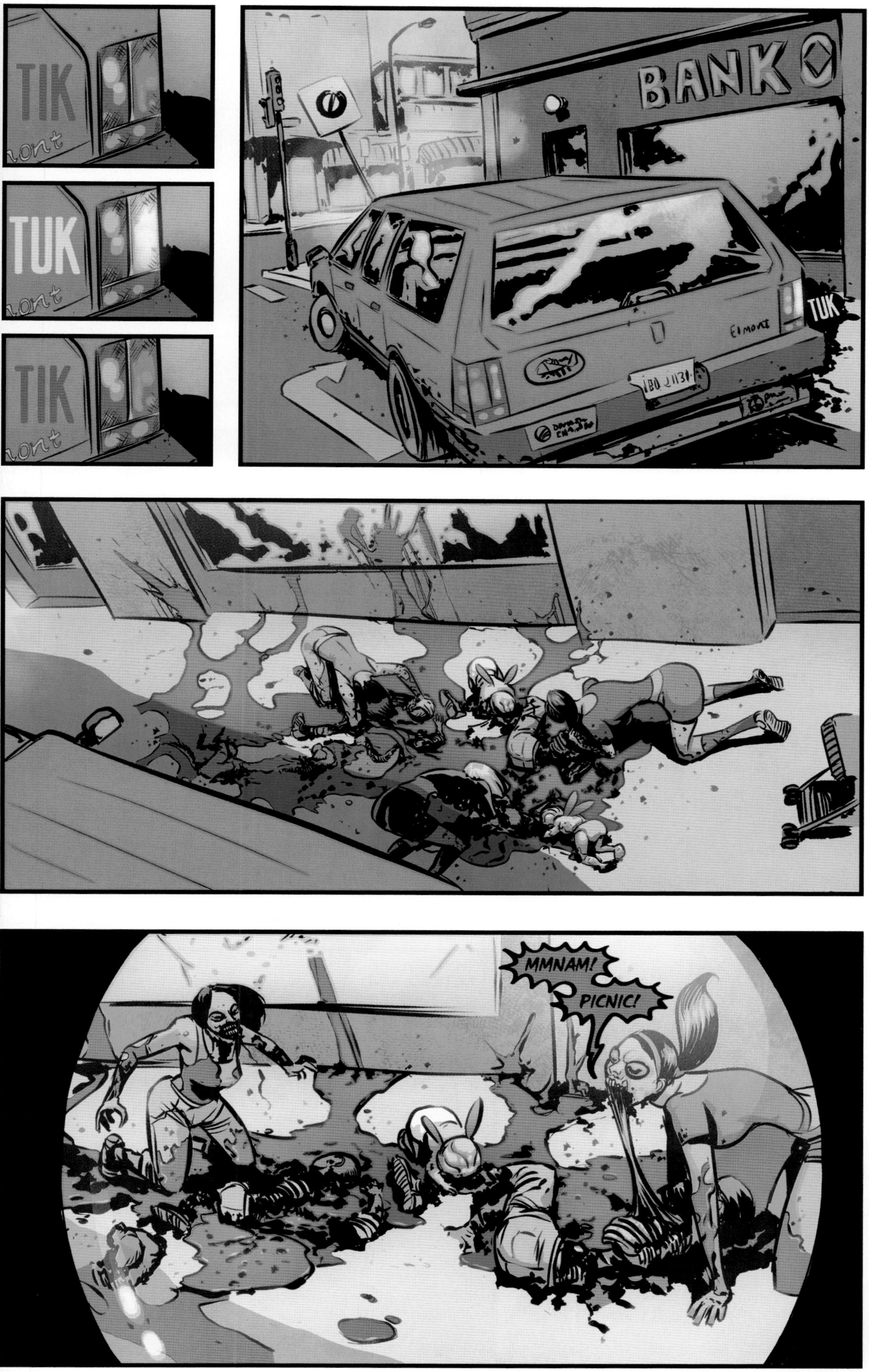

TIK
TUK
TIK
BANK
TUK
MMNAM!
PICNIC!

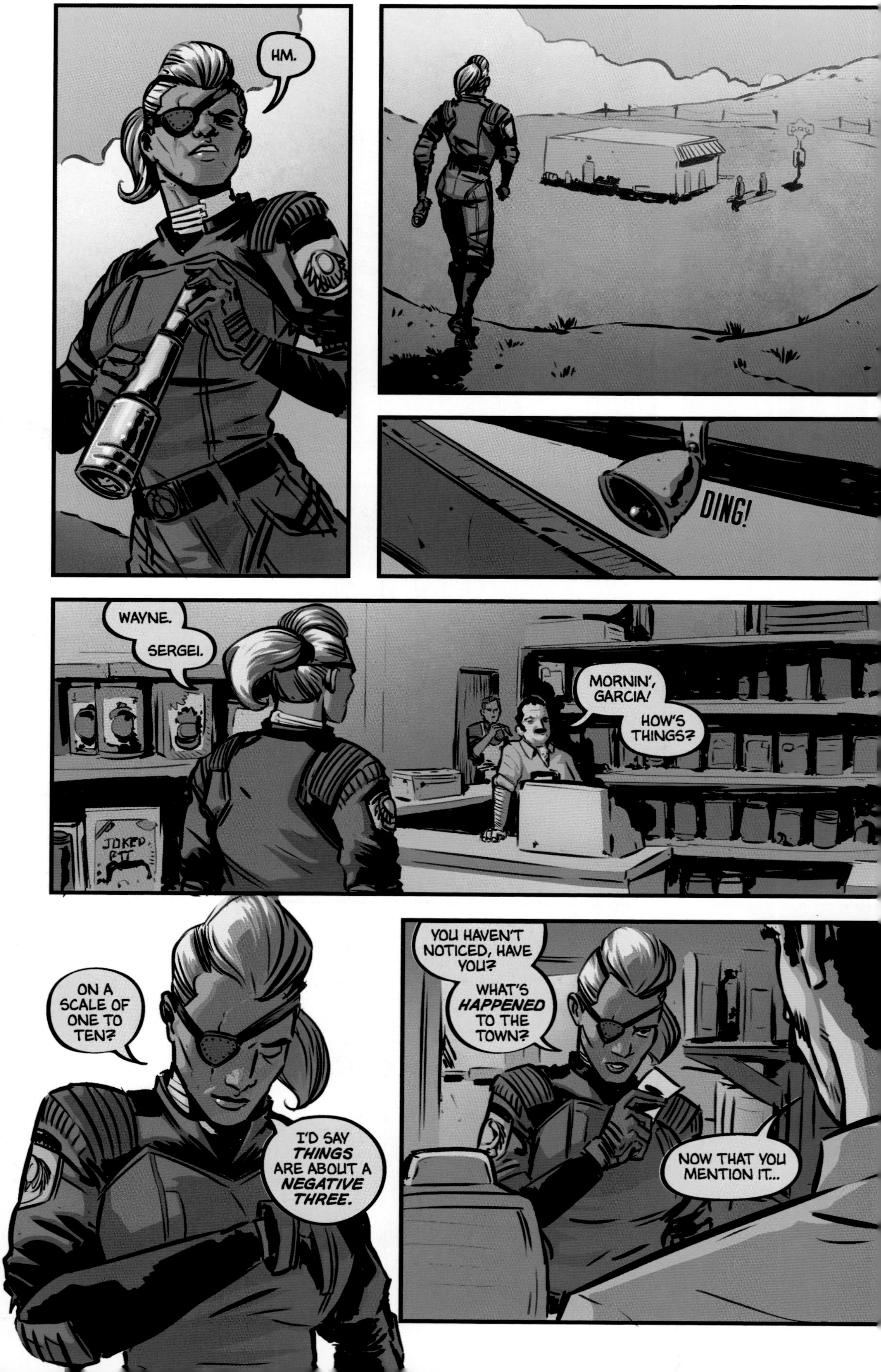
HM.
DING!
WAYNE.
SERGEI.
MORNIN', GARCIA!
HOW'S THINGS?
ON A SCALE OF ONE TO TEN?
I'D SAY *THINGS* ARE ABOUT A *NEGATIVE THREE.*
YOU HAVEN'T NOTICED, HAVE YOU?
WHAT'S *HAPPENED* TO THE TOWN?
NOW THAT YOU MENTION IT...

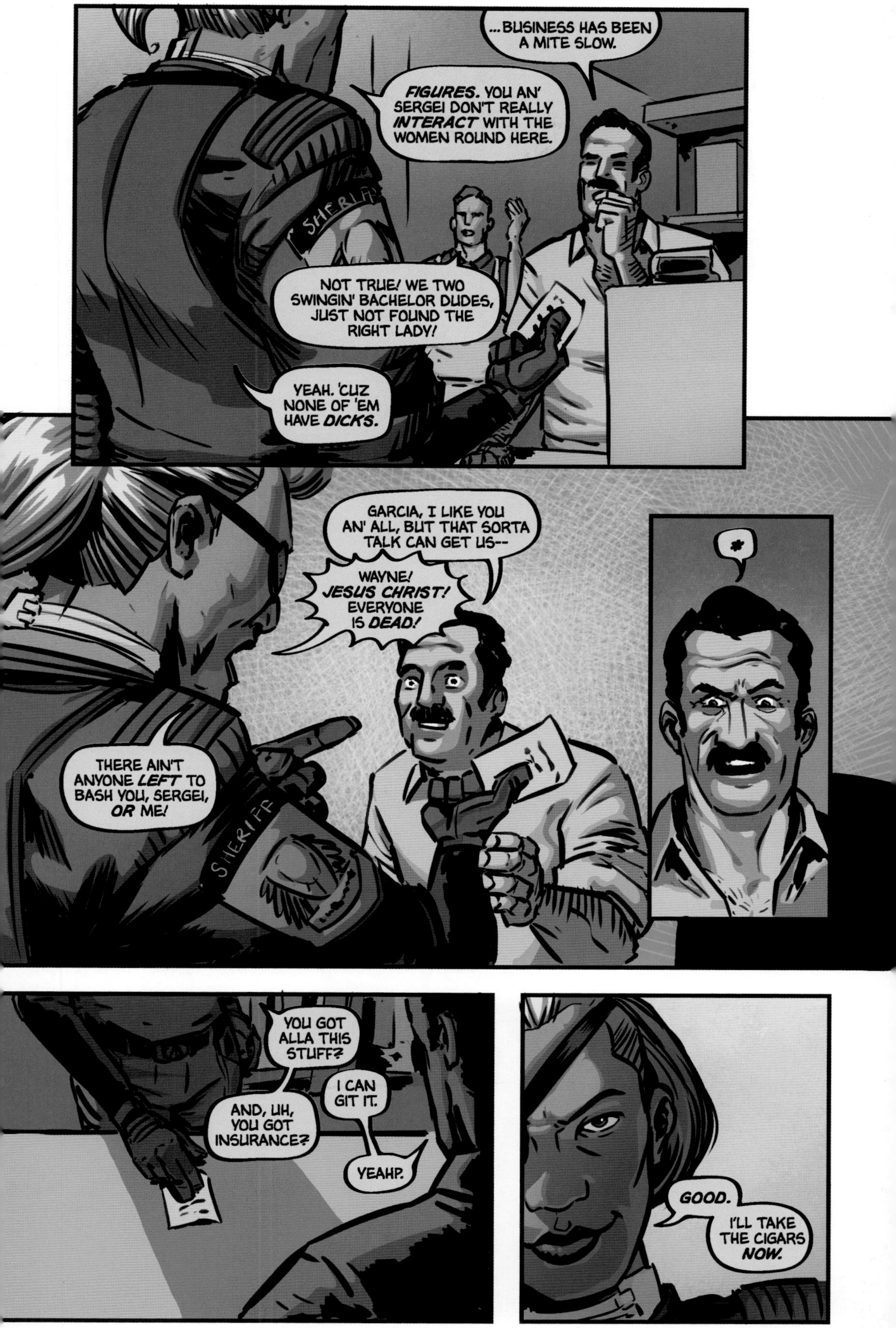
...BUSINESS HAS BEEN A MITE SLOW.
FIGURES. YOU AN' SERGEI DON'T REALLY INTERACT WITH THE WOMEN ROUND HERE.
NOT TRUE! WE TWO SWINGIN' BACHELOR DUDES, JUST NOT FOUND THE RIGHT LADY!
YEAH. 'CUZ NONE OF 'EM HAVE DICKS.
SHERIFF
GARCIA, I LIKE YOU AN' ALL, BUT THAT SORTA TALK CAN GET US--
WAYNE! JESUS CHRIST! EVERYONE IS DEAD!
THERE AIN'T ANYONE LEFT TO BASH YOU, SERGEI, OR ME!
SHERIFF
YOU GOT ALLA THIS STUFF?
I CAN GIT IT.
AND, UH, YOU GOT INSURANCE?
YEAHP.
GOOD.
I'LL TAKE THE CIGARS NOW.

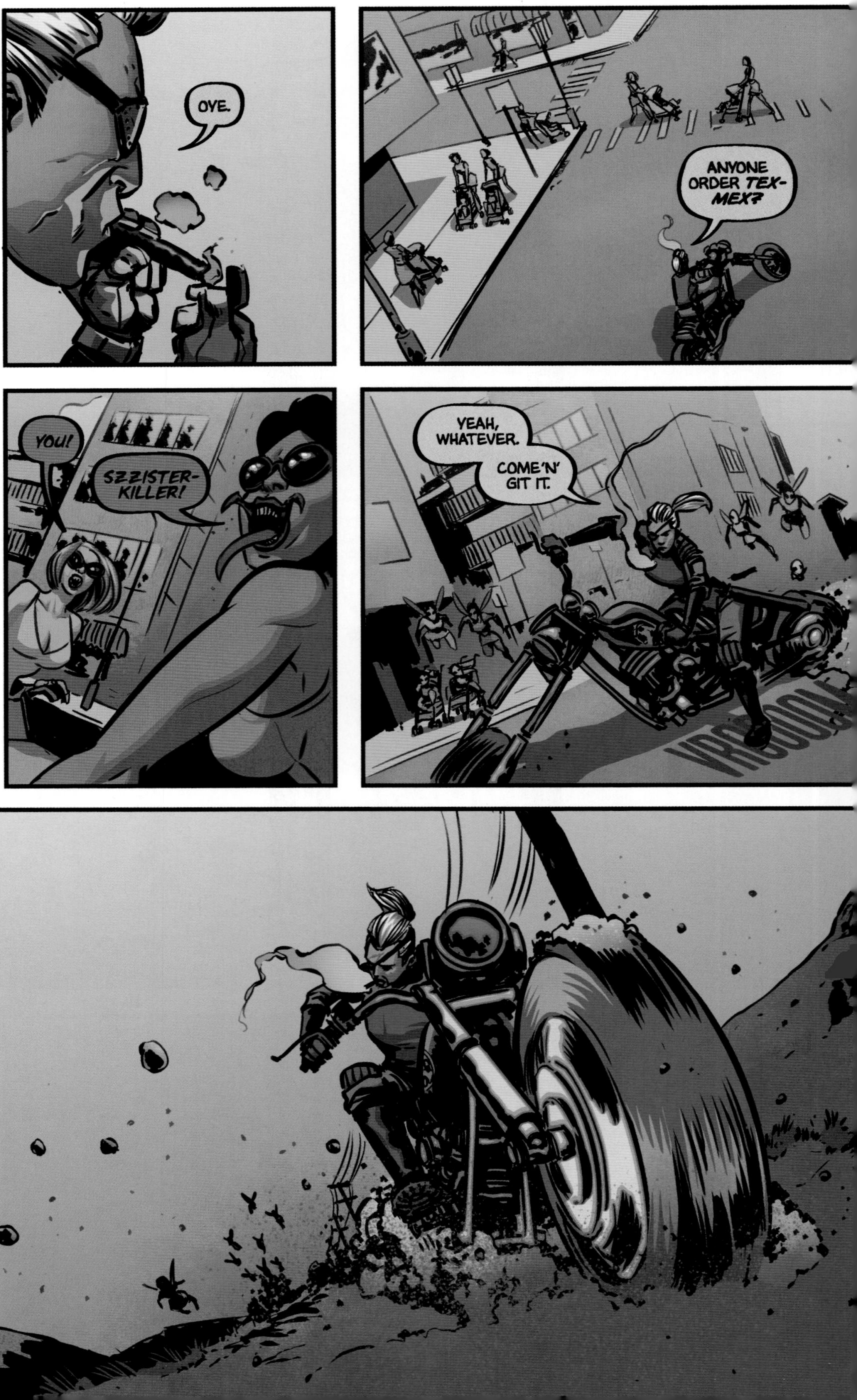
OYE.
ANYONE ORDER TEX-MEX?
YOU!
SZZISTER-KILLER!
YEAH, WHATEVER.
COME'N' GIT IT.

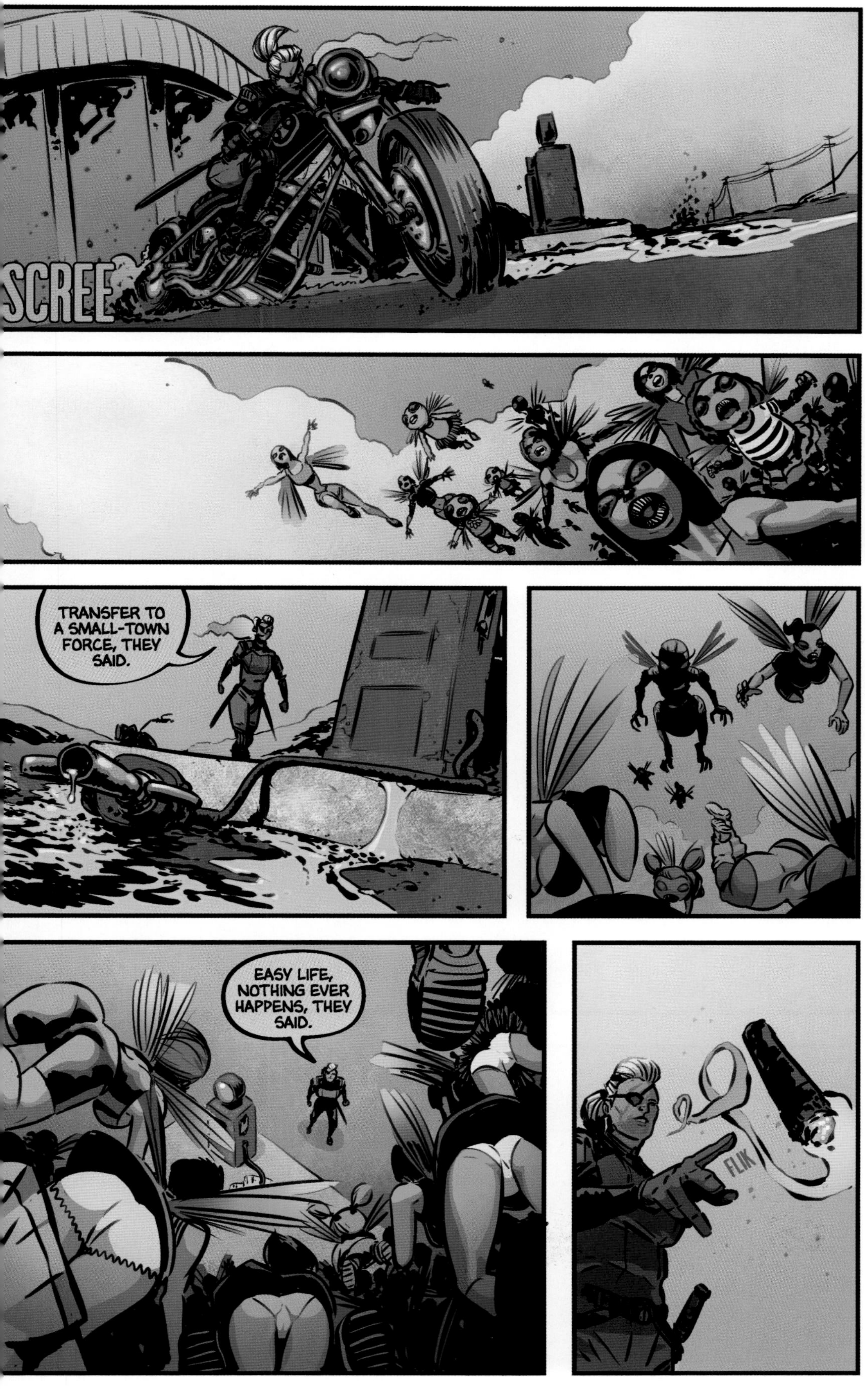
SCREE
TRANSFER TO A SMALL-TOWN FORCE, THEY SAID.
EASY LIFE, NOTHING EVER HAPPENS, THEY SAID.
FLIK

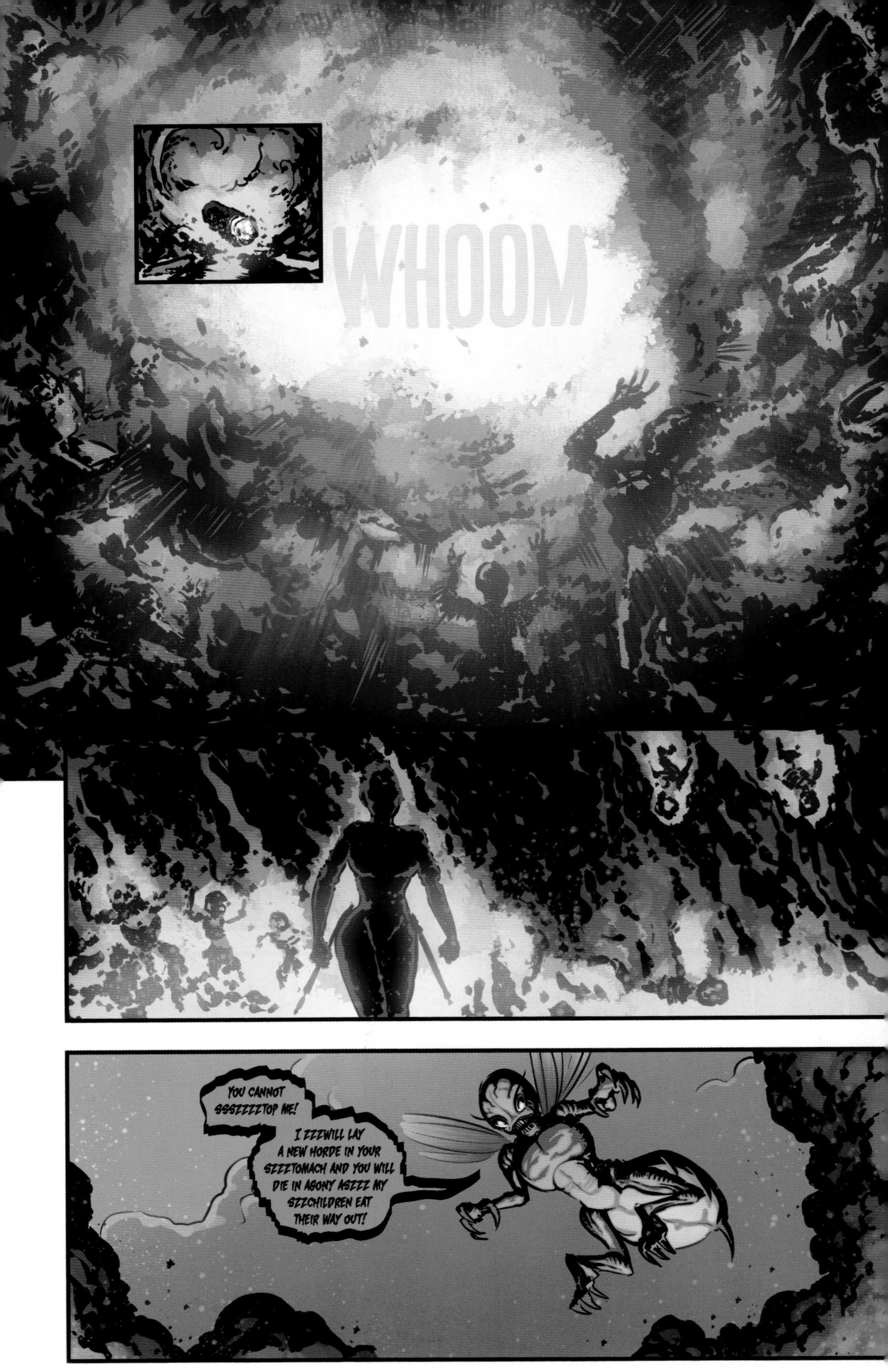
WHOOM
YOU CANNOT SSSZZZZTOP ME!
I ZZZWILL LAY A NEW HORDE IN YOUR SZZZTOMACH AND YOU WILL DIE IN AGONY ASZZZ MY SZZCHILDREN EAT THEIR WAY OUT!

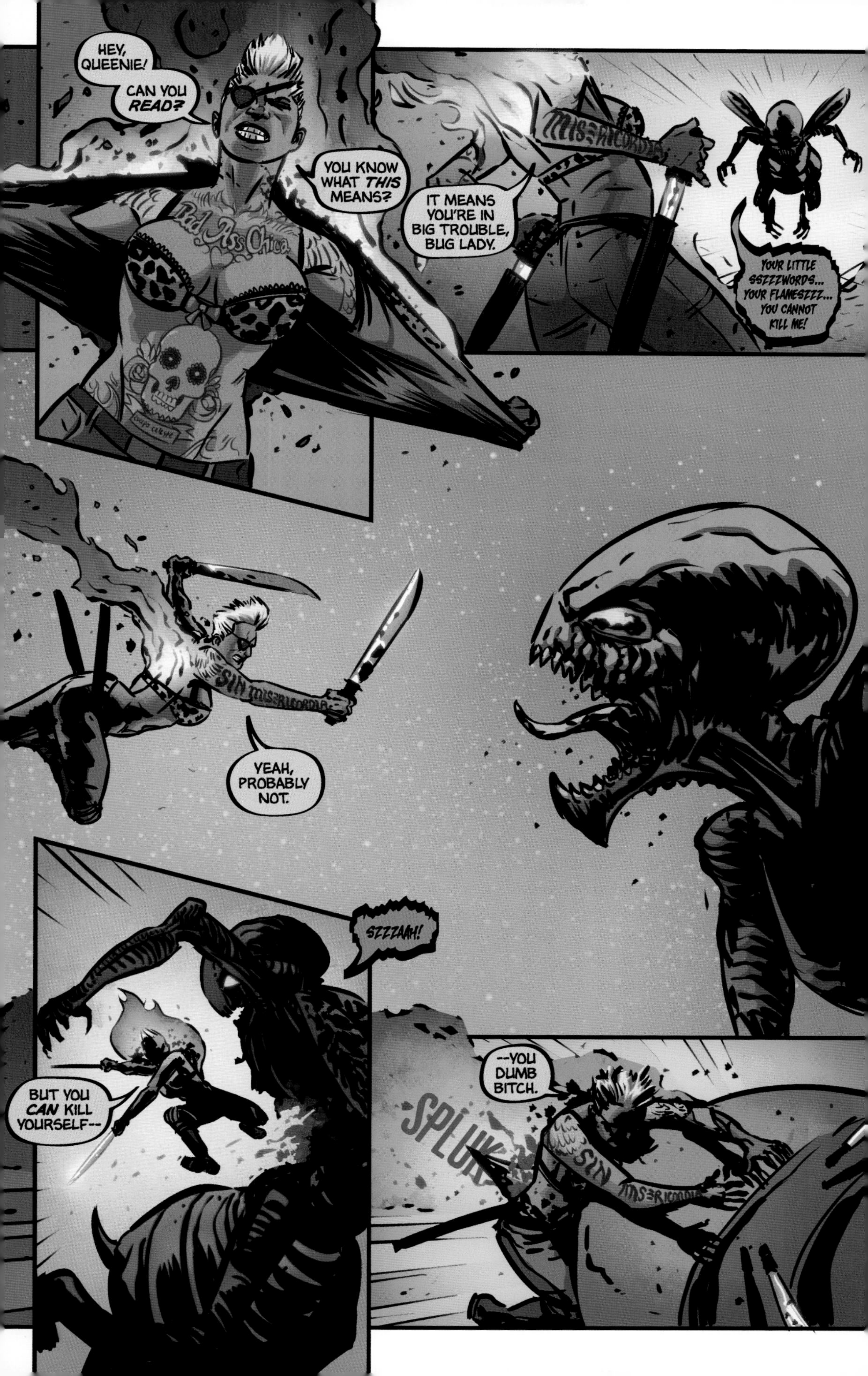
HEY, QUEENIE!
CAN YOU READ?
Bad Ass Chica
YOU KNOW WHAT THIS MEANS?
IT MEANS YOU'RE IN BIG TROUBLE, BUG LADY.
YOUR LITTLE SSZZZWORDS... YOUR FLAMESZZZ... YOU CANNOT KILL ME!
SIN
YEAH, PROBABLY NOT.
SZZZAAH!
BUT YOU CAN KILL YOURSELF--
--YOU DUMB BITCH.
SPLUK

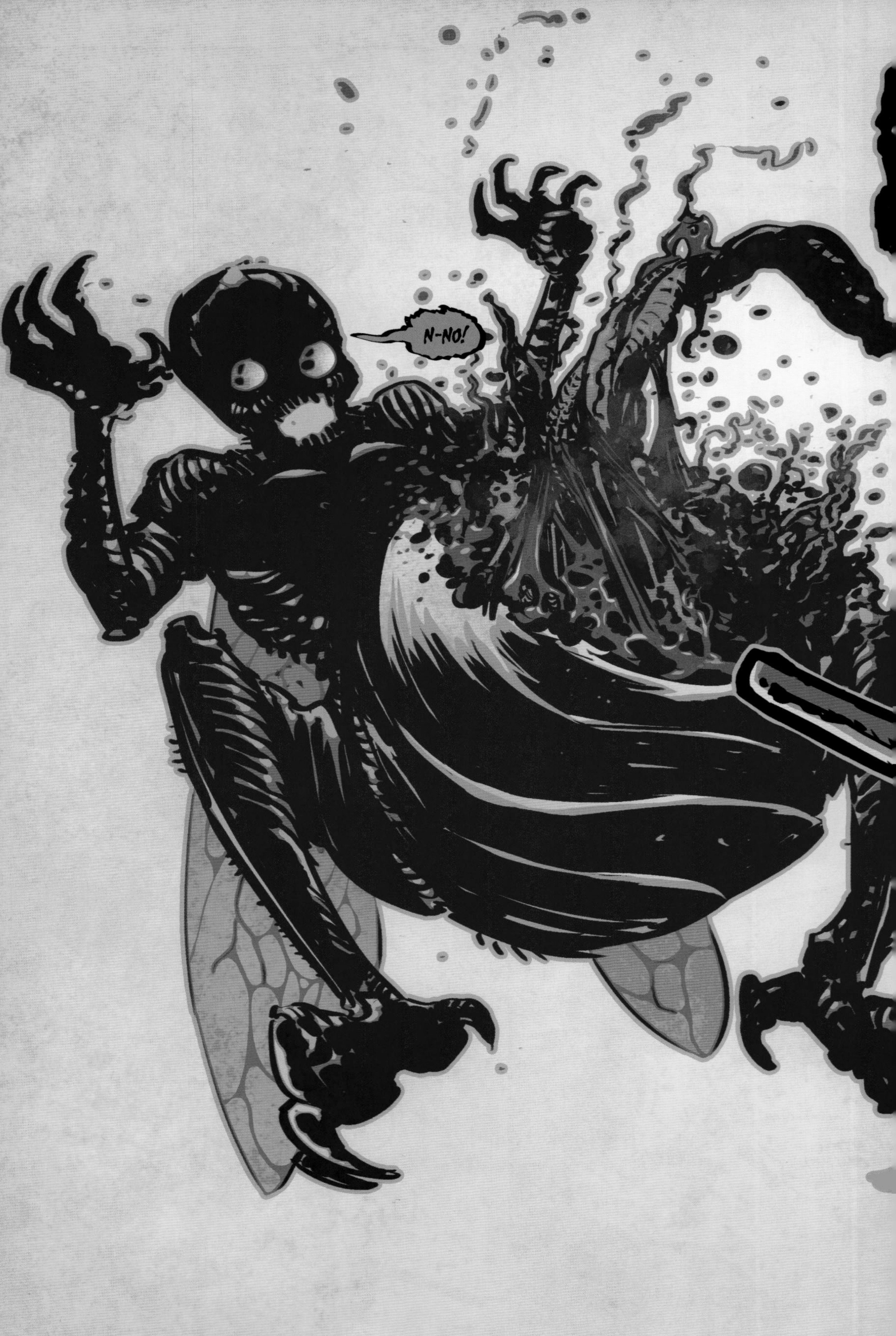
N-NO!

GRIND HOUSE
DOORS OPEN AT MIDNIGHT
DOUBLE FEATURE

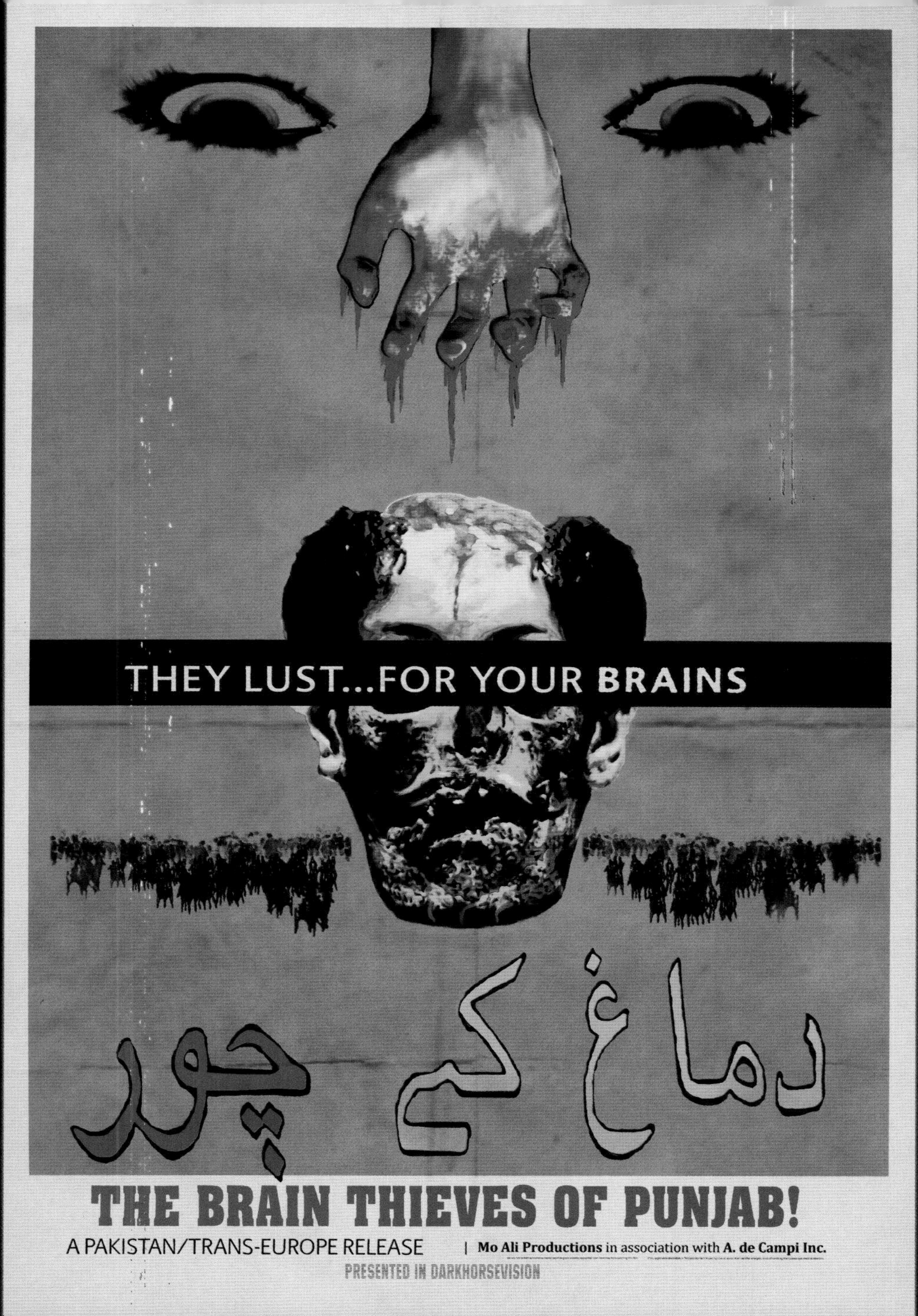
THEY LUST...FOR YOUR BRAINS
دماغ کے چور
THE BRAIN THIEVES OF PUNJAB!
A PAKISTAN/TRANS-EUROPE RELEASE | Mo Ali Productions in association with A. de Campi Inc.
PRESENTED IN DARKHORSEVISION

COMING SOON

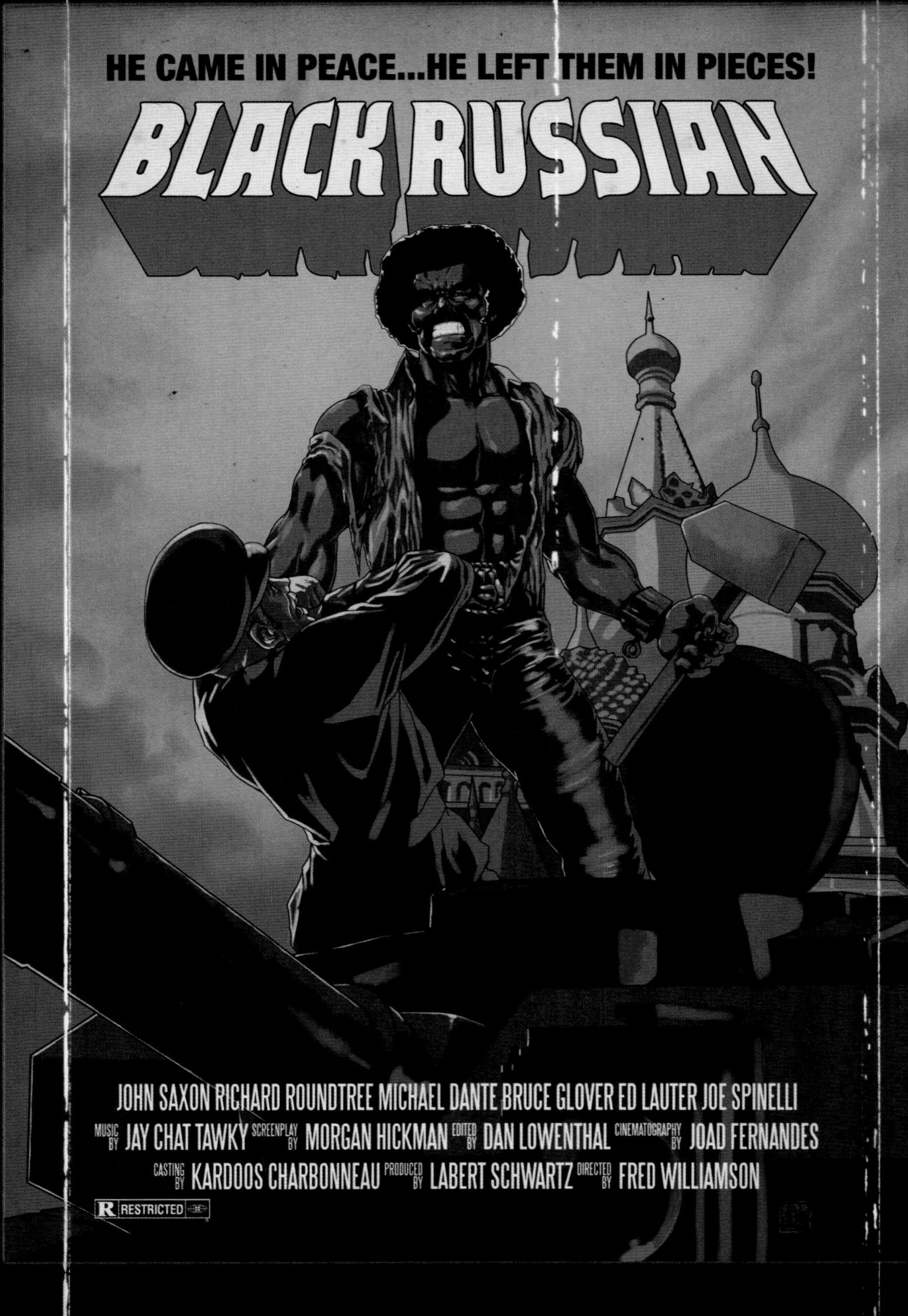
HE CAME IN PEACE...HE LEFT THEM IN PIECES!
BLACK RUSSIAN
JOHN SAXON RICHARD ROUNDTREE MICHAEL DANTE BRUCE GLOVER ED LAUTER JOE SPINELLI
MUSIC BY JAY CHAT TAWKY SCREENPLAY BY MORGAN HICKMAN EDITED BY DAN LOWENTHAL CINEMATOGRAPHY BY JOAD FERNANDES
CASTING BY KARDOOS CHARBONNEAU PRODUCED BY LABERT SCHWARTZ DIRECTED BY FRED WILLIAMSON
R RESTRICTED

ERIC KIM

FROM THE CREATOR OF **SMOKE & ASHES**

HOT GIRLS DOING HARD TIME IN OUTER SPACE!

PRISON SHIP ANTARES

DARK HORSE COMICS PRESENTS AN ALEX DE CAMPI PRODUCTION "PRISON SHIP ANTARES"

THE OX   EASY ANNIE   SPANISH FLY   COOKIE   TANESHA   SOLITARY   THE "ABC" GUARDS and WARDEN KALINKA

FILM EDITOR BRENDAN WRIGHT A.C.E.   ASSISTANT EDITOR IAN TUCKER   PRODUCTION DESIGNER JIMMY PRESLER   CGI ARTIST RYAN JORGENSEN

PRODUCED BY MIKE RICHARDSON   SCREENPLAY BY ALEX DE CAMPI   DIRECTED BY SIMON FRASER

12·04·13

PRISON SHIP ANTARES ™

SCRIPT AND LETTERS
ALEX DE CAMPI

ART AND TITLE PAGE
SIMON FRASER

COLORS
SIMON FRASER
WITH VICTORIA LAU
AND GARY CALDWELL

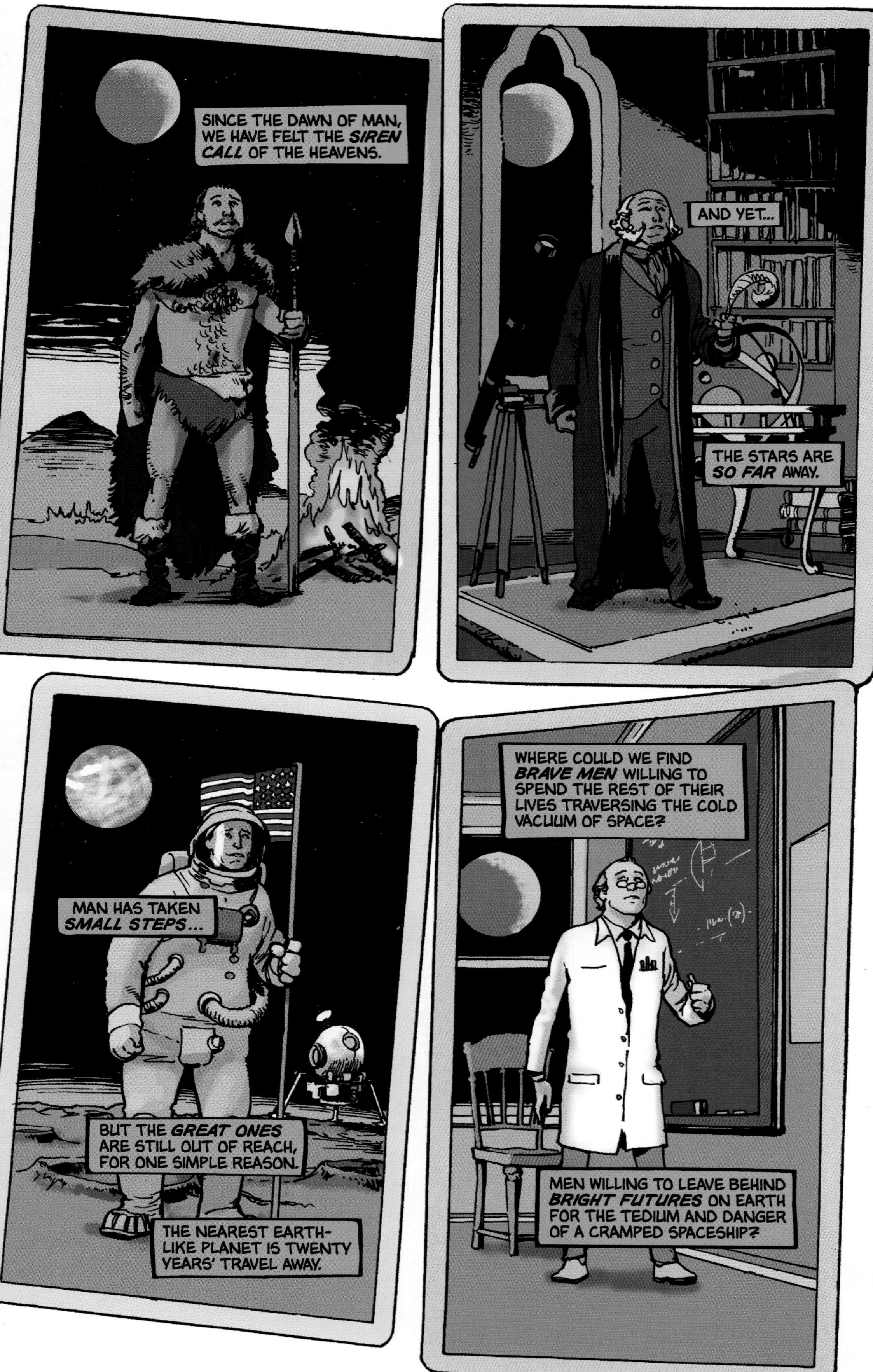
SINCE THE DAWN OF MAN, WE HAVE FELT THE SIREN CALL OF THE HEAVENS.
AND YET...
THE STARS ARE SO FAR AWAY.
MAN HAS TAKEN SMALL STEPS...
BUT THE GREAT ONES ARE STILL OUT OF REACH, FOR ONE SIMPLE REASON.
THE NEAREST EARTH-LIKE PLANET IS TWENTY YEARS' TRAVEL AWAY.
WHERE COULD WE FIND BRAVE MEN WILLING TO SPEND THE REST OF THEIR LIVES TRAVERSING THE COLD VACUUM OF SPACE?
MEN WILLING TO LEAVE BEHIND BRIGHT FUTURES ON EARTH FOR THE TEDIUM AND DANGER OF A CRAMPED SPACESHIP?

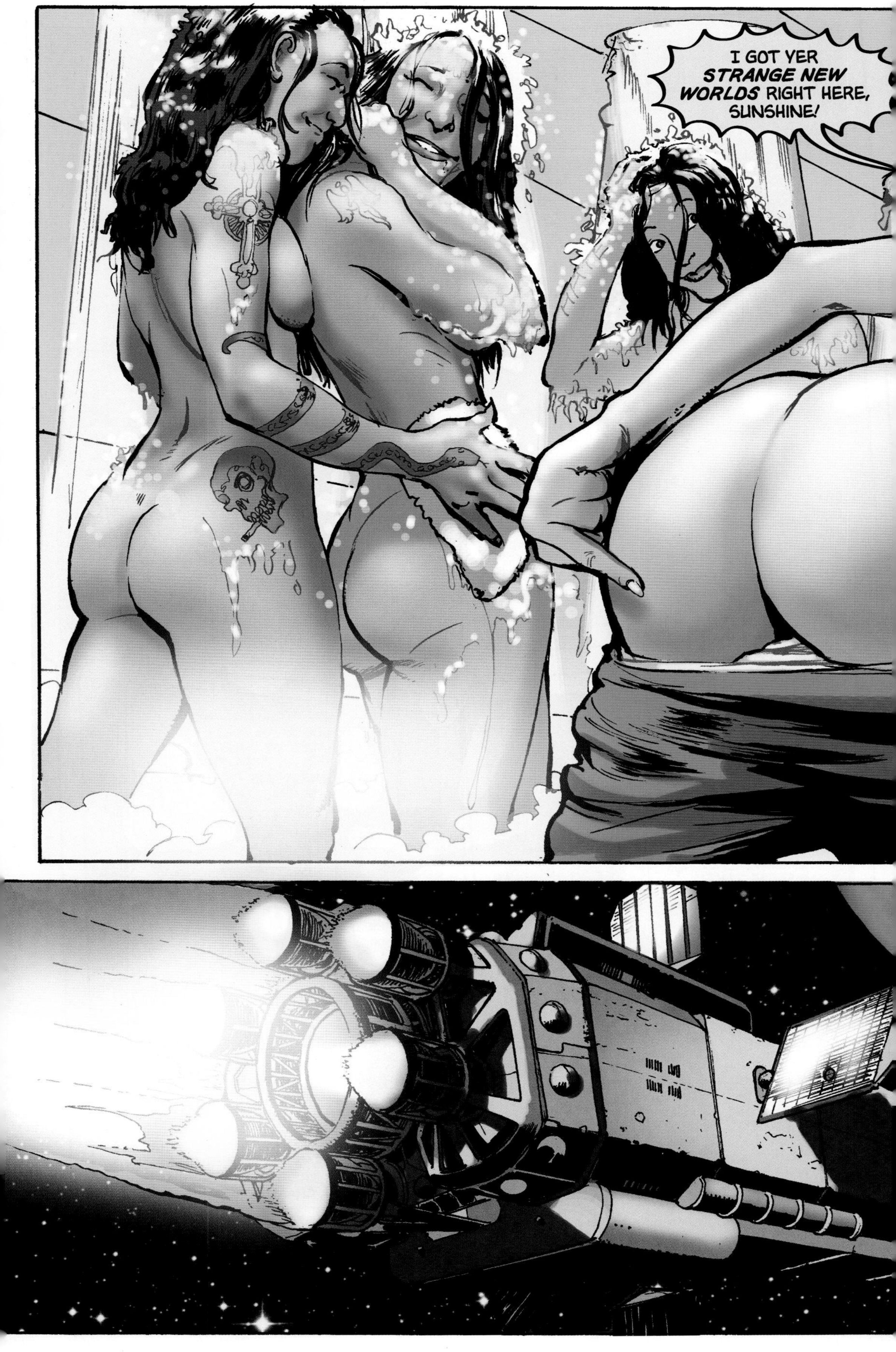
I GOT YER STRANGE NEW WORLDS RIGHT HERE, SUNSHINE!

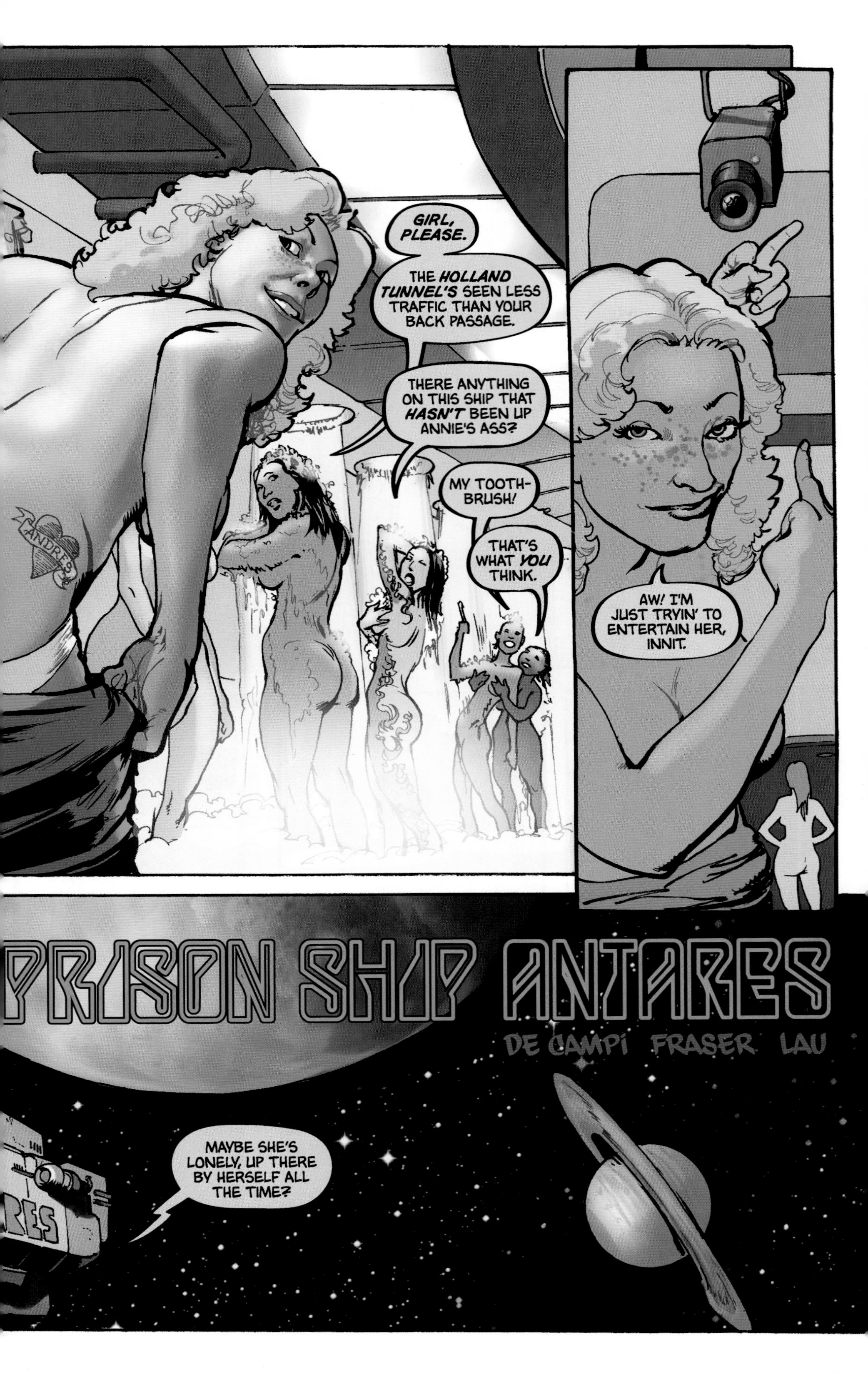
GIRL, PLEASE.
THE HOLLAND TUNNEL'S SEEN LESS TRAFFIC THAN YOUR BACK PASSAGE.
THERE ANYTHING ON THIS SHIP THAT HASN'T BEEN UP ANNIE'S ASS?
MY TOOTH-BRUSH!
THAT'S WHAT YOU THINK.
ANDRES
AW! I'M JUST TRYIN' TO ENTERTAIN HER, INNIT.
PRISON SHIP ANTARES
DE CAMPI FRASER LAU
MAYBE SHE'S LONELY, UP THERE BY HERSELF ALL THE TIME?
RES

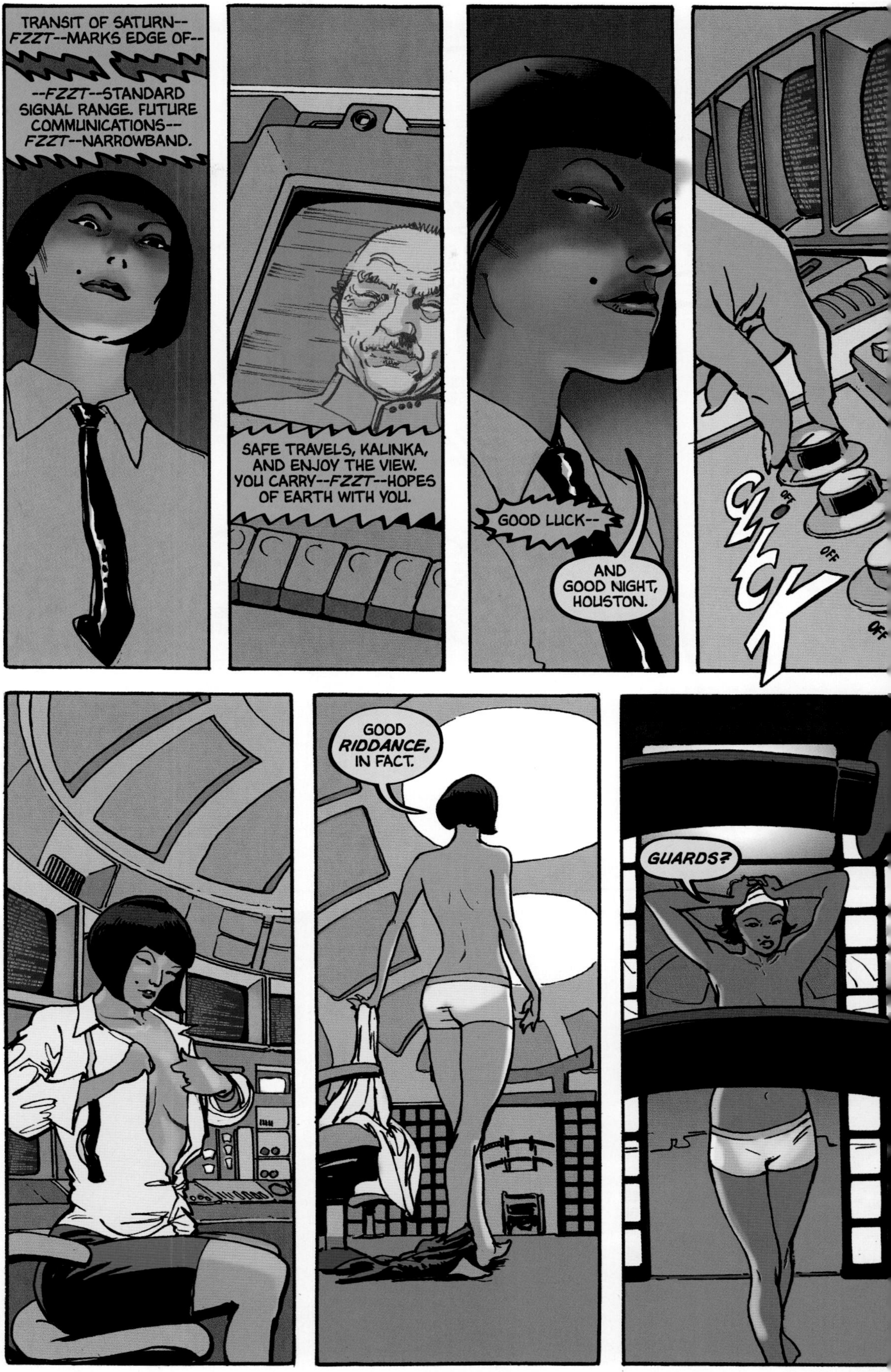
TRANSIT OF SATURN-- FZZT--MARKS EDGE OF--
--FZZT--STANDARD SIGNAL RANGE. FUTURE COMMUNICATIONS-- FZZT--NARROWBAND.
SAFE TRAVELS, KALINKA, AND ENJOY THE VIEW. YOU CARRY--FZZT--HOPES OF EARTH WITH YOU.
GOOD LUCK--
AND GOOD NIGHT, HOUSTON.
CLICK
OFF
OFF
OFF
GOOD RIDDANCE, IN FACT.
GUARDS?

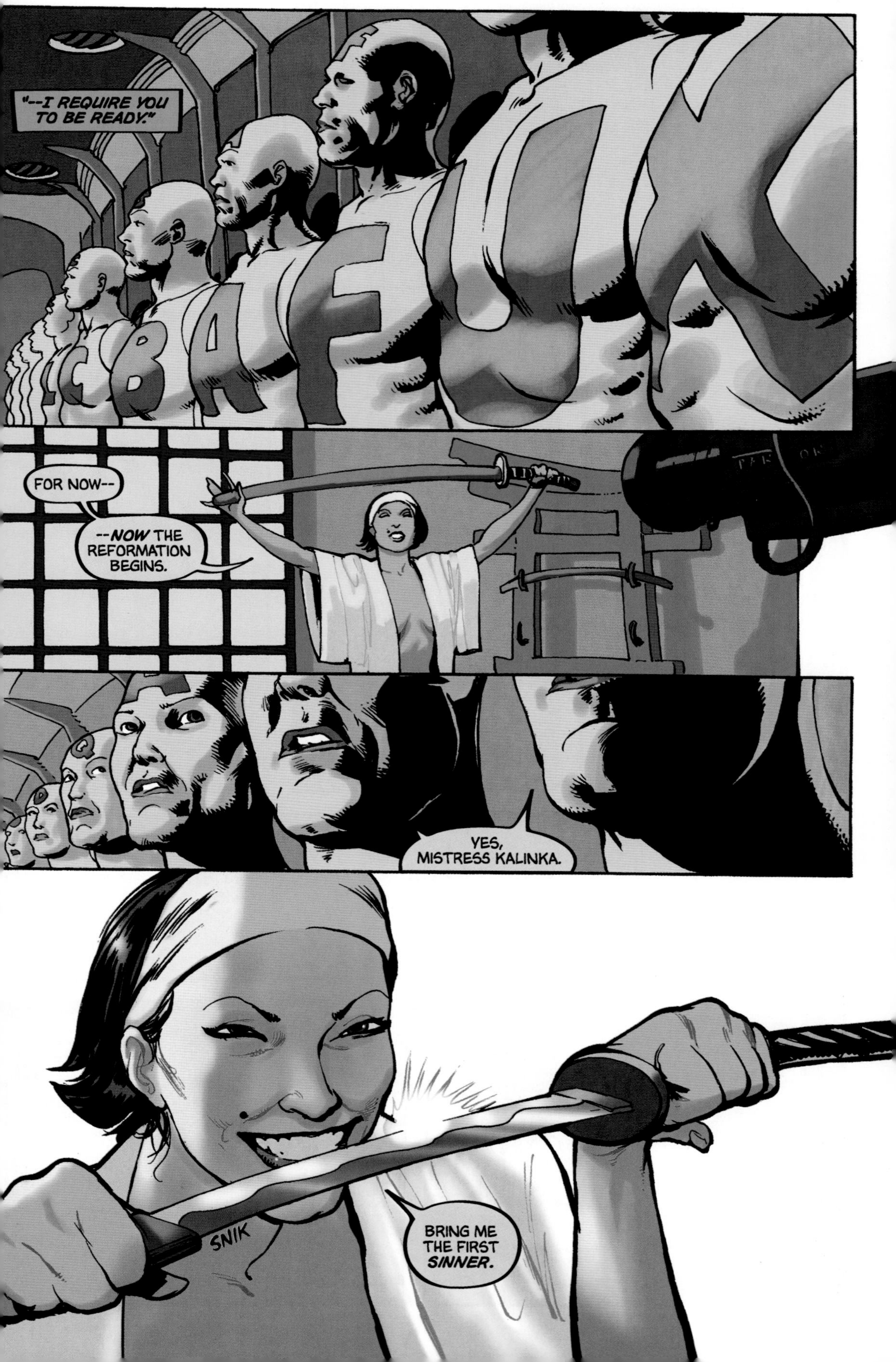
"--I REQUIRE YOU TO BE READY."
FOR NOW--
--*NOW* THE REFORMATION BEGINS.
YES, MISTRESS KALINKA.
SNIK
BRING ME THE FIRST *SINNER*.

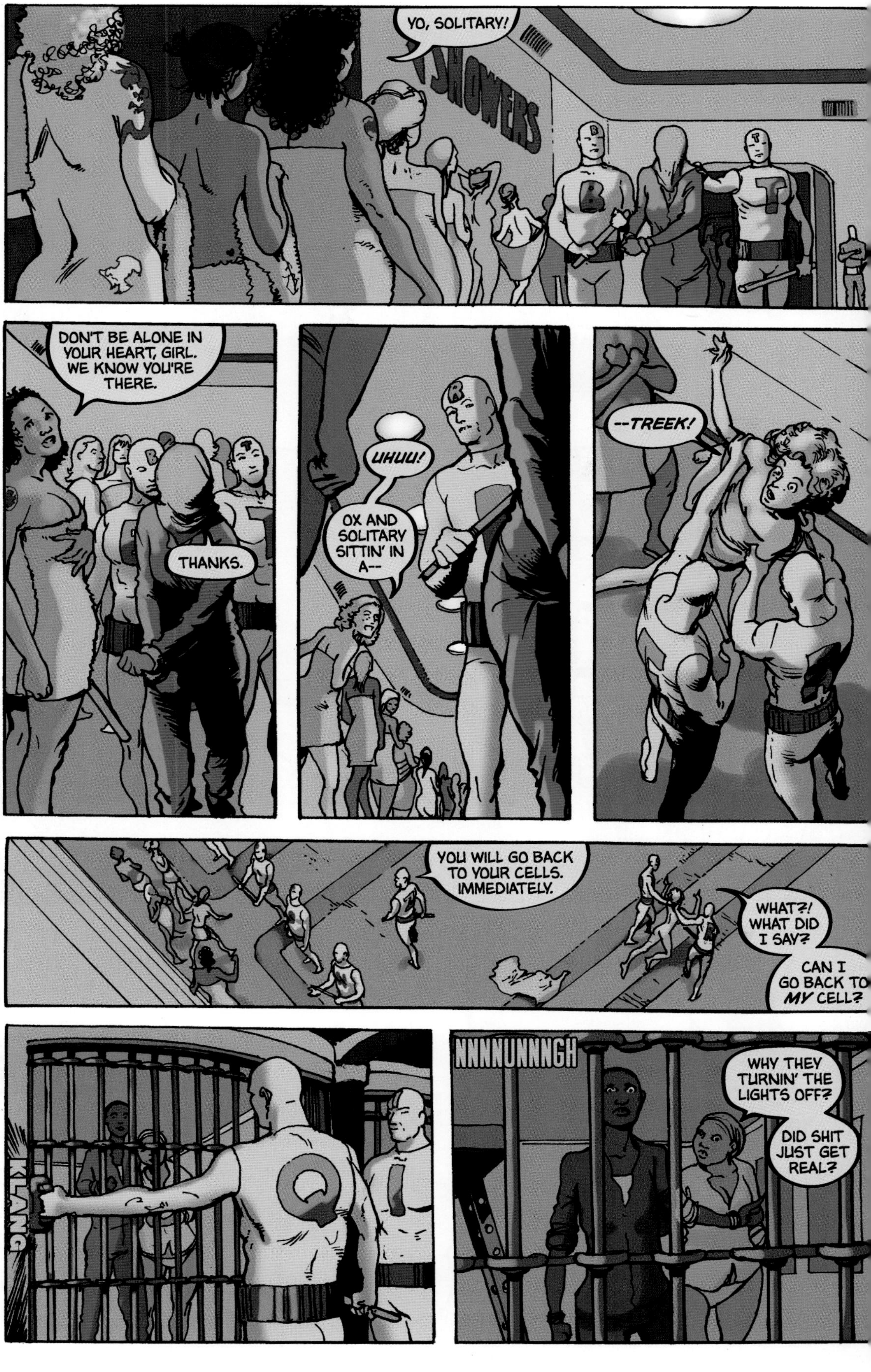
YO, SOLITARY!
SHOWERS
DON'T BE ALONE IN YOUR HEART, GIRL. WE KNOW YOU'RE THERE.
THANKS.
UHUU!
OX AND SOLITARY SITTIN' IN A--
--TREEK!
YOU WILL GO BACK TO YOUR CELLS. IMMEDIATELY.
WHAT?! WHAT DID I SAY?
CAN I GO BACK TO *MY* CELL?
KLANG
NNNNUNNNGH
WHY THEY TURNIN' THE LIGHTS OFF?
DID SHIT JUST GET REAL?

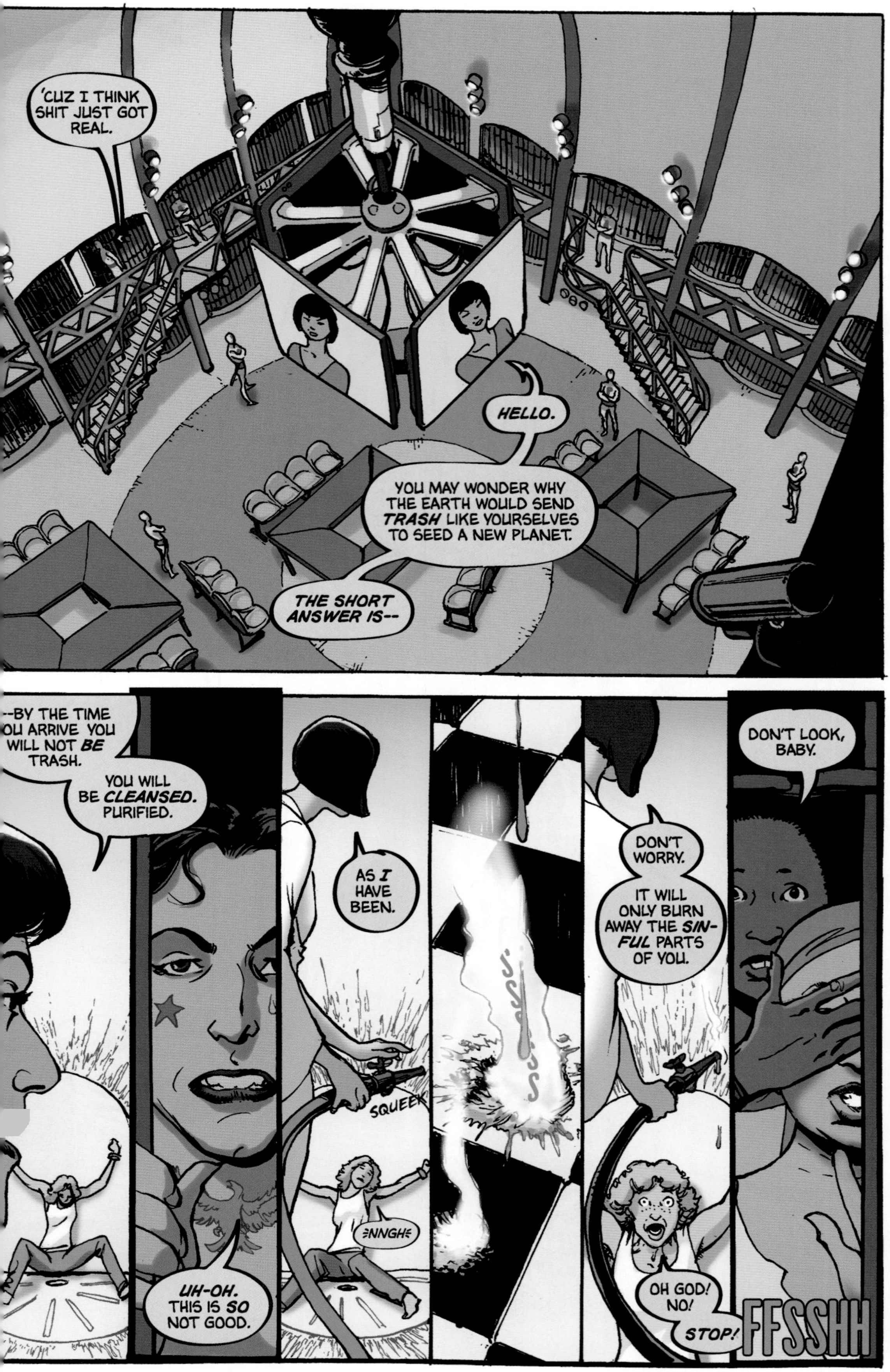
'CUZ I THINK SHIT JUST GOT REAL.
HELLO.
YOU MAY WONDER WHY THE EARTH WOULD SEND TRASH LIKE YOURSELVES TO SEED A NEW PLANET.
THE SHORT ANSWER IS--
--BY THE TIME YOU ARRIVE YOU WILL NOT BE TRASH.
YOU WILL BE CLEANSED. PURIFIED.
UH-OH. THIS IS SO NOT GOOD.
AS I HAVE BEEN.
SQUEEK
NNGH
DON'T WORRY.
IT WILL ONLY BURN AWAY THE SINFUL PARTS OF YOU.
OH GOD! NO!
STOP!
DON'T LOOK, BABY.
FFSSHH

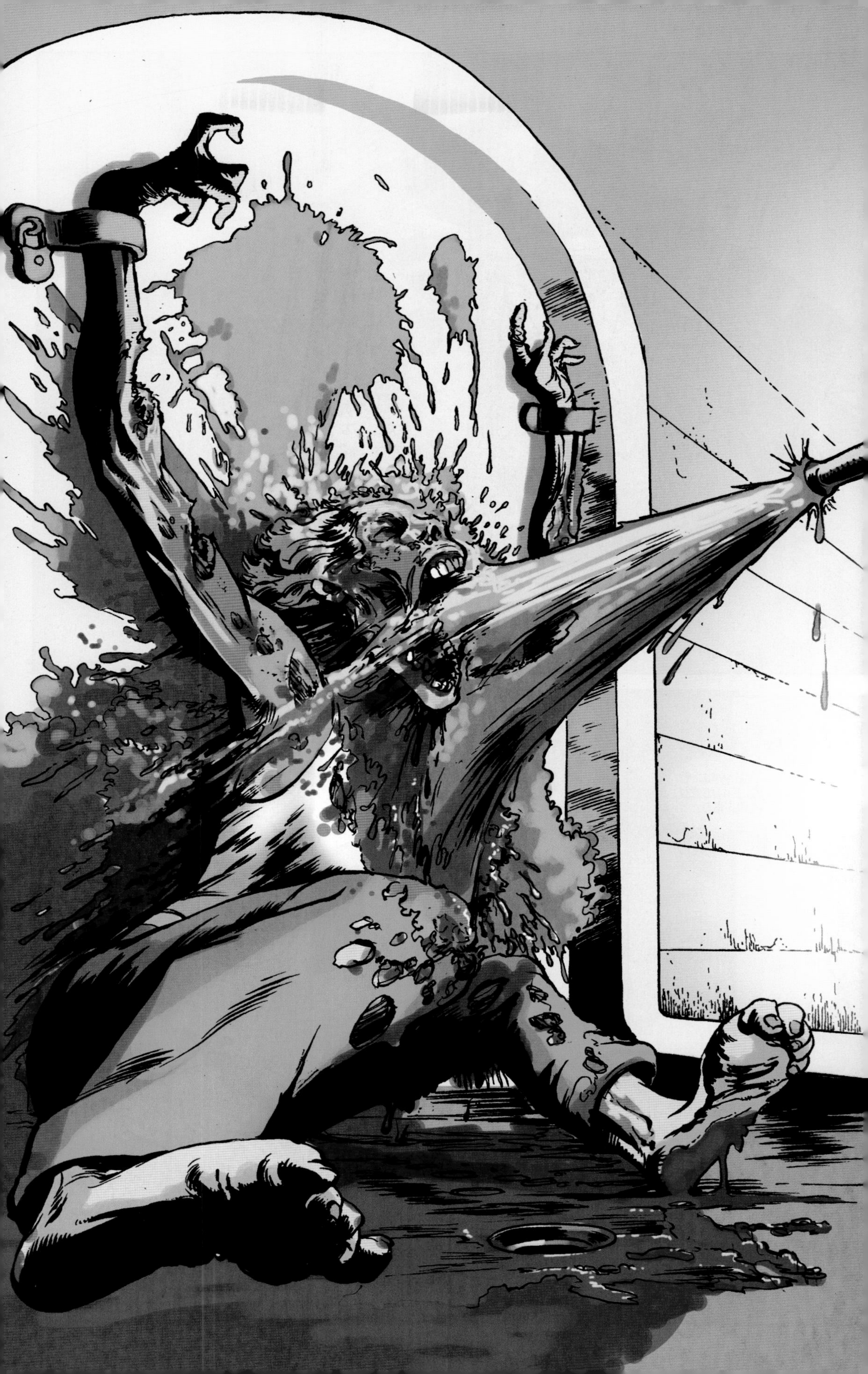

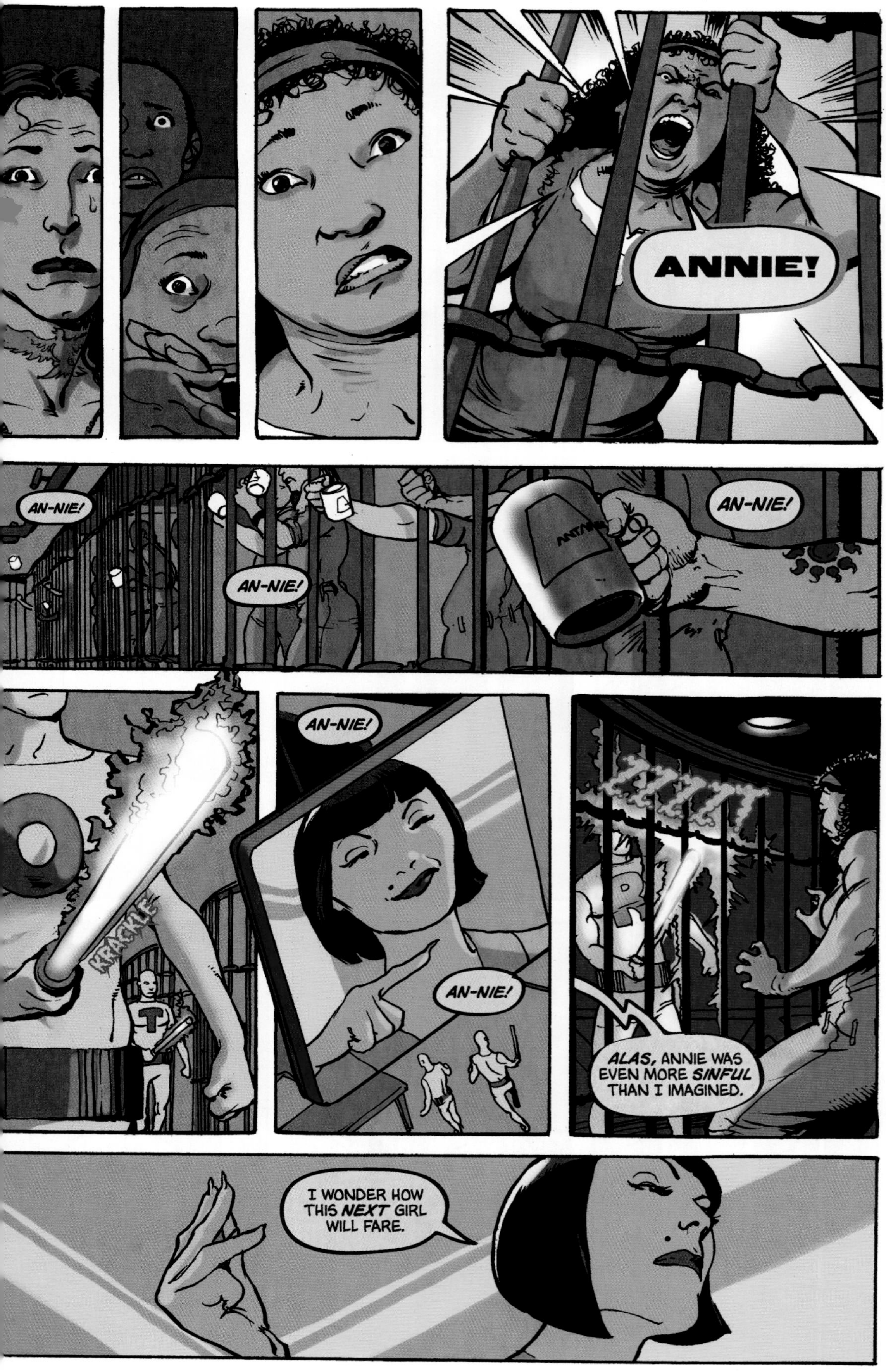
ANNIE!
AN-NIE!
AN-NIE!
AN-NIE!
KRACKLE
AN-NIE!
AN-NIE!
ALAS, ANNIE WAS EVEN MORE SINFUL THAN I IMAGINED.
I WONDER HOW THIS NEXT GIRL WILL FARE.

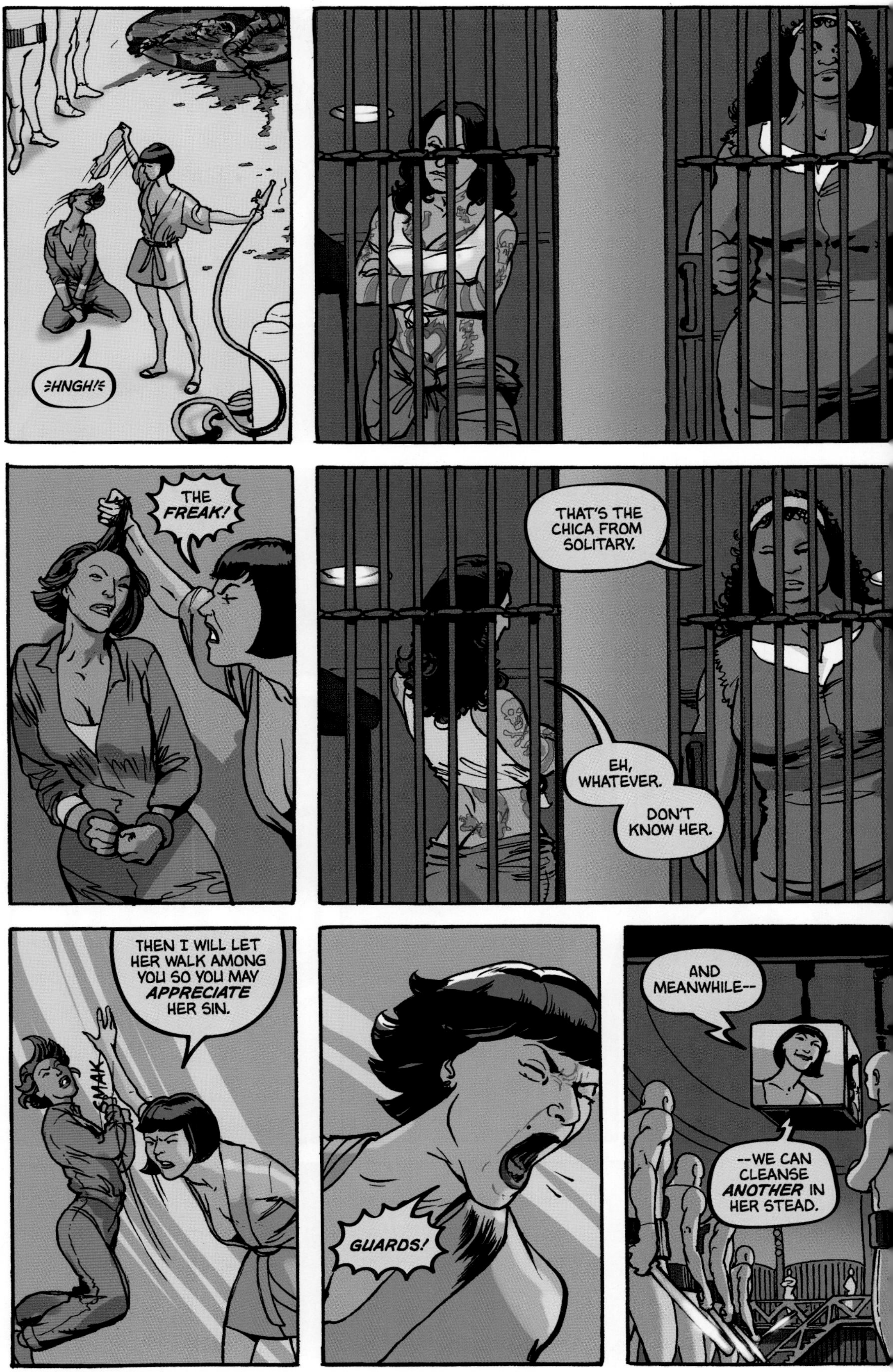

HNGH!
THE FREAK!
THAT'S THE CHICA FROM SOLITARY.
EH, WHATEVER.
DON'T KNOW HER.
THEN I WILL LET HER WALK AMONG YOU SO YOU MAY APPRECIATE HER SIN.
SMAK
GUARDS!
AND MEANWHILE--
--WE CAN CLEANSE ANOTHER IN HER STEAD.

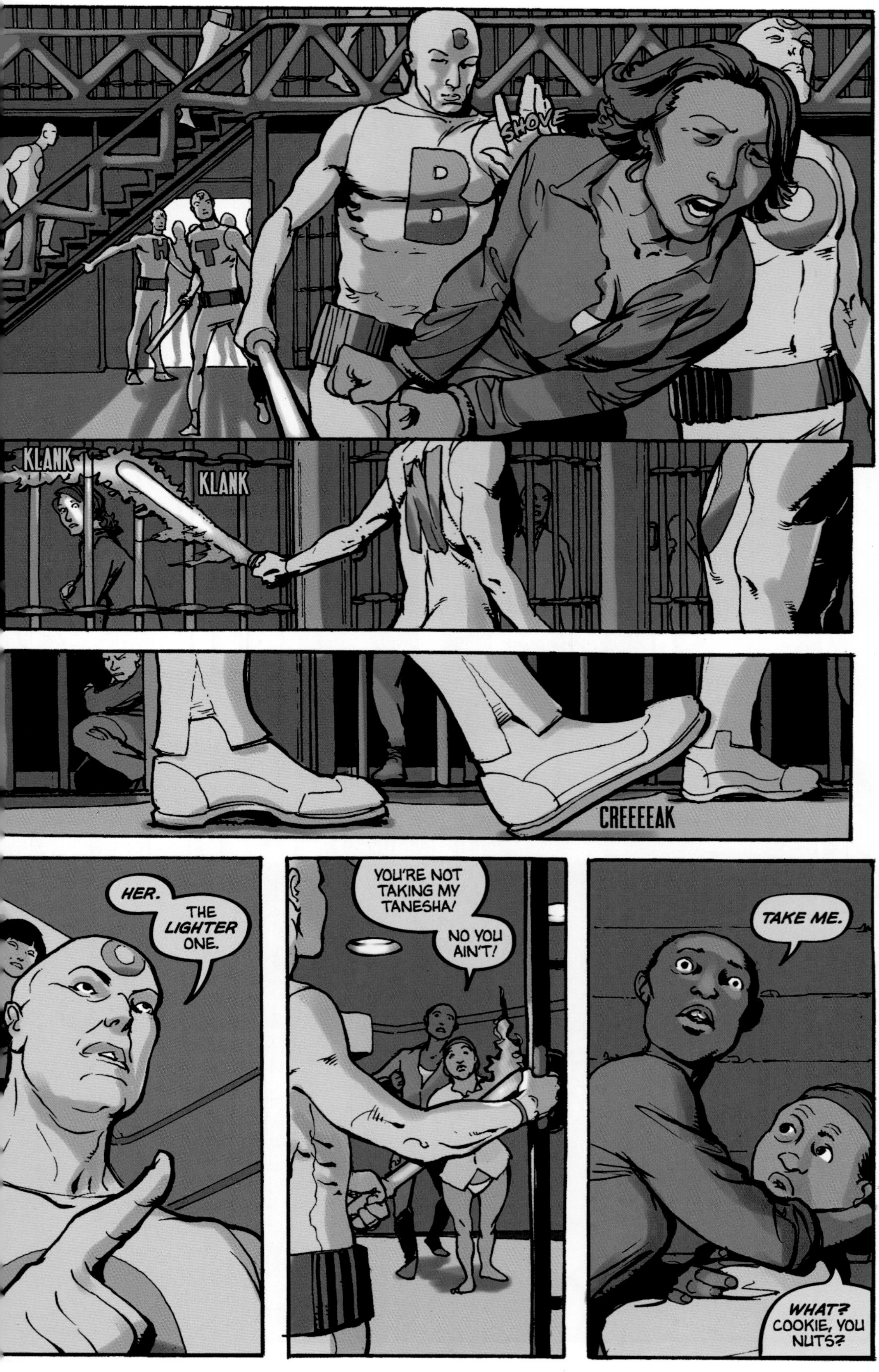
SHOVE
KLANK
KLANK
CREEEEAK
HER.
THE LIGHTER ONE.
YOU'RE NOT TAKING MY TANESHA!
NO YOU AIN'T!
TAKE ME.
WHAT? COOKIE, YOU NUTS?

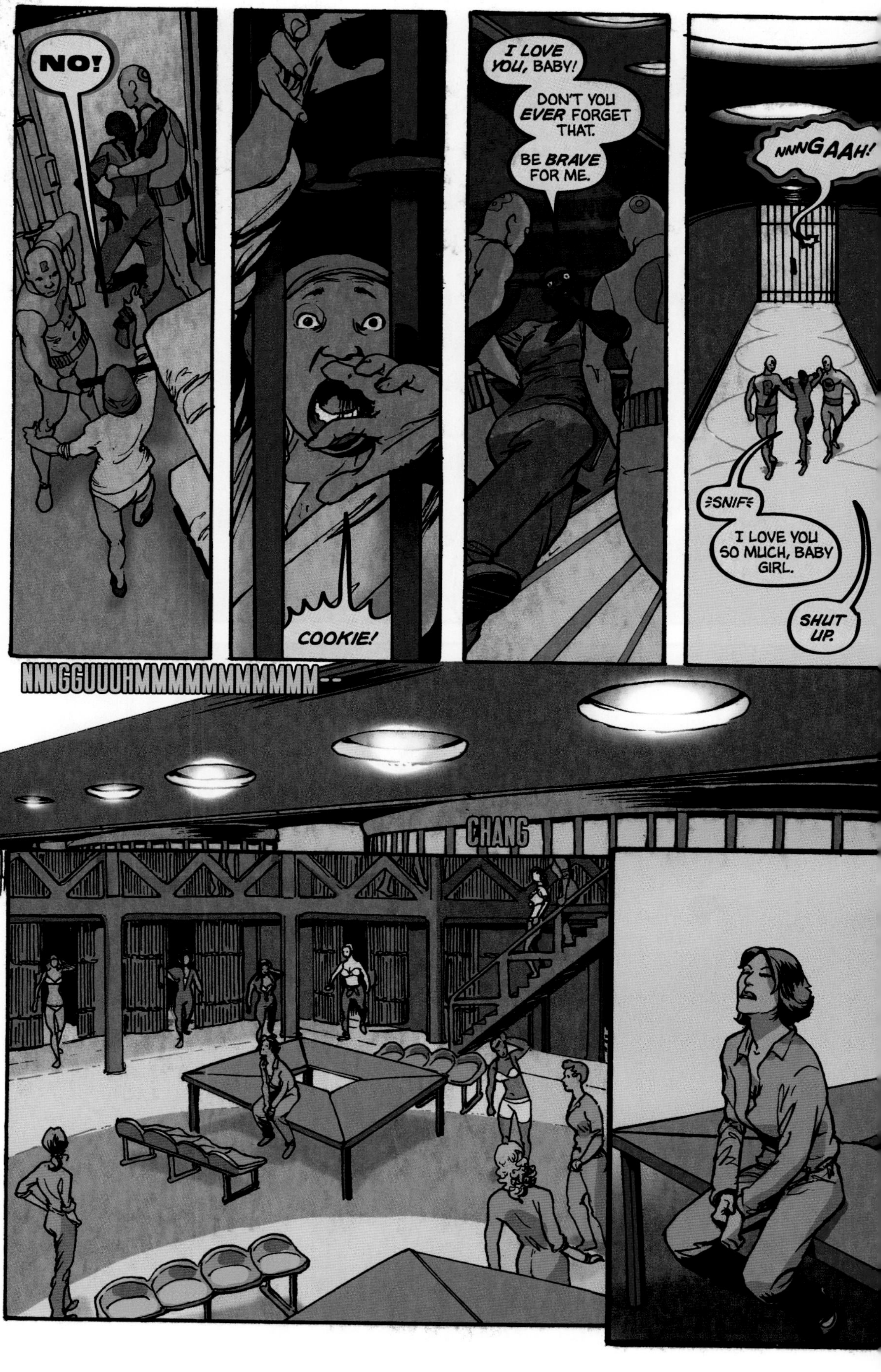
NO!
COOKIE!
I LOVE YOU, BABY!
DON'T YOU EVER FORGET THAT.
BE BRAVE FOR ME.
NNNGAAH!
SNIF
I LOVE YOU SO MUCH, BABY GIRL.
SHUT UP.
NNNGGUUUHMMMMMMMMMMMM
CHANG

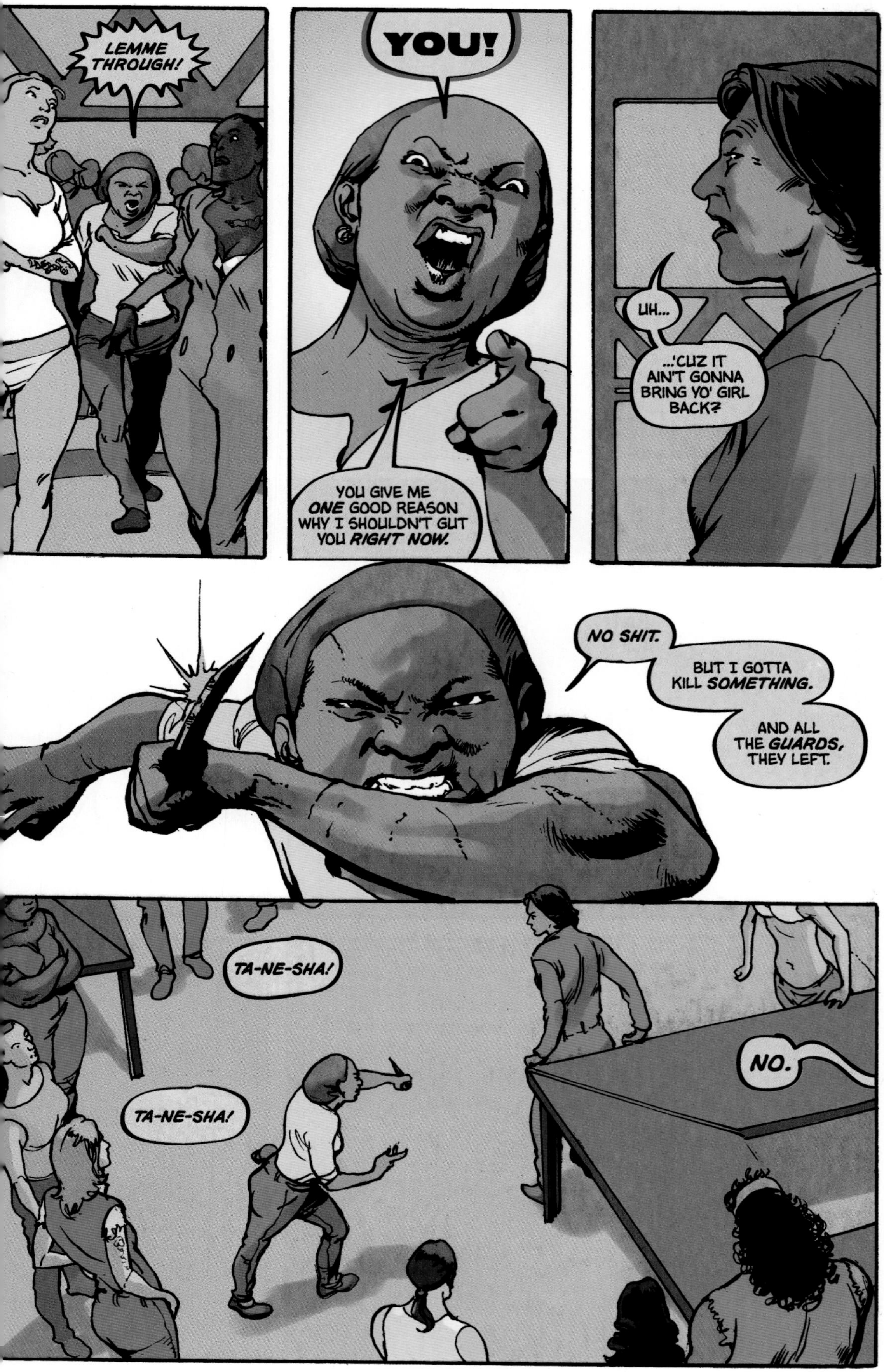
LEMME THROUGH!
YOU!
YOU GIVE ME ONE GOOD REASON WHY I SHOULDN'T GUT YOU RIGHT NOW.
UH...
...'CUZ IT AIN'T GONNA BRING YO' GIRL BACK?
NO SHIT.
BUT I GOTTA KILL SOMETHING.
AND ALL THE GUARDS, THEY LEFT.
TA-NE-SHA!
TA-NE-SHA!
NO.

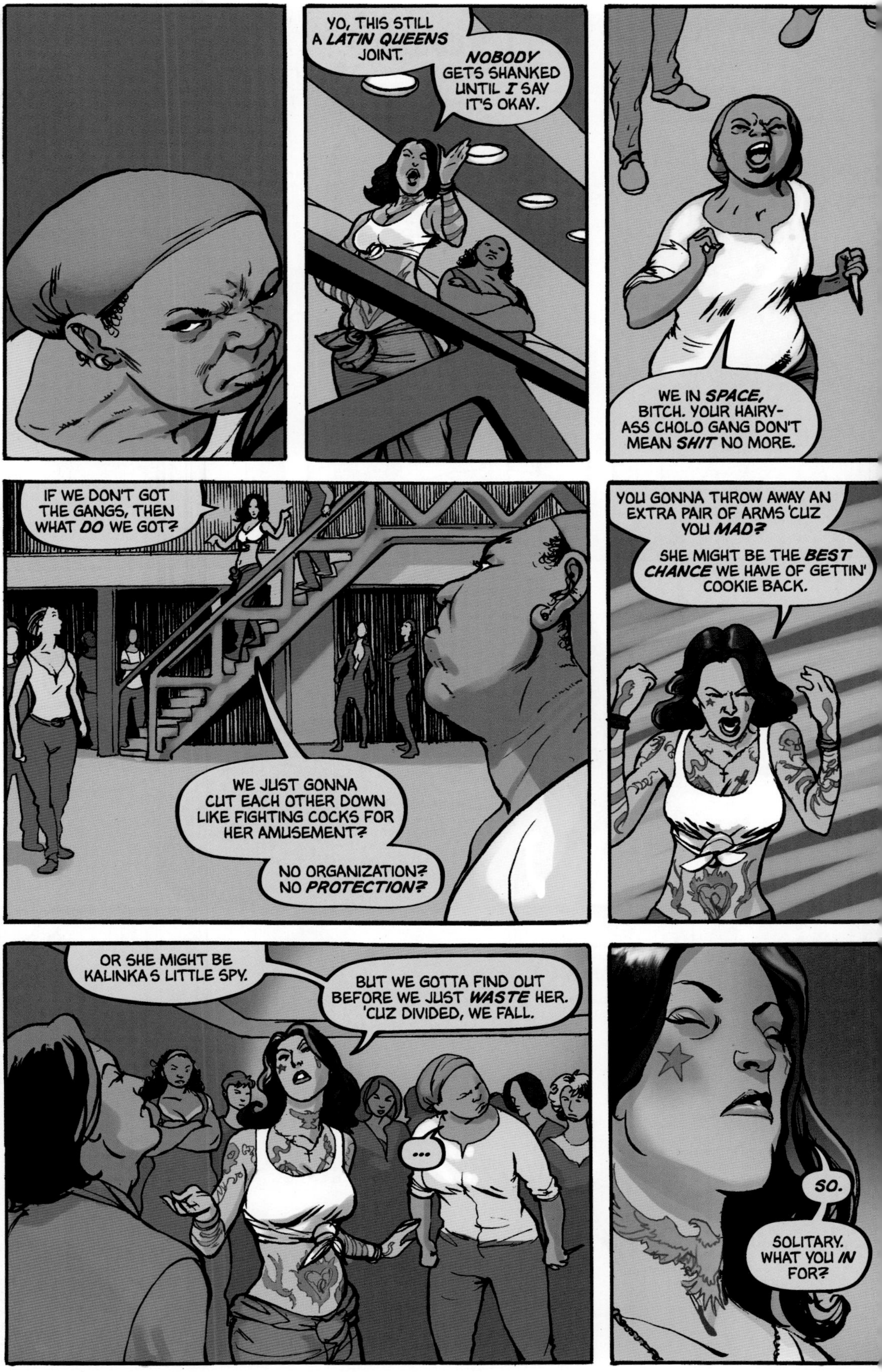

YO, THIS STILL A LATIN QUEENS JOINT.
NOBODY GETS SHANKED UNTIL I SAY IT'S OKAY.
WE IN SPACE, BITCH. YOUR HAIRY-ASS CHOLO GANG DON'T MEAN SHIT NO MORE.
IF WE DON'T GOT THE GANGS, THEN WHAT DO WE GOT?
WE JUST GONNA CUT EACH OTHER DOWN LIKE FIGHTING COCKS FOR HER AMUSEMENT?
NO ORGANIZATION? NO PROTECTION?
YOU GONNA THROW AWAY AN EXTRA PAIR OF ARMS 'CUZ YOU MAD?
SHE MIGHT BE THE BEST CHANCE WE HAVE OF GETTIN' COOKIE BACK.
OR SHE MIGHT BE KALINKA'S LITTLE SPY.
BUT WE GOTTA FIND OUT BEFORE WE JUST WASTE HER. 'CUZ DIVIDED, WE FALL.
...
SO.
SOLITARY. WHAT YOU IN FOR?

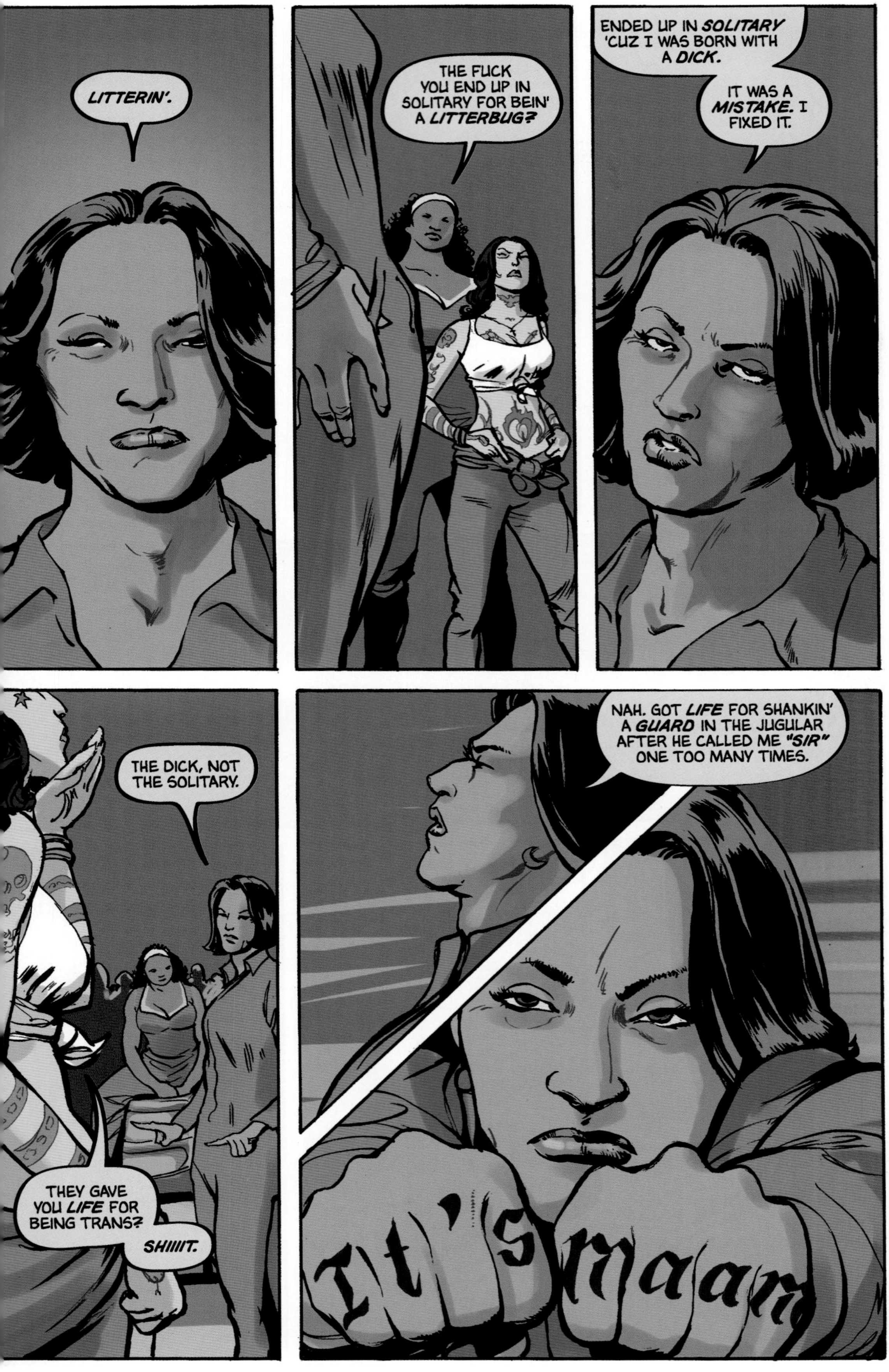
LITTERIN'.
THE FUCK YOU END UP IN SOLITARY FOR BEIN' A LITTERBUG?
ENDED UP IN SOLITARY 'CUZ I WAS BORN WITH A DICK.
IT WAS A MISTAKE. I FIXED IT.
THE DICK, NOT THE SOLITARY.
THEY GAVE YOU LIFE FOR BEING TRANS?
SHIIIIT.
NAH. GOT LIFE FOR SHANKIN' A GUARD IN THE JUGULAR AFTER HE CALLED ME "SIR" ONE TOO MANY TIMES.
It's maam

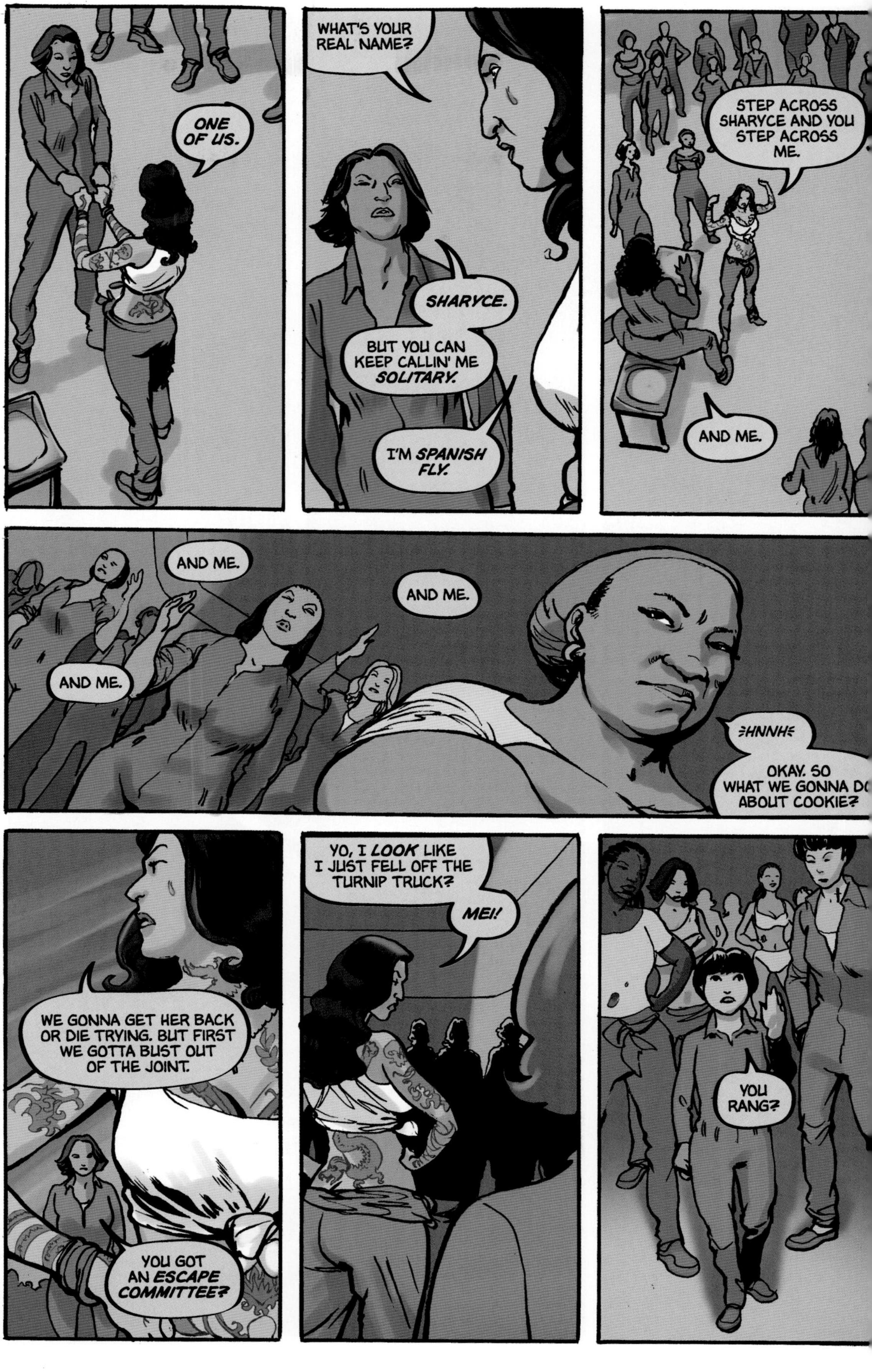
ONE OF US.
WHAT'S YOUR REAL NAME?
SHARYCE.
BUT YOU CAN KEEP CALLIN' ME SOLITARY.
I'M SPANISH FLY.
STEP ACROSS SHARYCE AND YOU STEP ACROSS ME.
AND ME.
AND ME.
AND ME.
AND ME.
HNNH
OKAY. SO WHAT WE GONNA DO ABOUT COOKIE?
WE GONNA GET HER BACK OR DIE TRYING. BUT FIRST WE GOTTA BUST OUT OF THE JOINT.
YOU GOT AN ESCAPE COMMITTEE?
YO, I LOOK LIKE I JUST FELL OFF THE TURNIP TRUCK?
MEI!
YOU RANG?

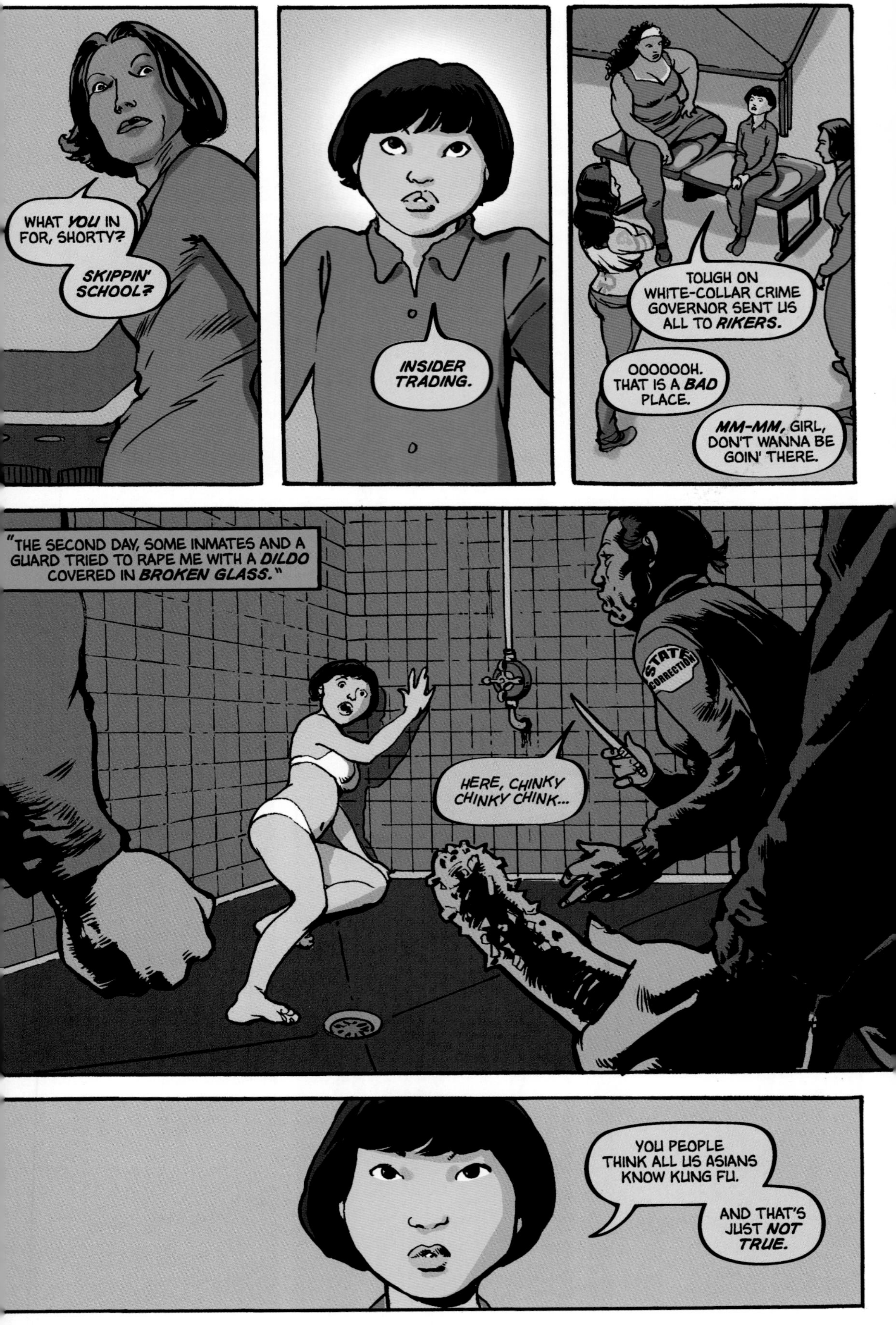
WHAT YOU IN FOR, SHORTY?
SKIPPIN' SCHOOL?
INSIDER TRADING.
TOUGH ON WHITE-COLLAR CRIME GOVERNOR SENT US ALL TO RIKERS.
OOOOOOH. THAT IS A BAD PLACE.
MM-MM, GIRL, DON'T WANNA BE GOIN' THERE.
"THE SECOND DAY, SOME INMATES AND A GUARD TRIED TO RAPE ME WITH A DILDO COVERED IN BROKEN GLASS."
STATE CORRECTION
HERE, CHINKY CHINKY CHINK...
YOU PEOPLE THINK ALL US ASIANS KNOW KUNG FU.
AND THAT'S JUST NOT TRUE.

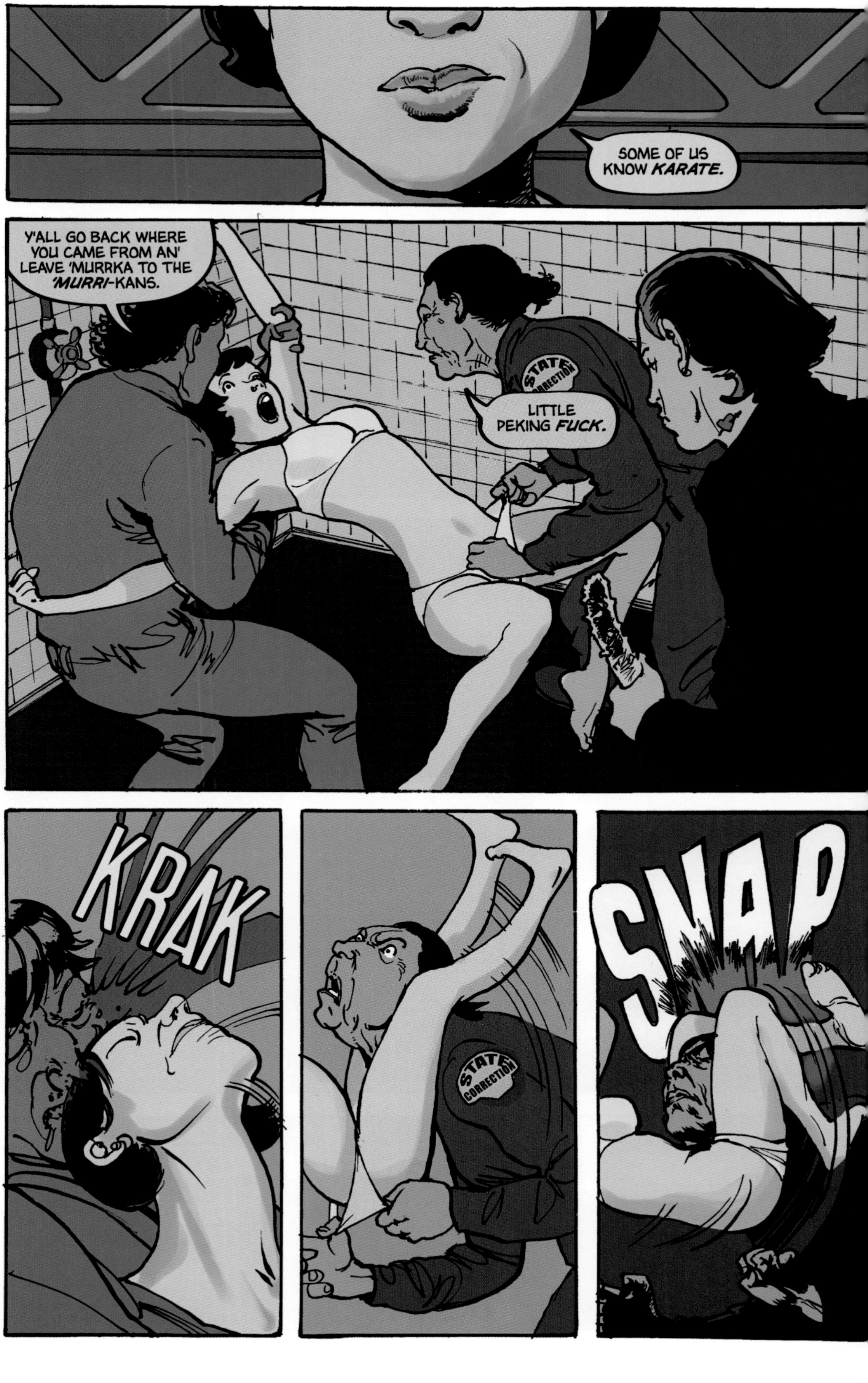
SOME OF US KNOW *KARATE.*
Y'ALL GO BACK WHERE YOU CAME FROM AN' LEAVE 'MURRKA TO THE *'MURRI*-KANS.
LITTLE PEKING *FUCK.*
STATE CORRECTION
KRAK
STATE CORRECTION
SNAP

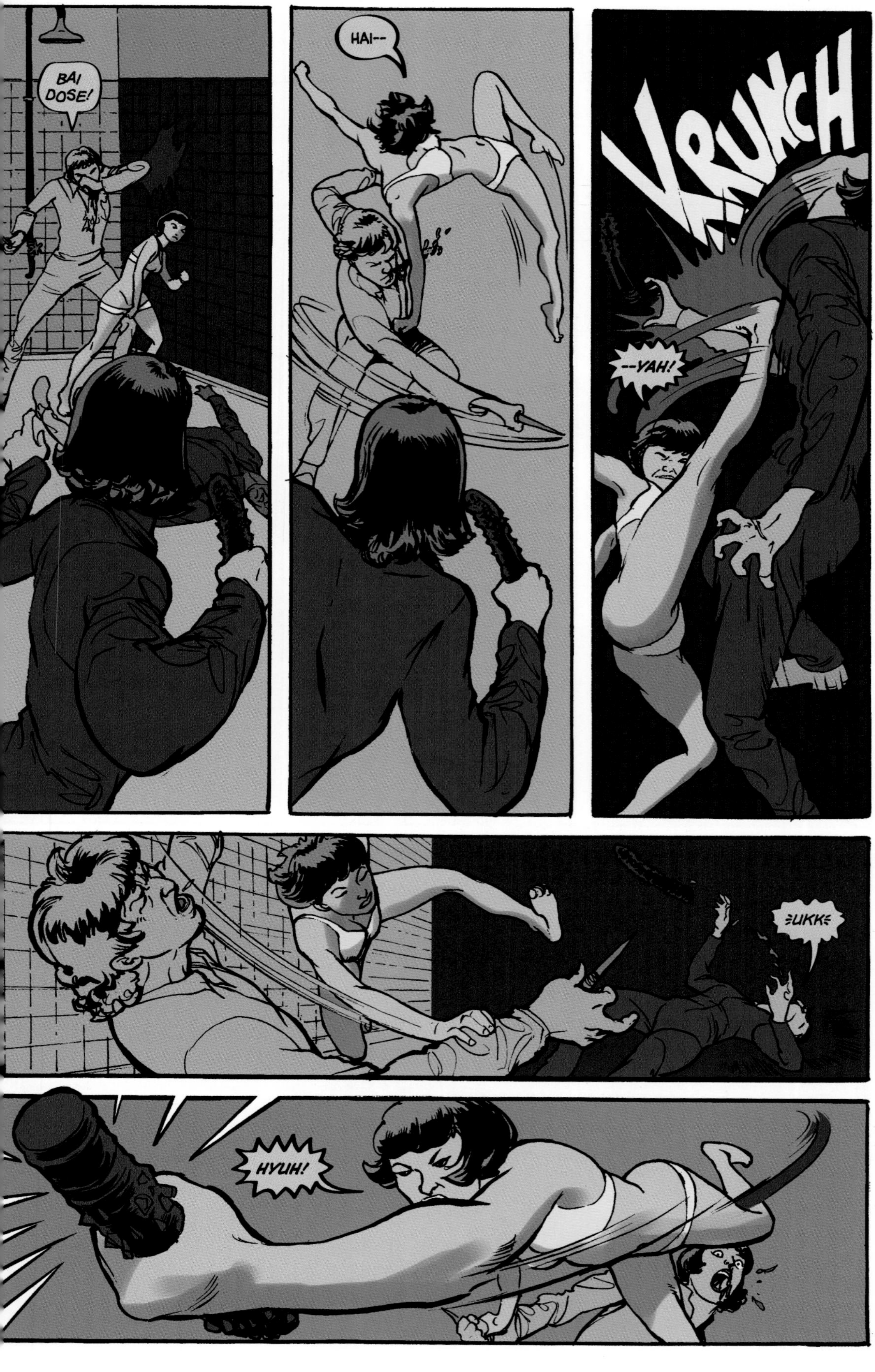
BAI DOSE!
HAI--
VRUNCH
--YAH!
UKK
HYUH!

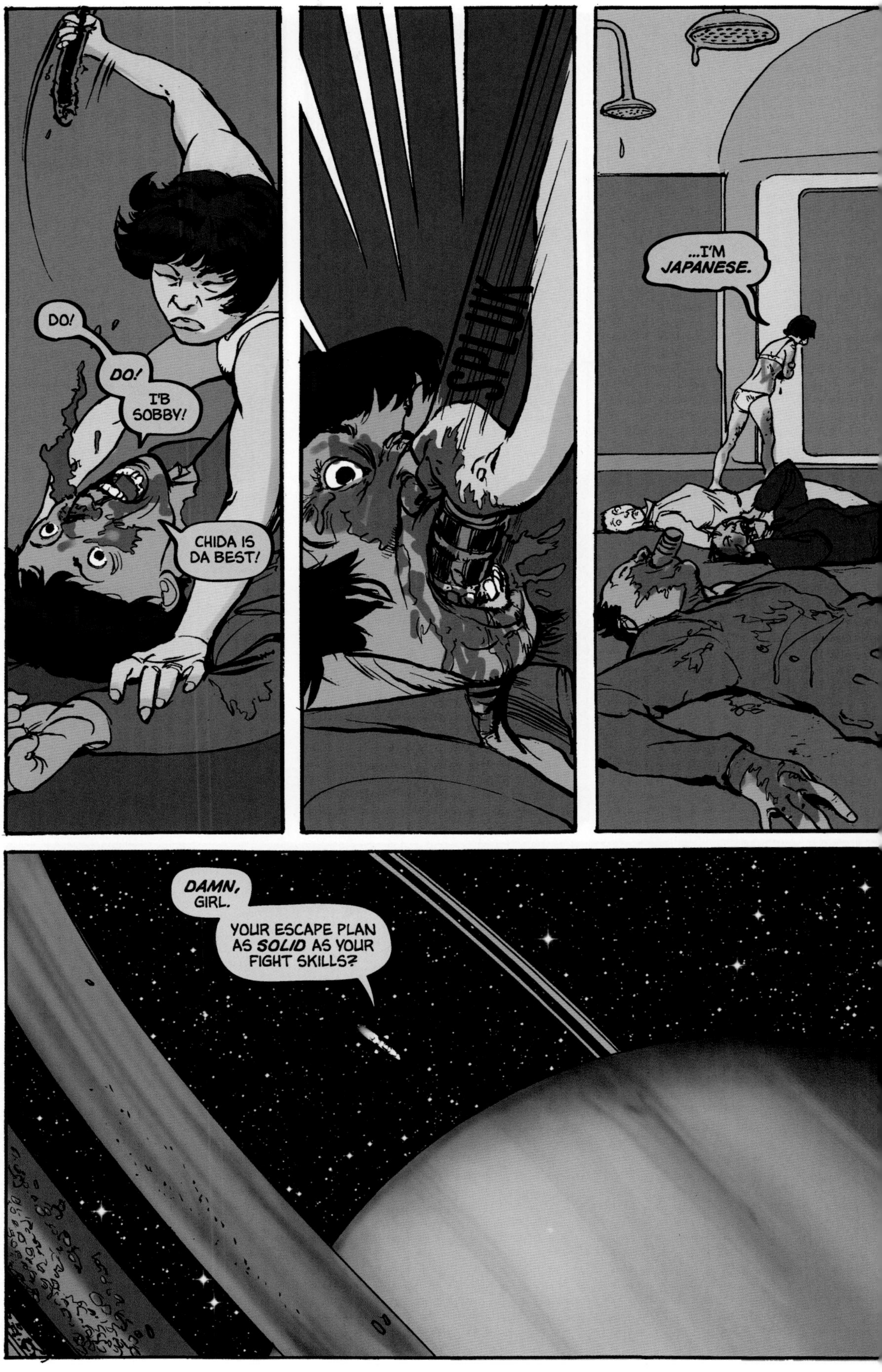
DO!
DO! I'B SOBBY!
CHIDA IS DA BEST!
SPLUK
...I'M JAPANESE.
DAMN, GIRL.
YOUR ESCAPE PLAN AS SOLID AS YOUR FIGHT SKILLS?

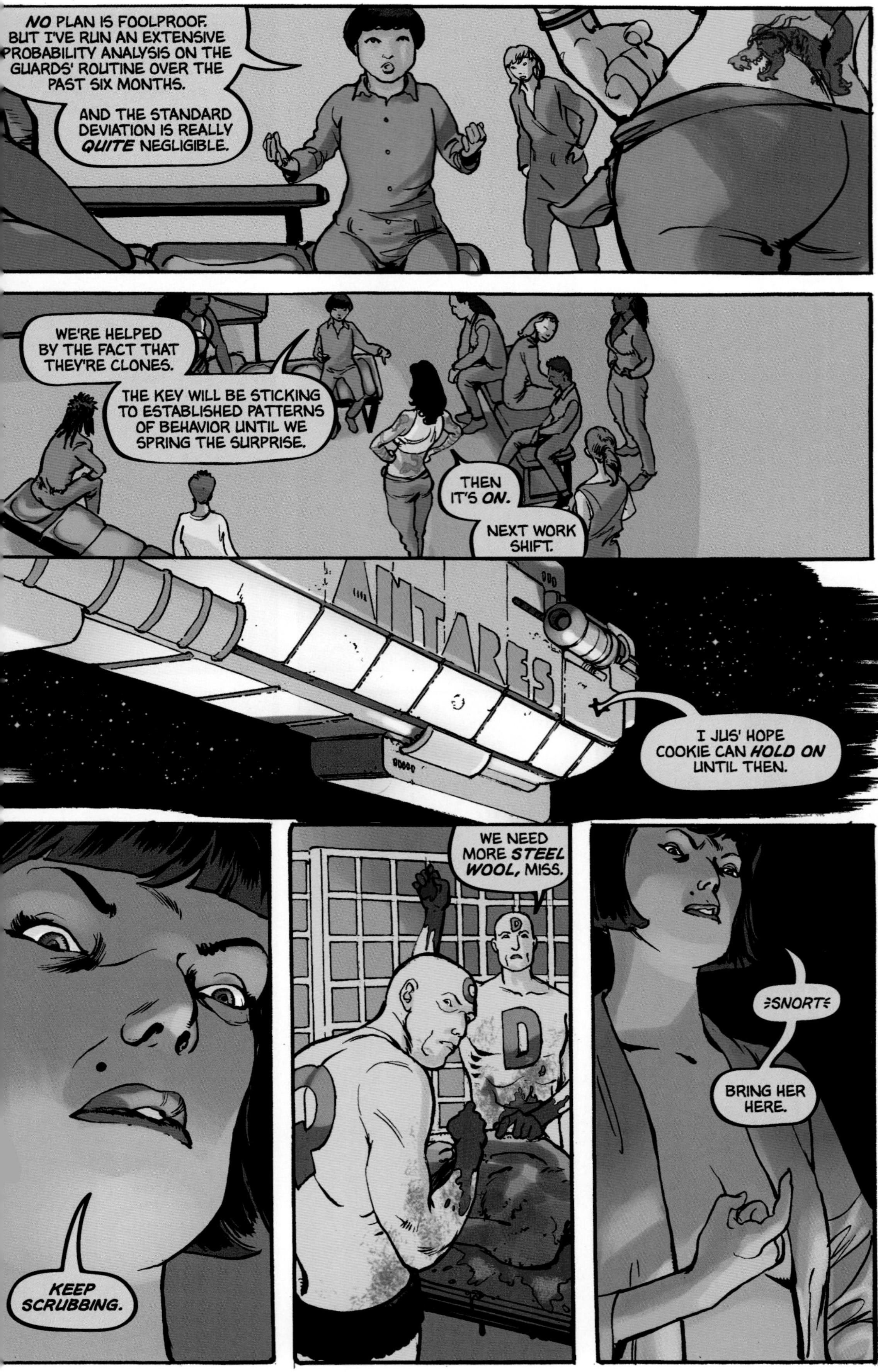
NO PLAN IS FOOLPROOF. BUT I'VE RUN AN EXTENSIVE PROBABILITY ANALYSIS ON THE GUARDS' ROUTINE OVER THE PAST SIX MONTHS.
AND THE STANDARD DEVIATION IS REALLY QUITE NEGLIGIBLE.
WE'RE HELPED BY THE FACT THAT THEY'RE CLONES.
THE KEY WILL BE STICKING TO ESTABLISHED PATTERNS OF BEHAVIOR UNTIL WE SPRING THE SURPRISE.
THEN IT'S ON.
NEXT WORK SHIFT.
ANTARES
I JUS' HOPE COOKIE CAN HOLD ON UNTIL THEN.
KEEP SCRUBBING.
WE NEED MORE STEEL WOOL, MISS.
D
SNORT
BRING HER HERE.

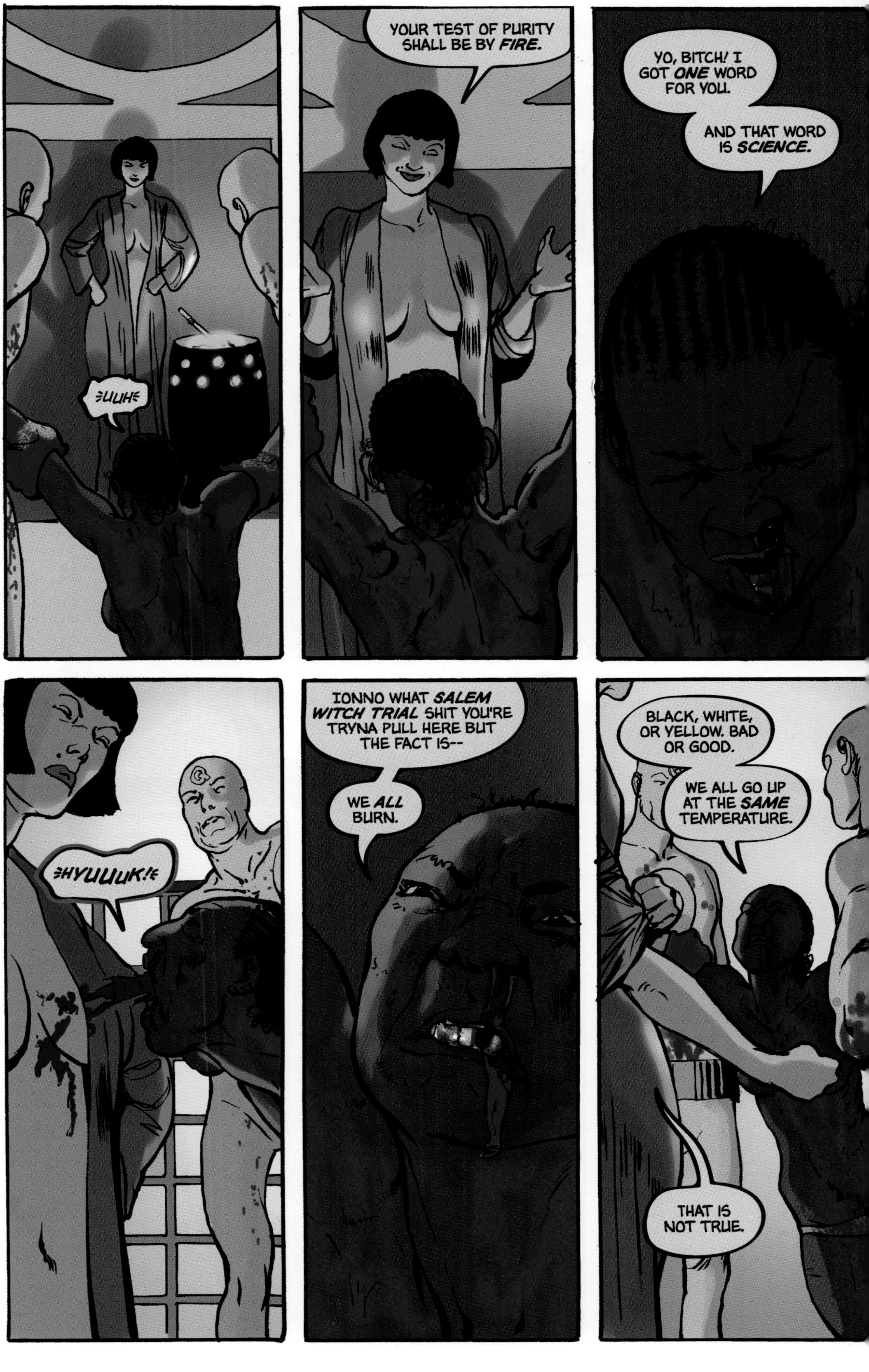
≈UUH≈
YOUR TEST OF PURITY SHALL BE BY *FIRE.*
YO, BITCH! I GOT *ONE* WORD FOR YOU.
AND THAT WORD IS *SCIENCE.*
≈HYUUUK!≈
IONNO WHAT *SALEM WITCH TRIAL* SHIT YOU'RE TRYNA PULL HERE BUT THE FACT IS--
WE *ALL* BURN.
BLACK, WHITE, OR YELLOW. BAD OR GOOD.
WE ALL GO UP AT THE *SAME* TEMPERATURE.
THAT IS NOT TRUE.

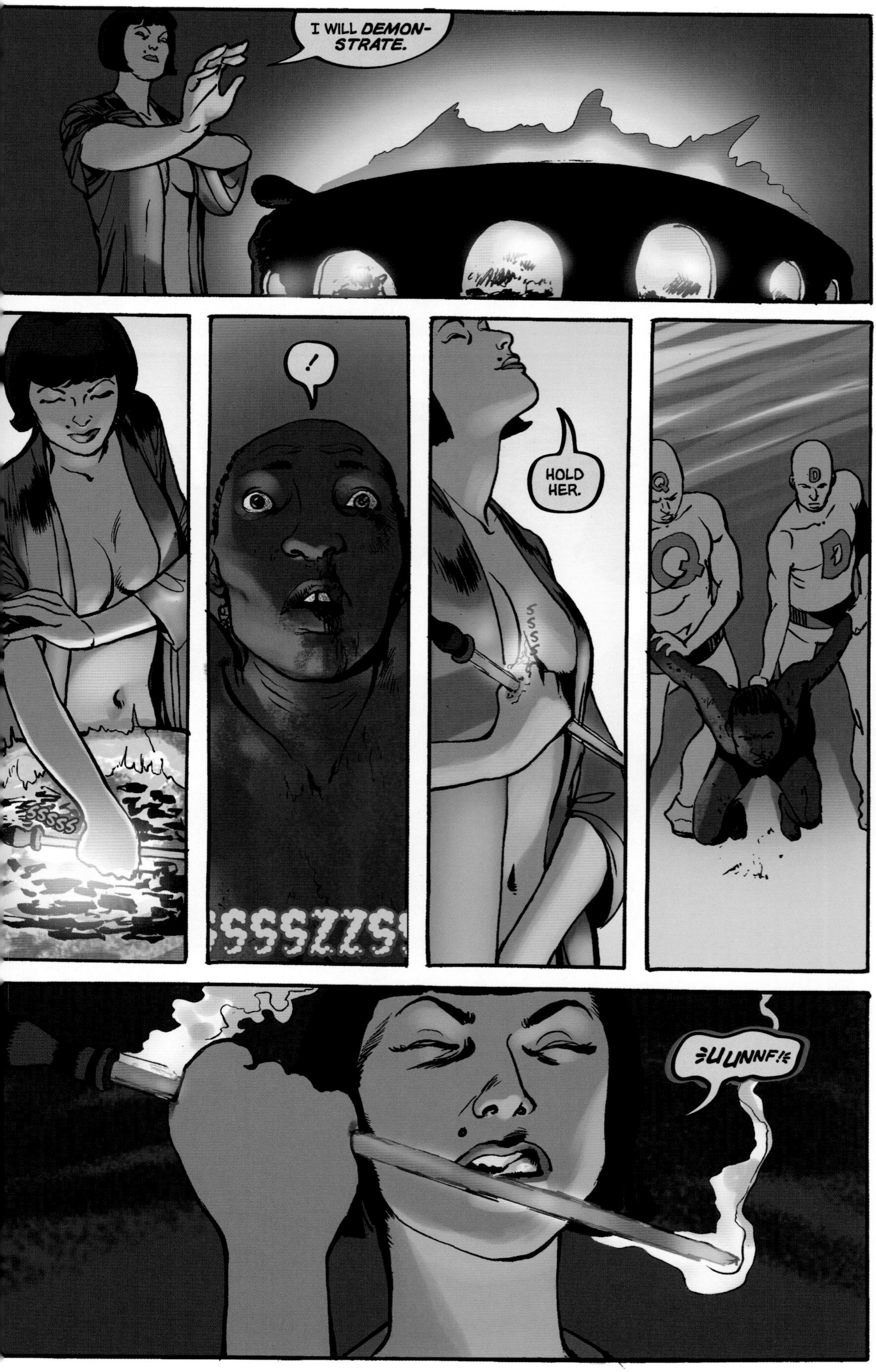
I WILL DEMON-STRATE.
SSSSS
!
SSSSZZSS
SSSS
HOLD HER.
UUNNF!

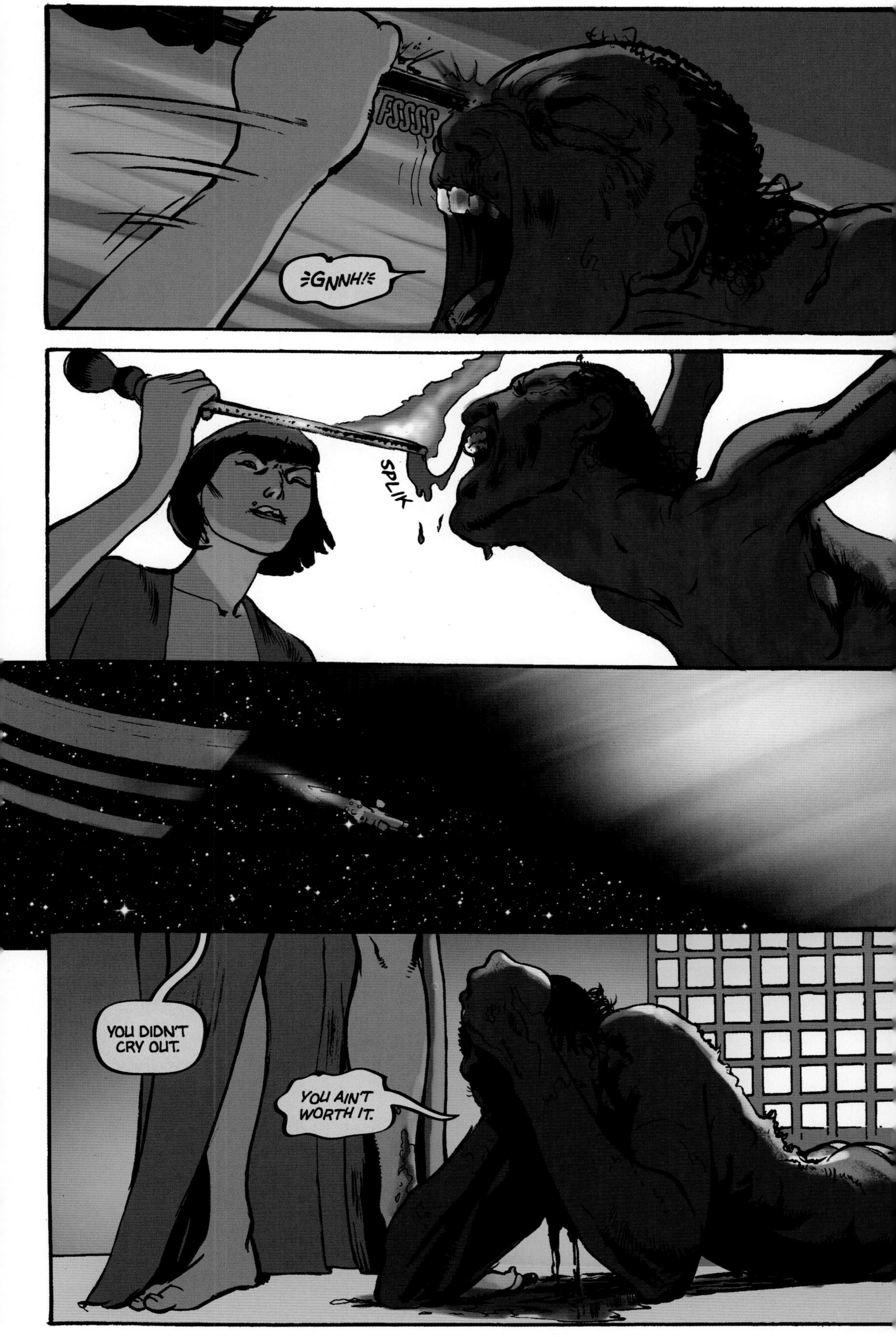
FSSSSS
GNNH!
SPLIK
YOU DIDN'T CRY OUT.
YOU AIN'T WORTH IT.

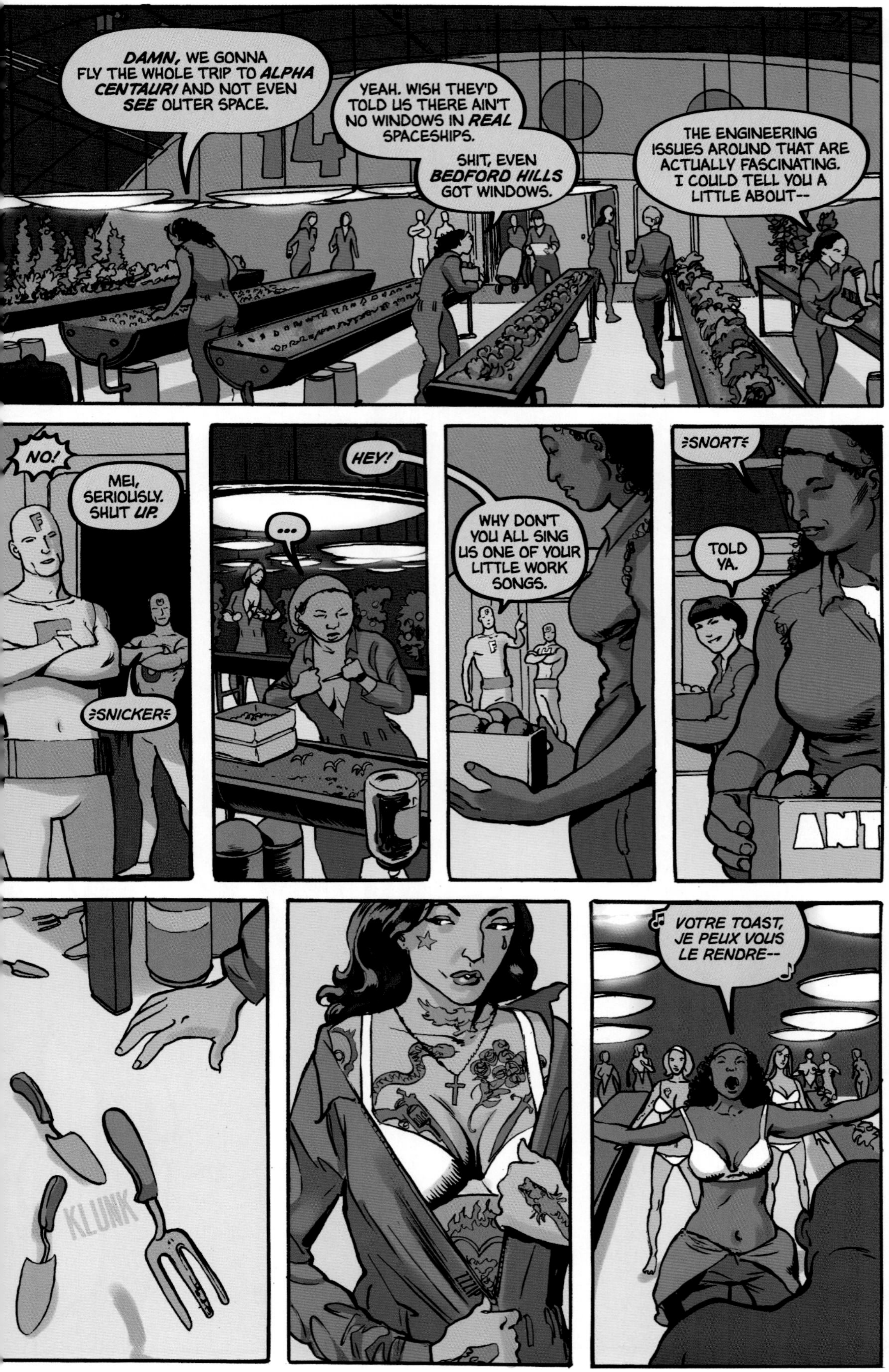
DAMN, WE GONNA FLY THE WHOLE TRIP TO ALPHA CENTAURI AND NOT EVEN SEE OUTER SPACE.
YEAH. WISH THEY'D TOLD US THERE AIN'T NO WINDOWS IN REAL SPACESHIPS.
SHIT, EVEN BEDFORD HILLS GOT WINDOWS.
THE ENGINEERING ISSUES AROUND THAT ARE ACTUALLY FASCINATING. I COULD TELL YOU A LITTLE ABOUT--
NO!
MEI, SERIOUSLY. SHUT UP.
SNICKER
HEY!
...
WHY DON'T YOU ALL SING US ONE OF YOUR LITTLE WORK SONGS.
SNORT
TOLD YA.
ANT
KLUNK
VOTRE TOAST, JE PEUX VOUS LE RENDRE--

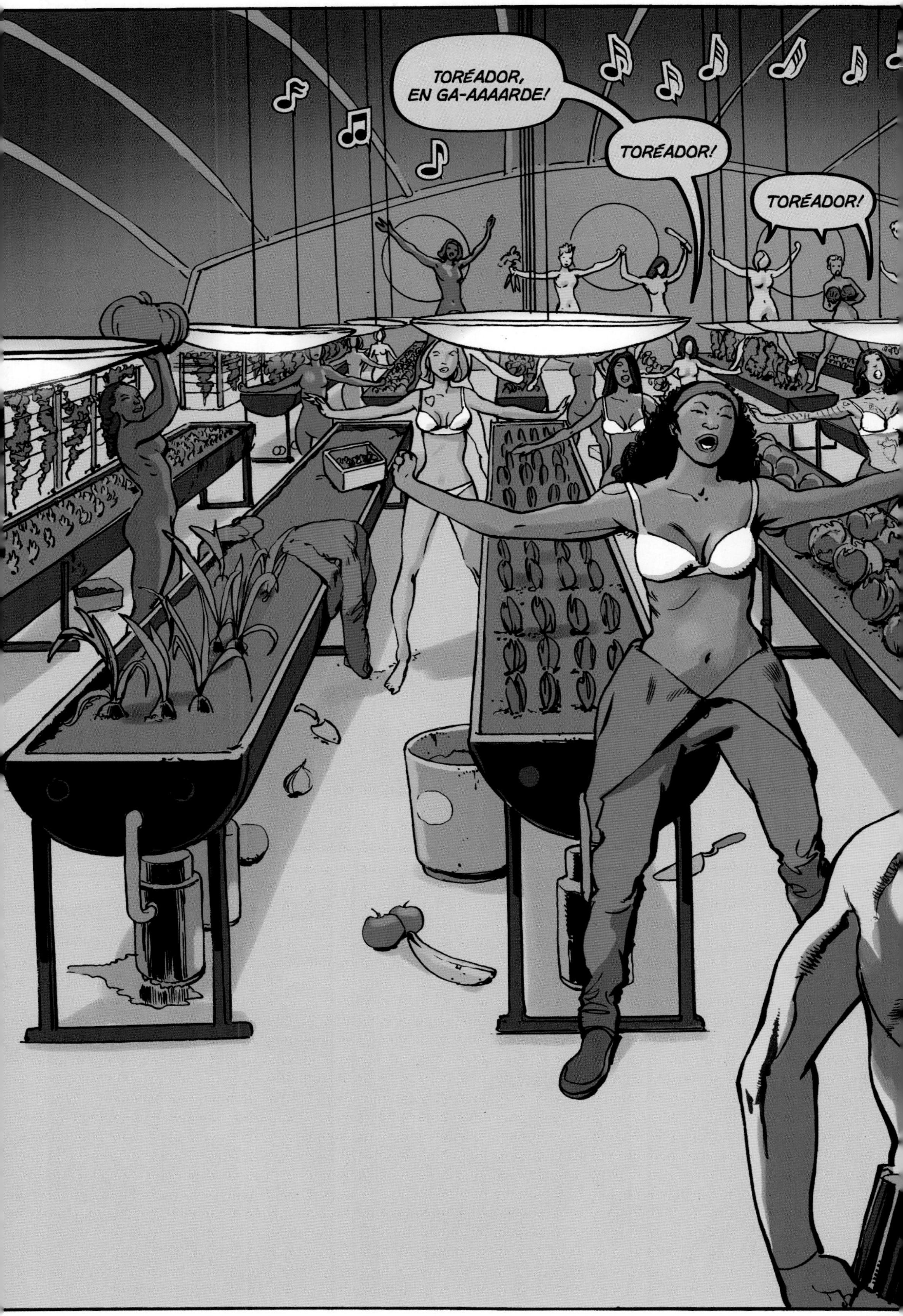
TORÉADOR, EN GA-AAAARDE!
TORÉADOR!
TORÉADOR!

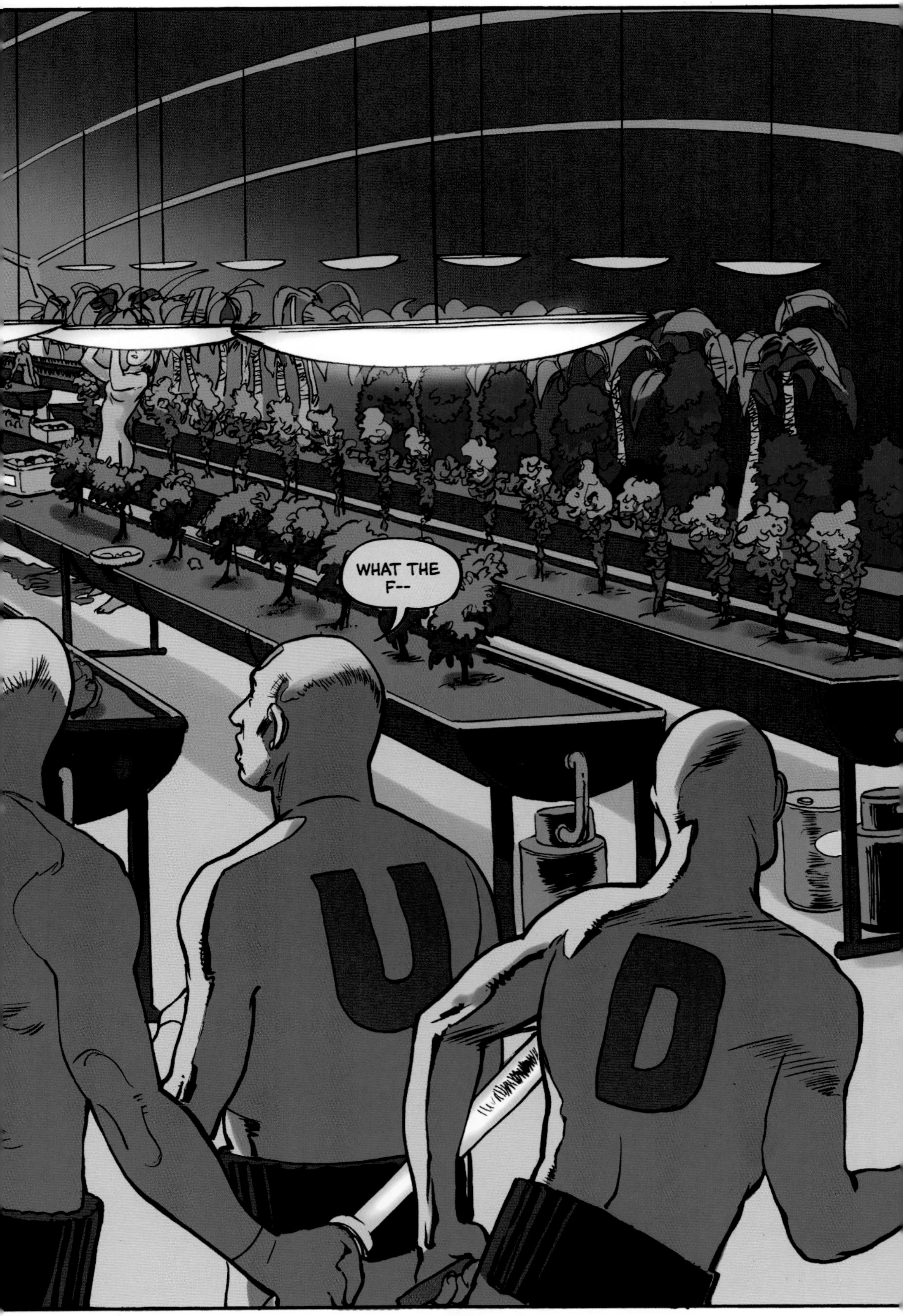
WHAT THE
F--

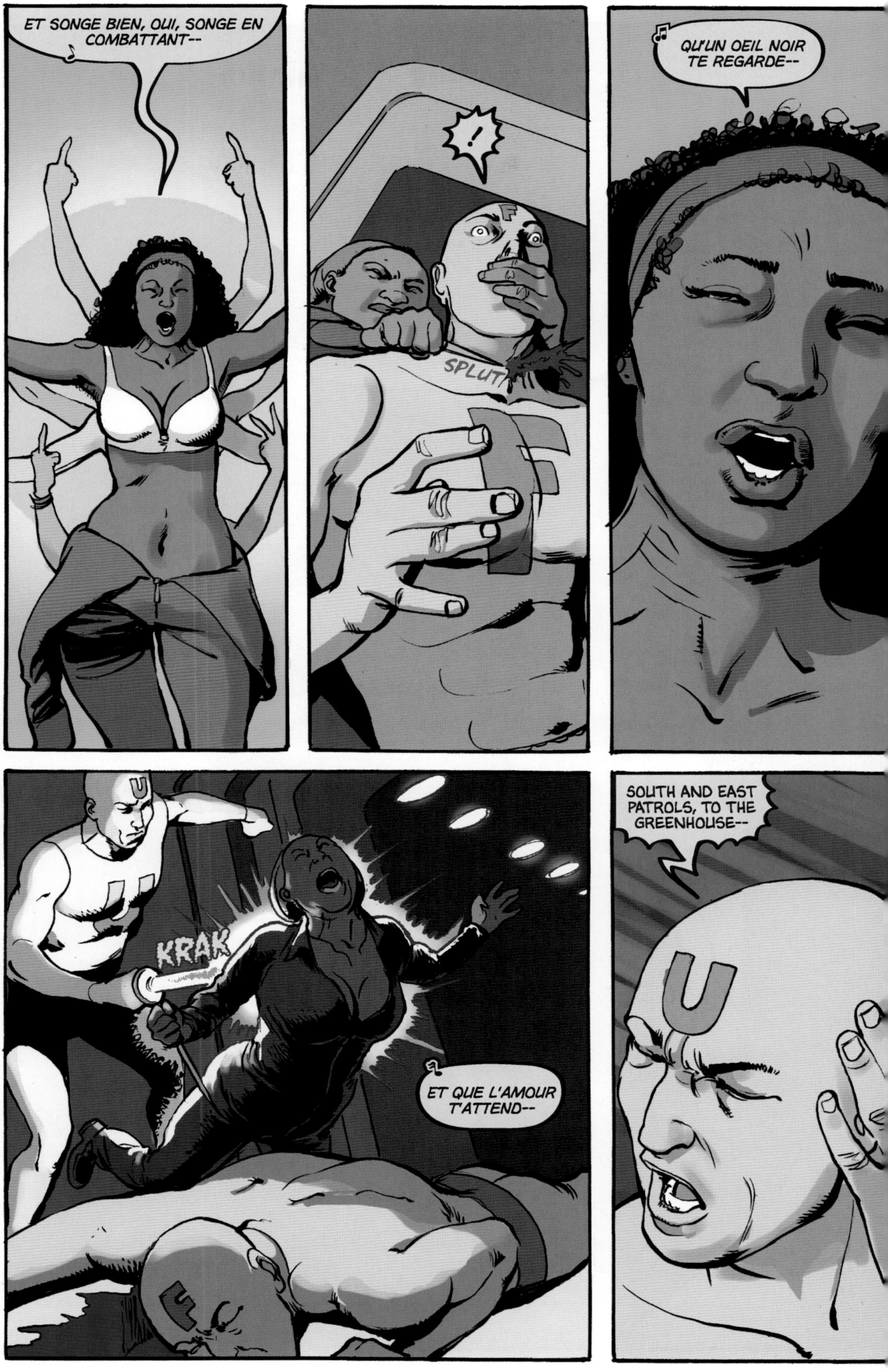
ET SONGE BIEN, OUI, SONGE EN COMBATTANT--
!
SPLUT
QU'UN OEIL NOIR TE REGARDE--
KRAK
ET QUE L'AMOUR T'ATTEND--
SOUTH AND EAST PATROLS, TO THE GREENHOUSE--

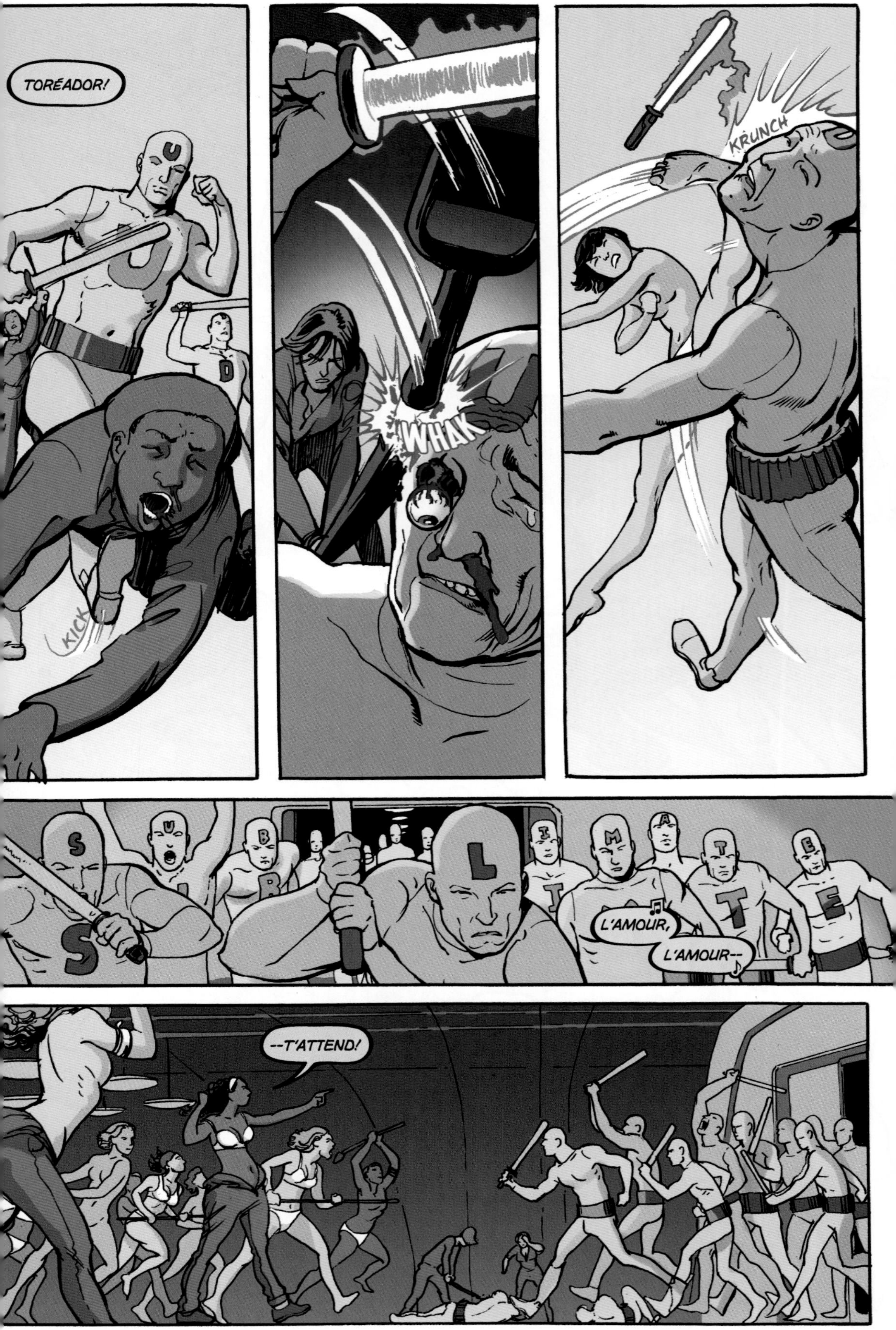

TORÉADOR!
KICK
WHAK
KRUNCH
L'AMOUR,
L'AMOUR--
--T'ATTEND!

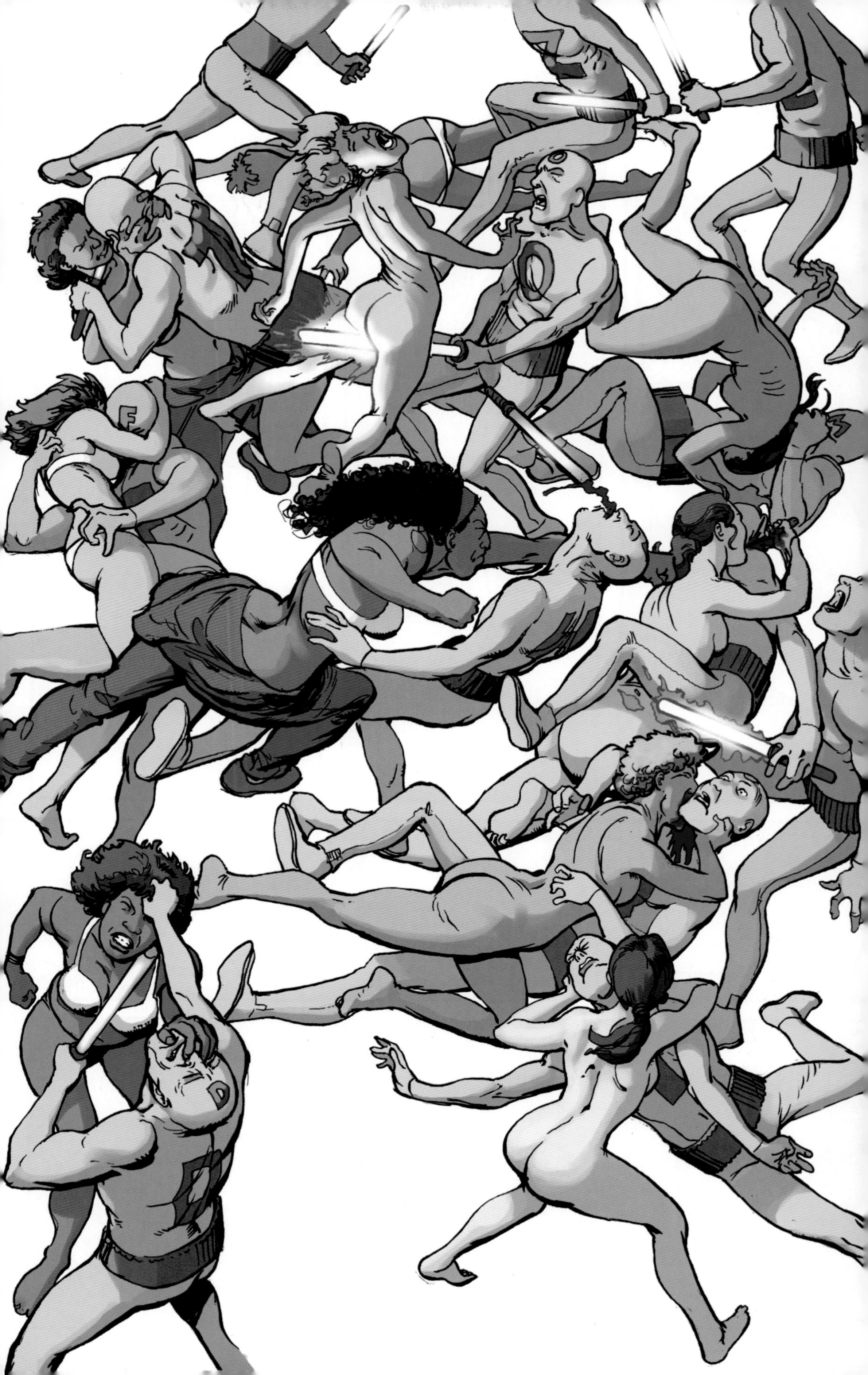

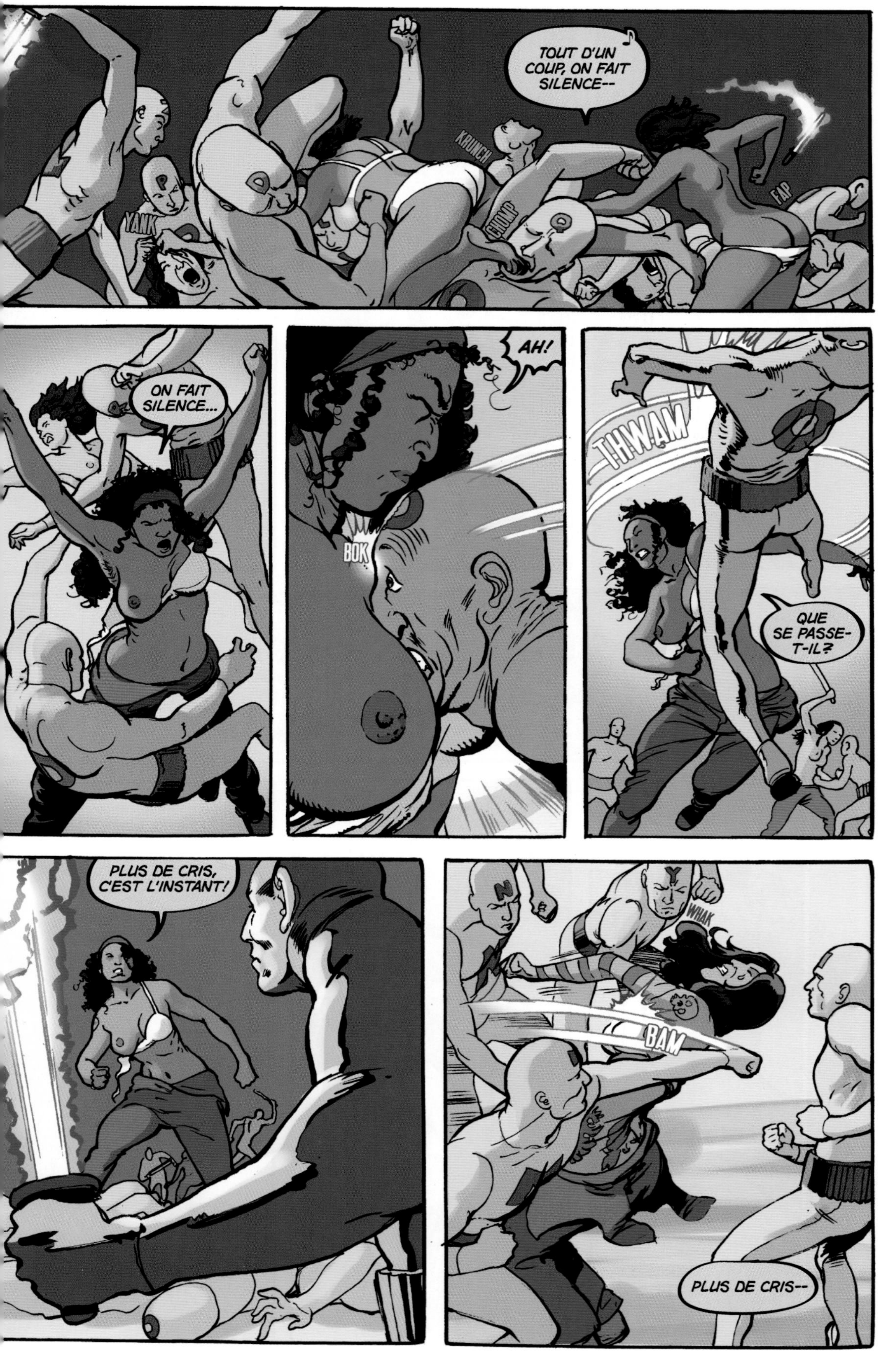
TOUT D'UN COUP, ON FAIT SILENCE--
YANK
KRUNCH
CHOMP
FAP
ON FAIT SILENCE...
AH!
BOK
THWAM
QUE SE PASSE-T-IL?
PLUS DE CRIS, C'EST L'INSTANT!
WHAK
BAM
PLUS DE CRIS--

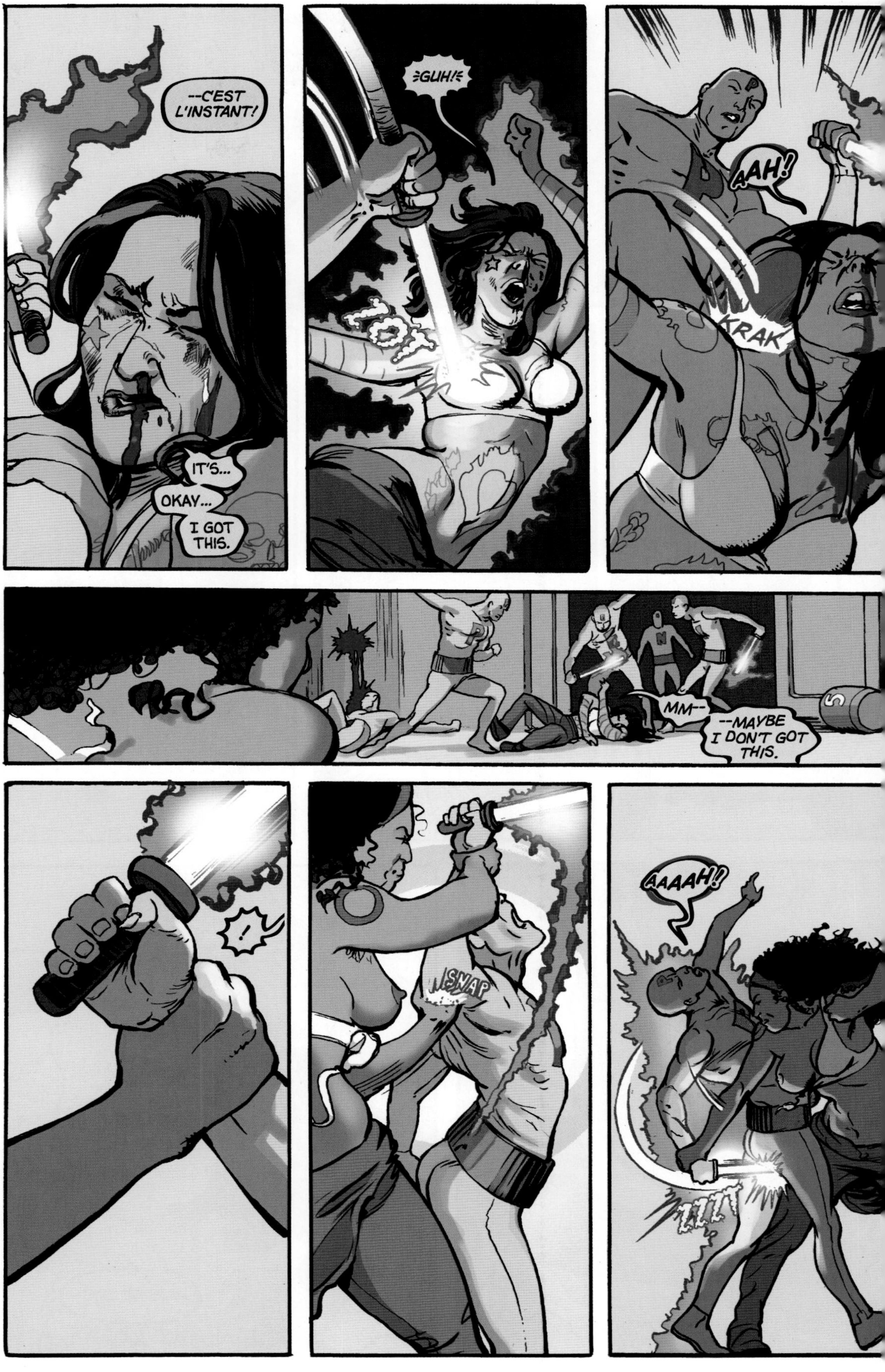
--C'EST L'INSTANT!
IT'S...
OKAY...
I GOT THIS.
GUH!
TOT
AAH!
KRAK
MM--
--MAYBE I DON'T GOT THIS.
!
SNAP
AAAAH!
ZZZT

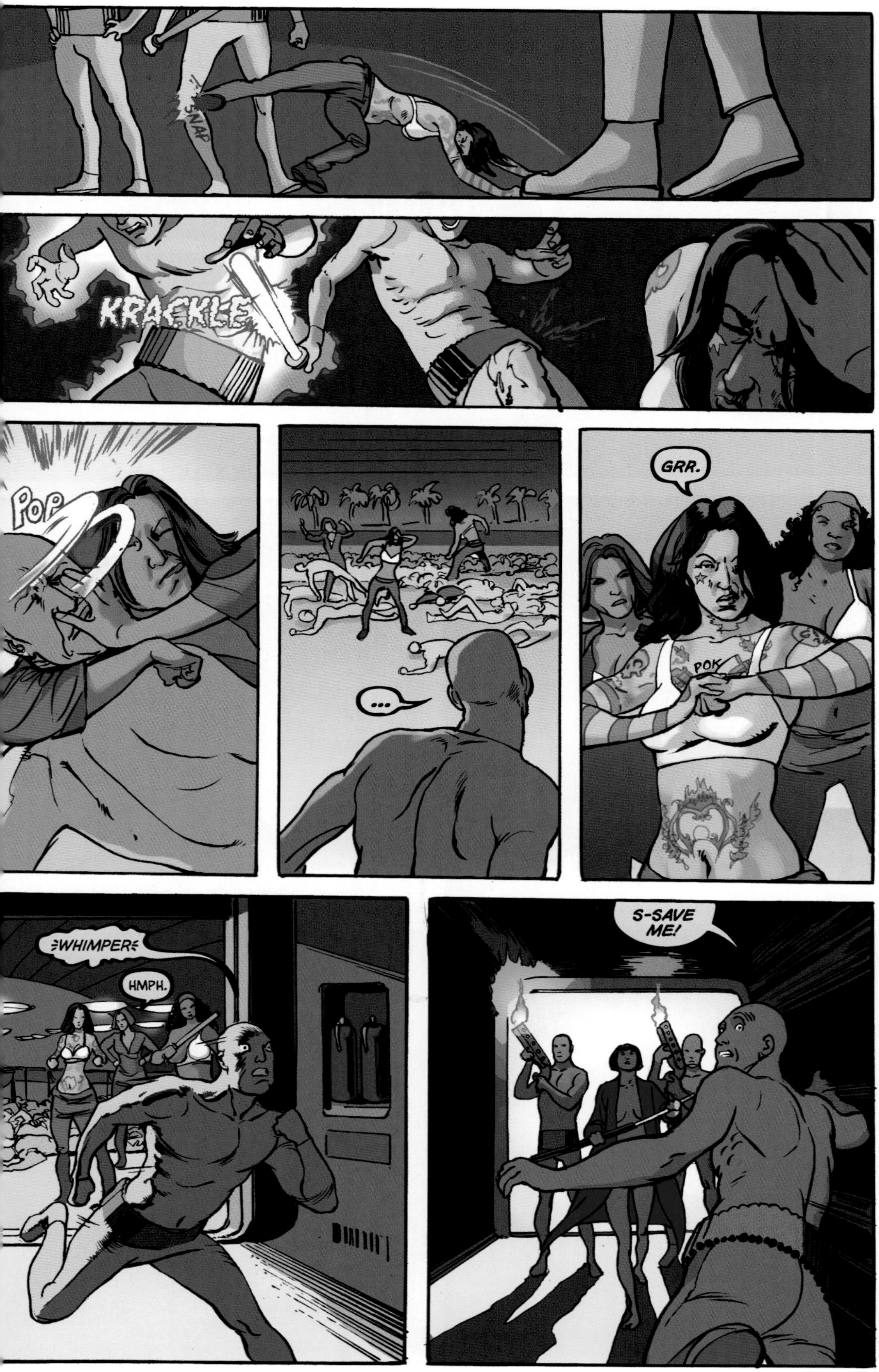
SNAP
KRACKLE
POP
...
GRR.
POK
≈WHIMPER≈
HMPH.
S-SAVE ME!

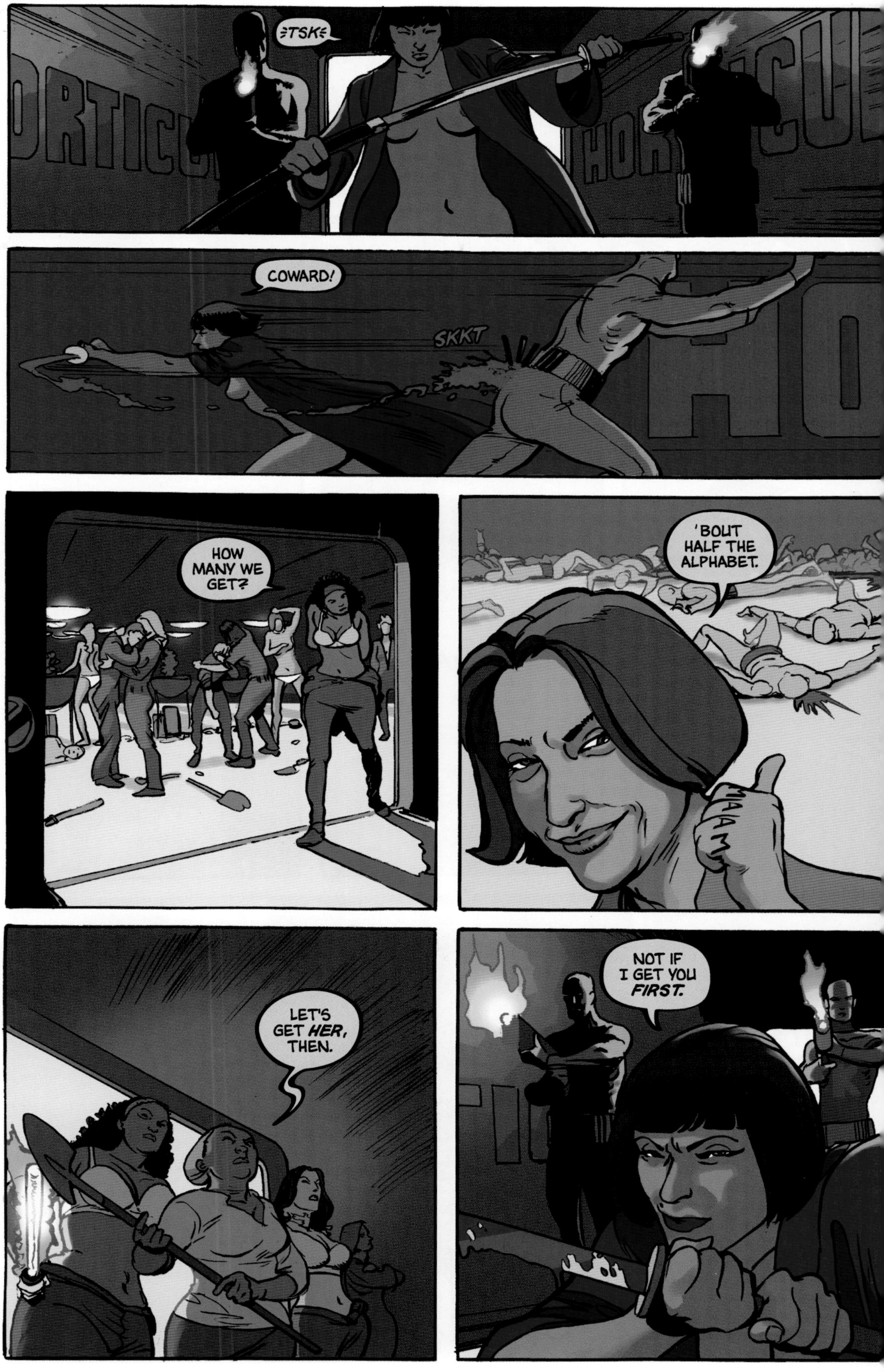
TSK
COWARD!
SKKT
HOW MANY WE GET?
'BOUT HALF THE ALPHABET.
MA'AM
LET'S GET HER, THEN.
NOT IF I GET YOU FIRST.

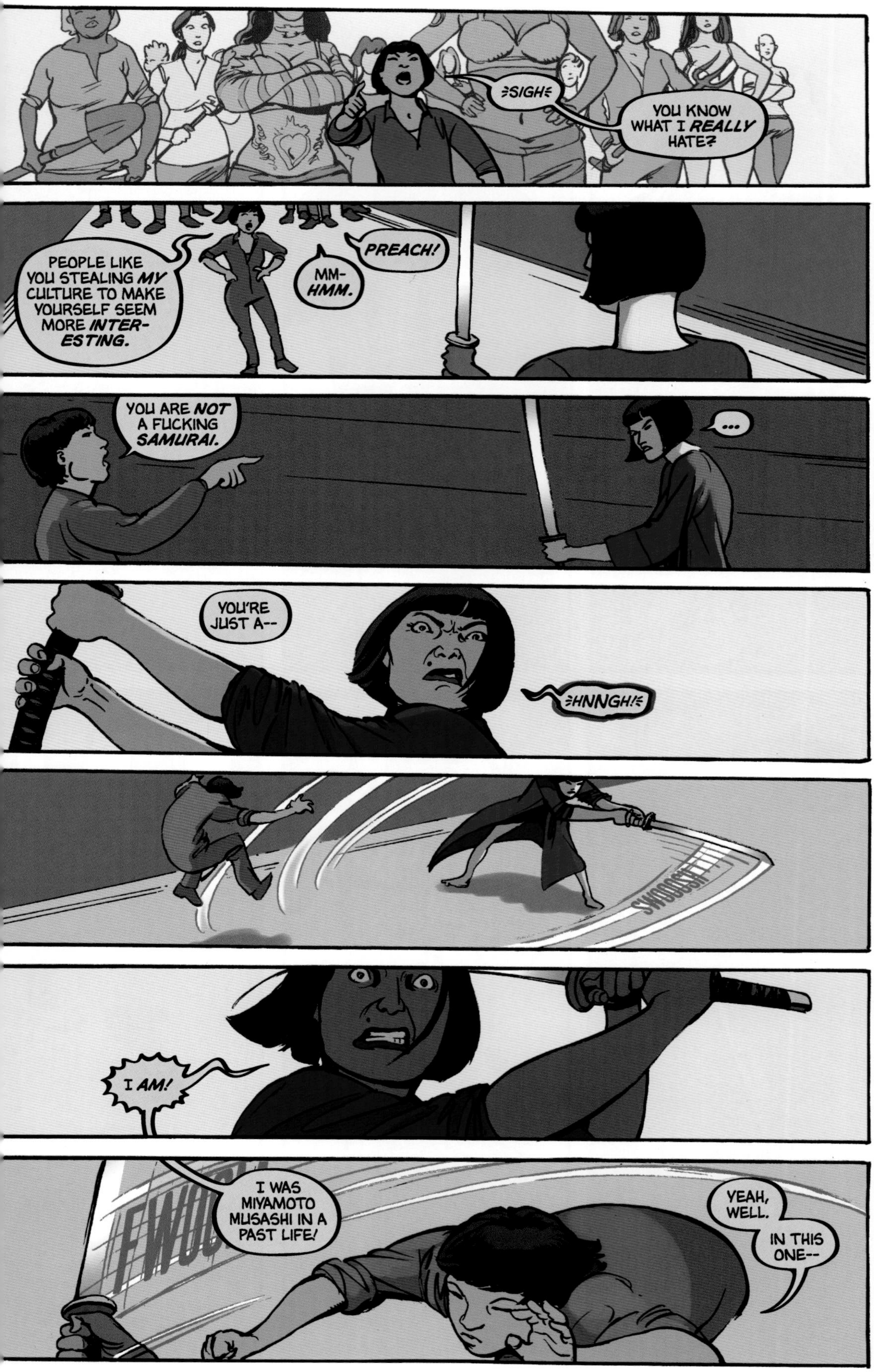
SIGH
YOU KNOW WHAT I REALLY HATE?
PEOPLE LIKE YOU STEALING MY CULTURE TO MAKE YOURSELF SEEM MORE INTER-ESTING.
MM-HMM.
PREACH!
YOU ARE NOT A FUCKING SAMURAI.
...
YOU'RE JUST A--
HNNGH!
SWOOSH
I AM!
FWOOSH
I WAS MIYAMOTO MUSASHI IN A PAST LIFE!
YEAH, WELL.
IN THIS ONE--

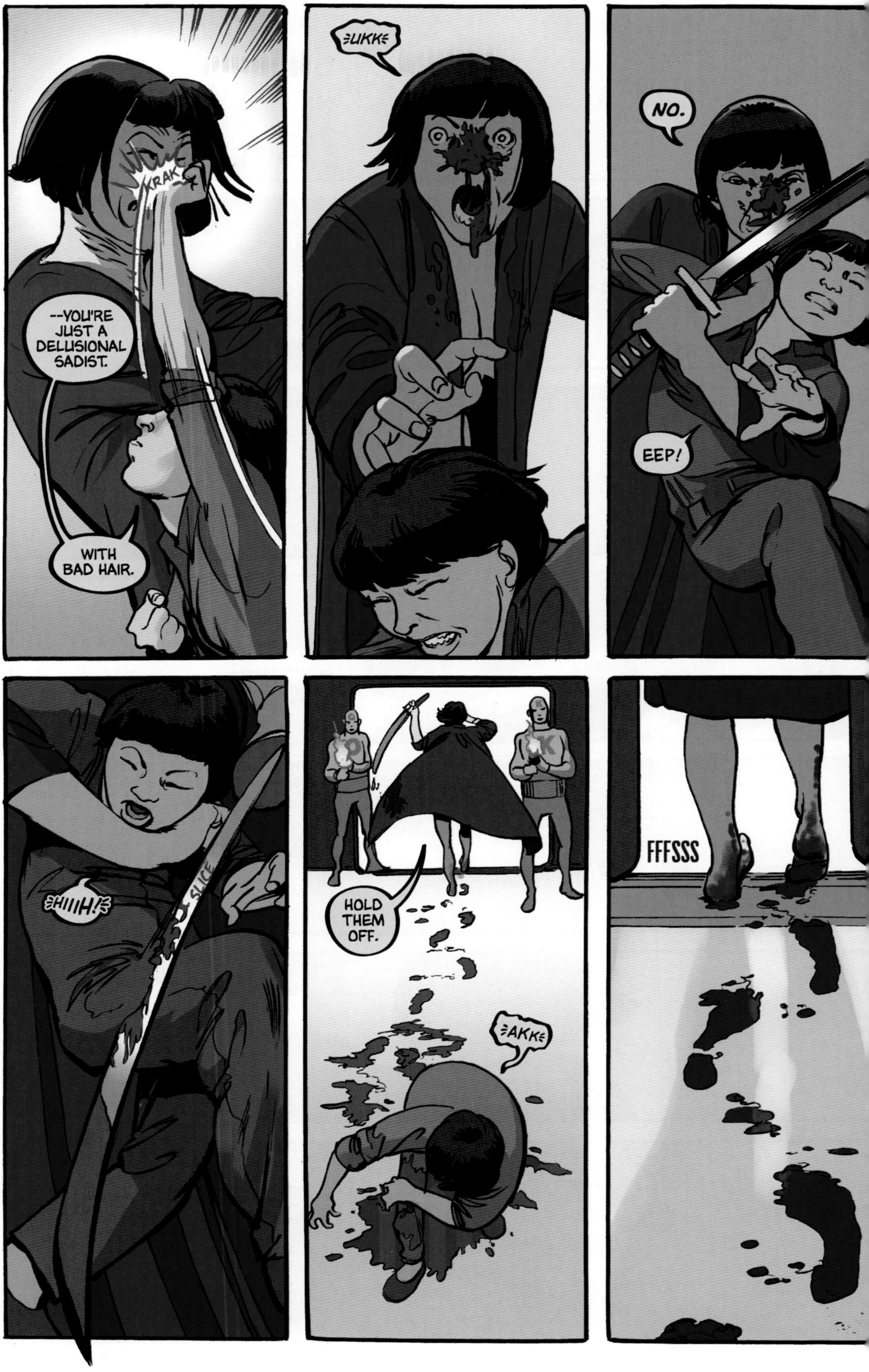

KRAK
--YOU'RE JUST A DELUSIONAL SADIST.
WITH BAD HAIR.
UKK
NO.
EEP!
HIIIH!
SLICE
HOLD THEM OFF.
AKK
FFFSSS

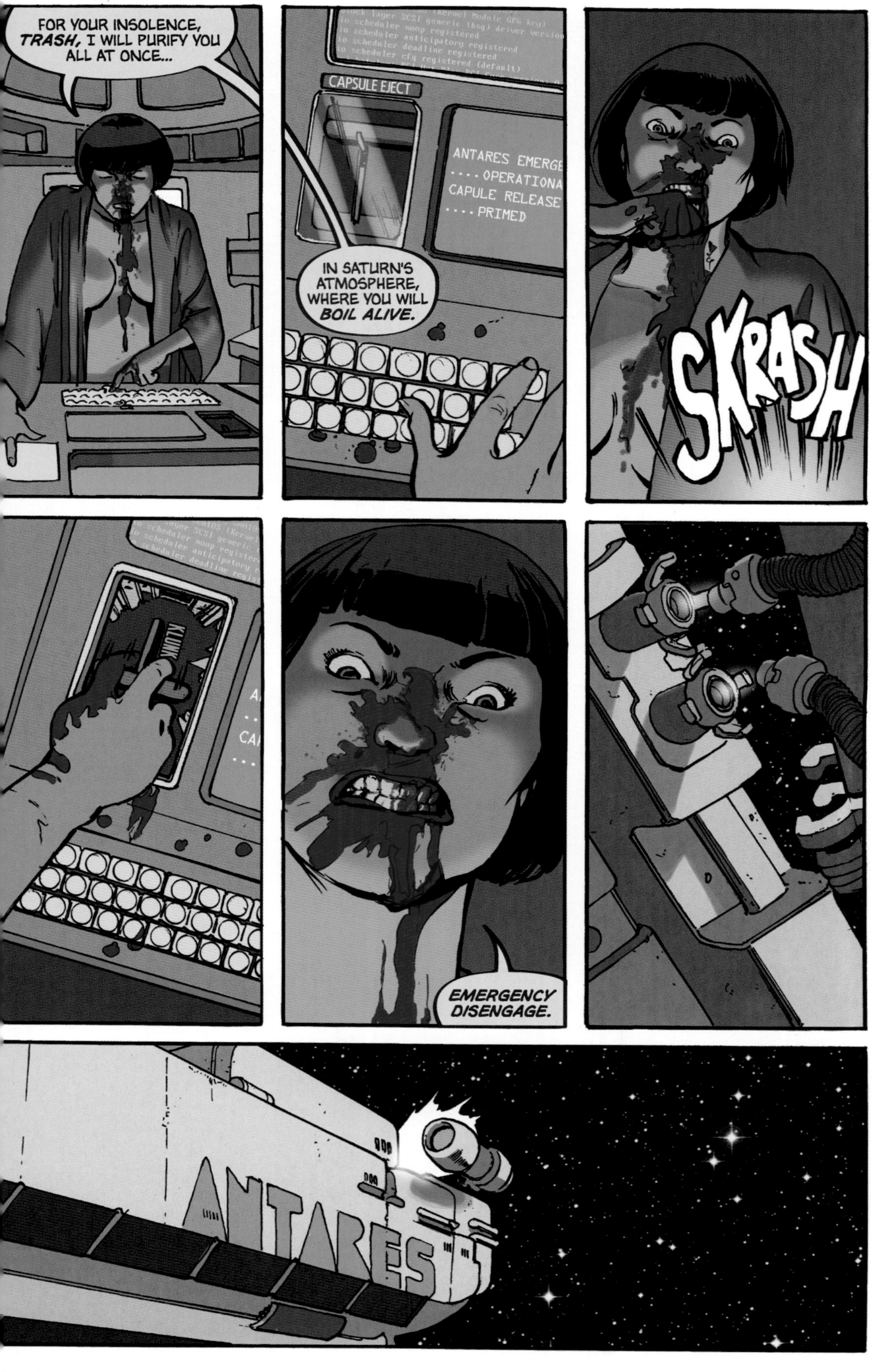

FOR YOUR INSOLENCE, *TRASH,* I WILL PURIFY YOU ALL AT ONCE...
CAPSULE EJECT
ANTARES EMERGE
....OPERATIONA
CAPULE RELEASE
....PRIMED
IN SATURN'S ATMOSPHERE, WHERE YOU WILL *BOIL ALIVE.*
SKRASH
KLUNK
EMERGENCY DISENGAGE.
ANTARES

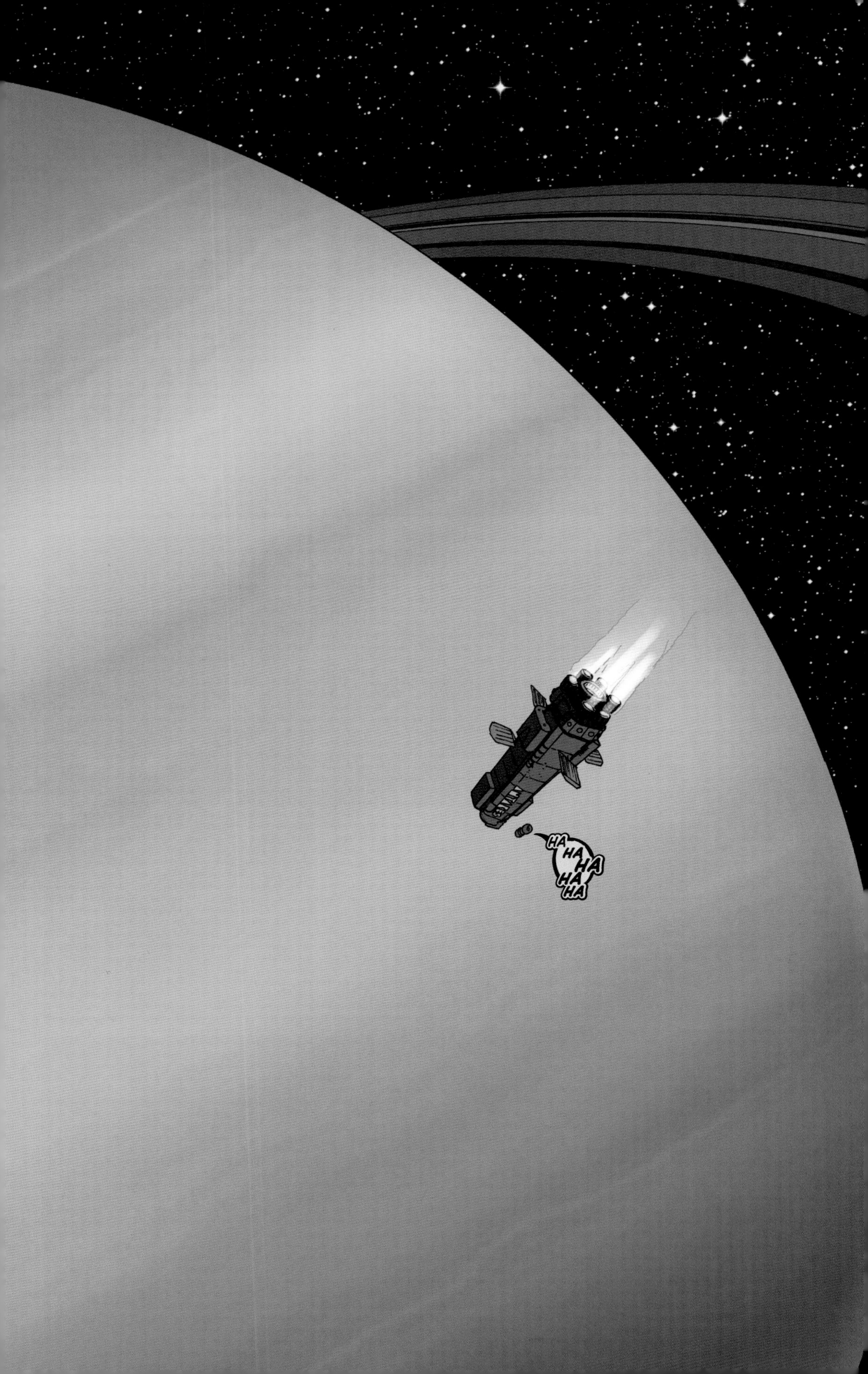
HA HA HA HA HA

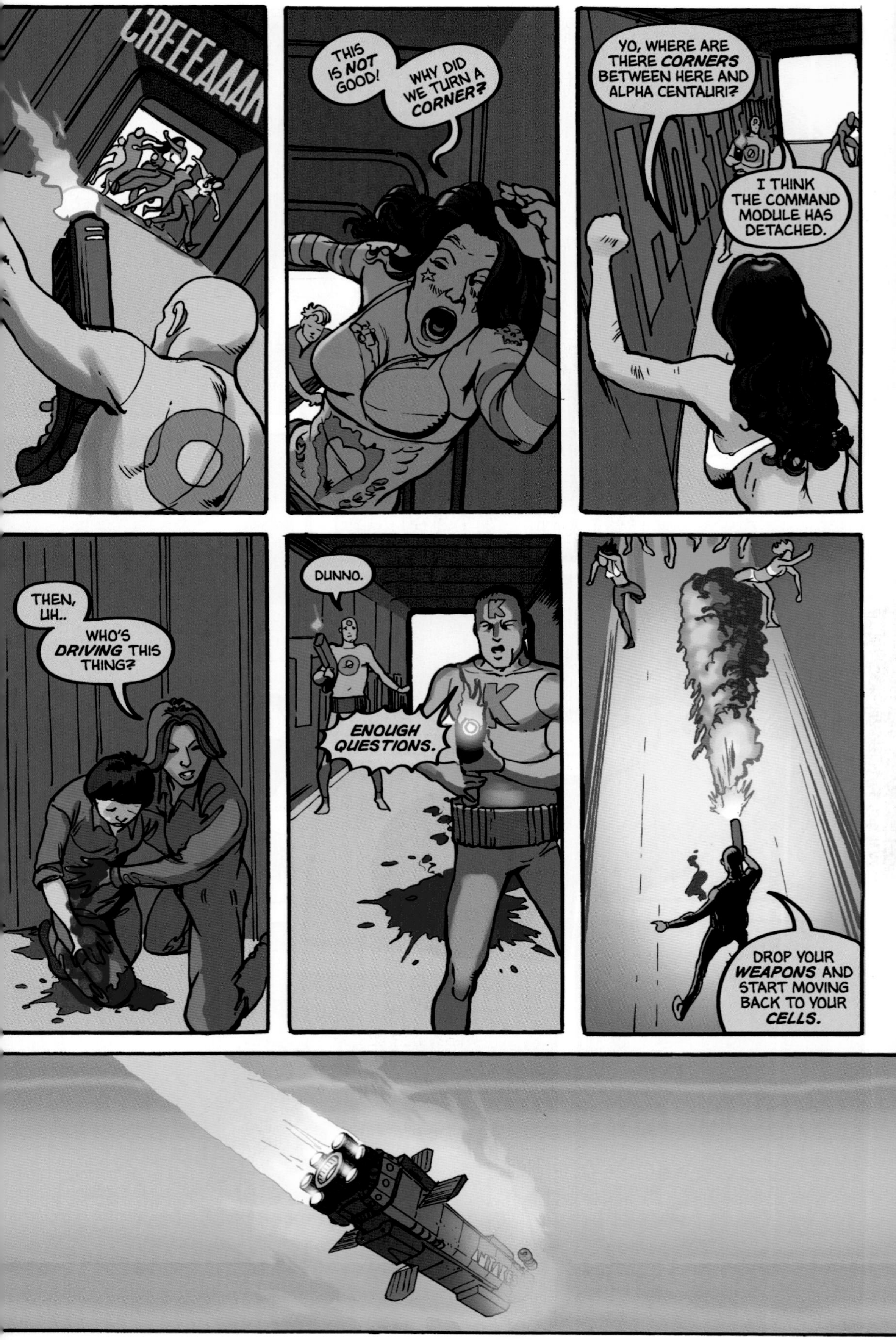
CREEEAAAK
THIS IS NOT GOOD!
WHY DID WE TURN A CORNER?
YO, WHERE ARE THERE CORNERS BETWEEN HERE AND ALPHA CENTAURI?
I THINK THE COMMAND MODULE HAS DETACHED.
THEN, UH..
WHO'S DRIVING THIS THING?
DUNNO.
ENOUGH QUESTIONS.
DROP YOUR WEAPONS AND START MOVING BACK TO YOUR CELLS.

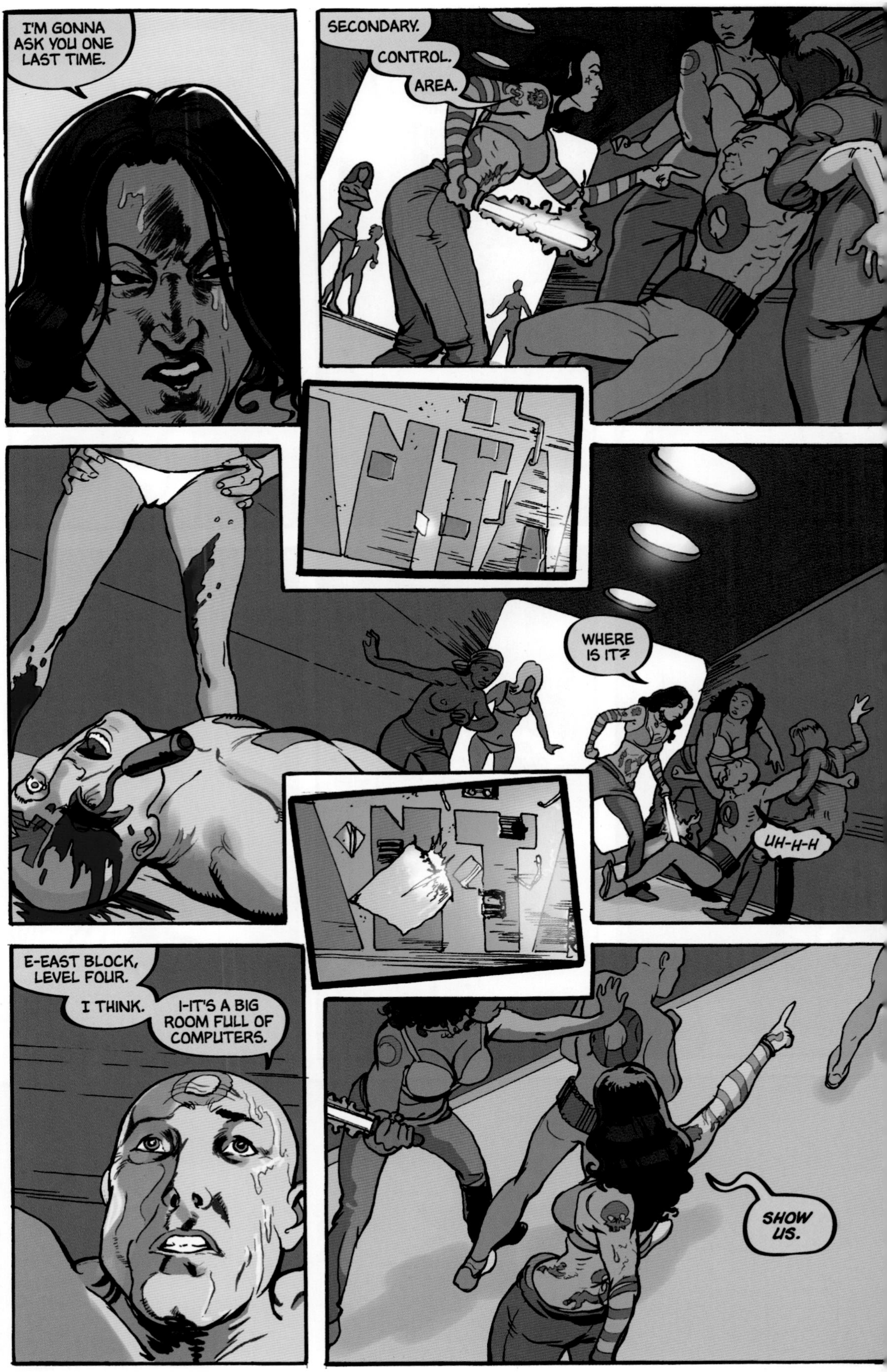
I'M GONNA ASK YOU ONE LAST TIME.
SECONDARY.
CONTROL.
AREA.
WHERE IS IT?
UH-H-H
E-EAST BLOCK, LEVEL FOUR.
I THINK.
I-IT'S A BIG ROOM FULL OF COMPUTERS.
SHOW US.

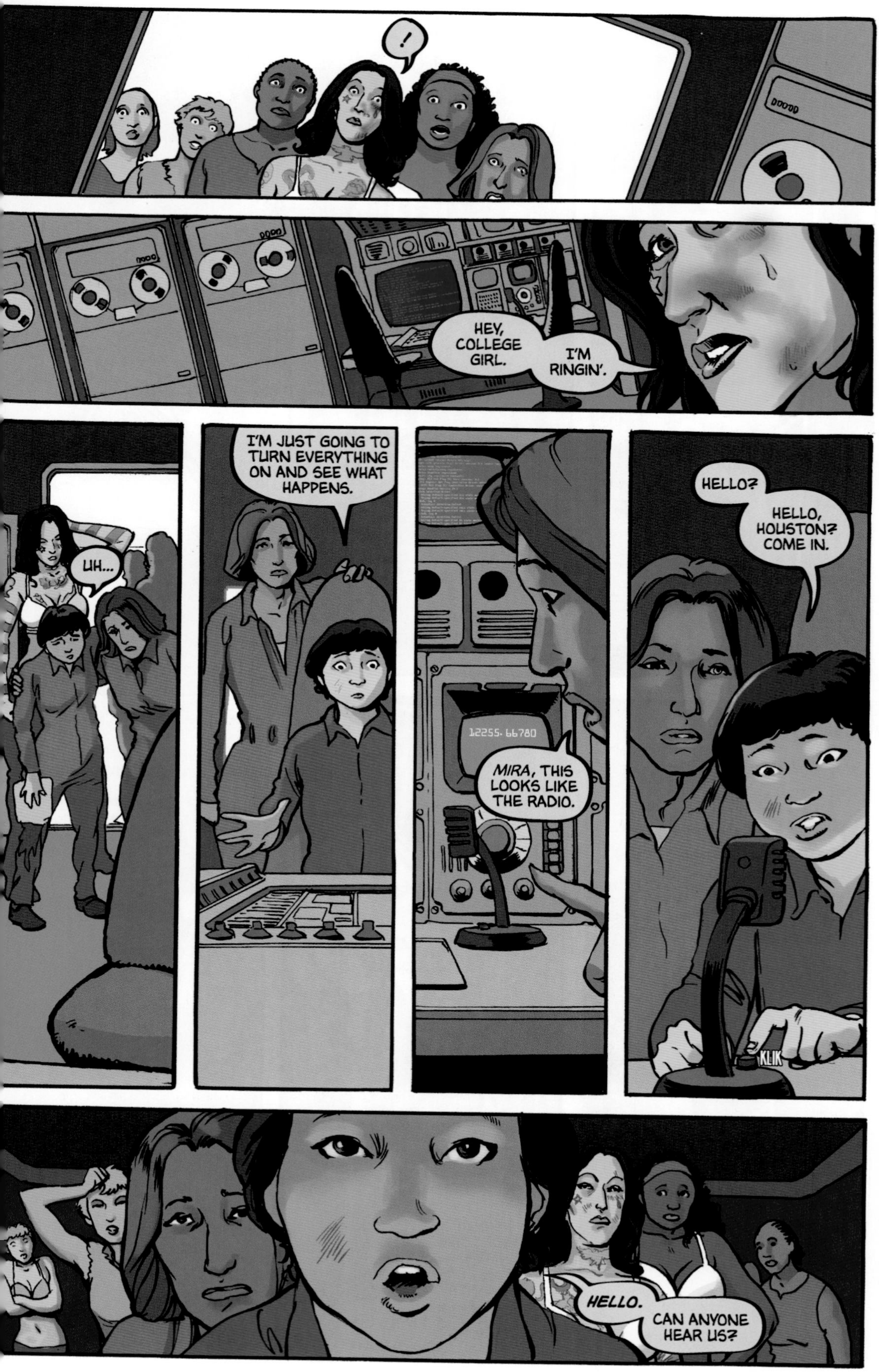
!
HEY, COLLEGE GIRL.
I'M RINGIN'.
UH...
I'M JUST GOING TO TURN EVERYTHING ON AND SEE WHAT HAPPENS.
12255. 66780
MIRA, THIS LOOKS LIKE THE RADIO.
HELLO?
HELLO, HOUSTON? COME IN.
KLIK
HELLO.
CAN ANYONE HEAR US?

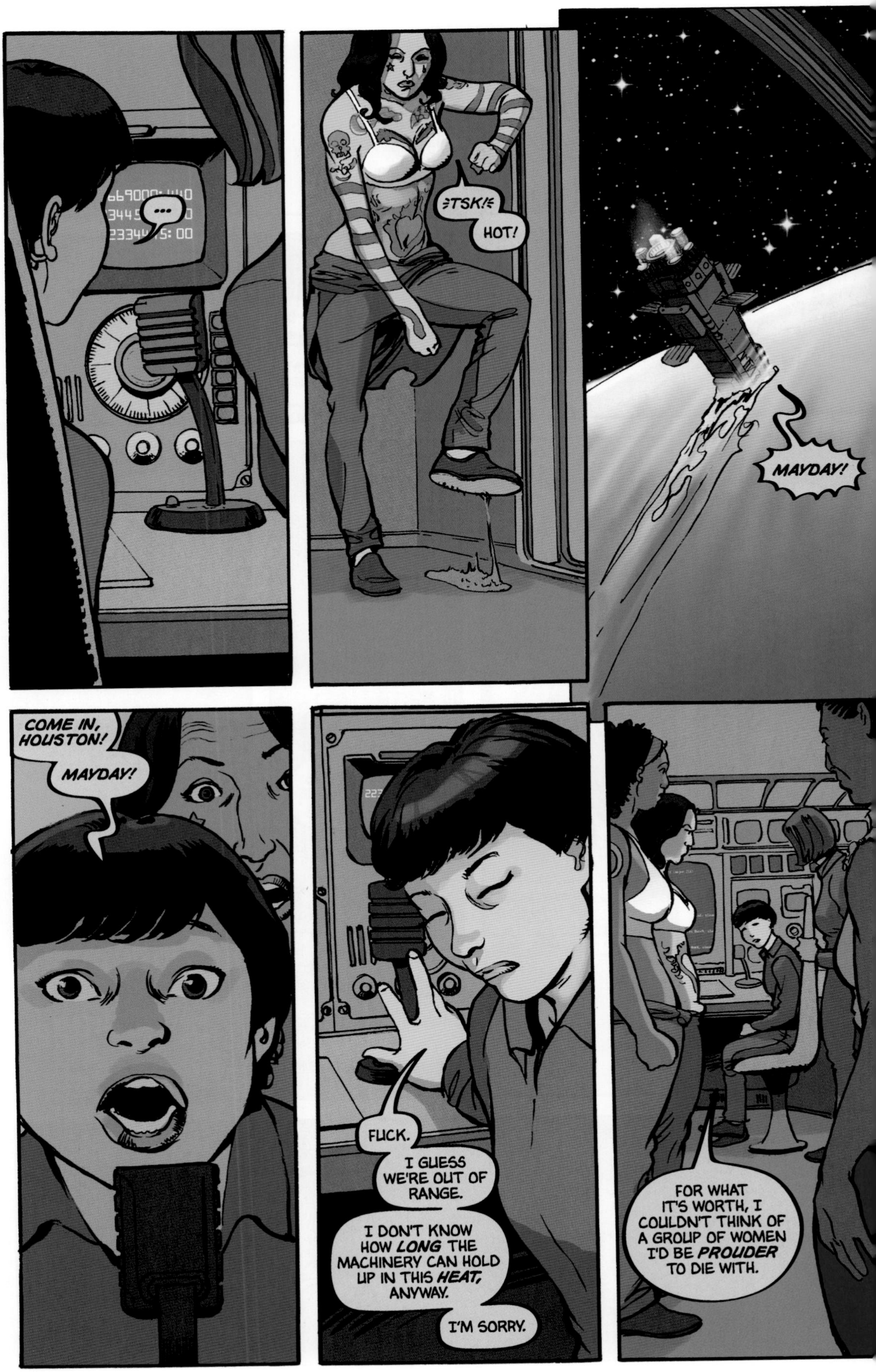
669000:1410
...
2334445:00
TSK!
HOT!
MAYDAY!
COME IN, HOUSTON!
MAYDAY!
FUCK.
I GUESS WE'RE OUT OF RANGE.
I DON'T KNOW HOW *LONG* THE MACHINERY CAN HOLD UP IN THIS *HEAT,* ANYWAY.
I'M SORRY.
FOR WHAT IT'S WORTH, I COULDN'T THINK OF A GROUP OF WOMEN I'D BE *PROUDER* TO DIE WITH.

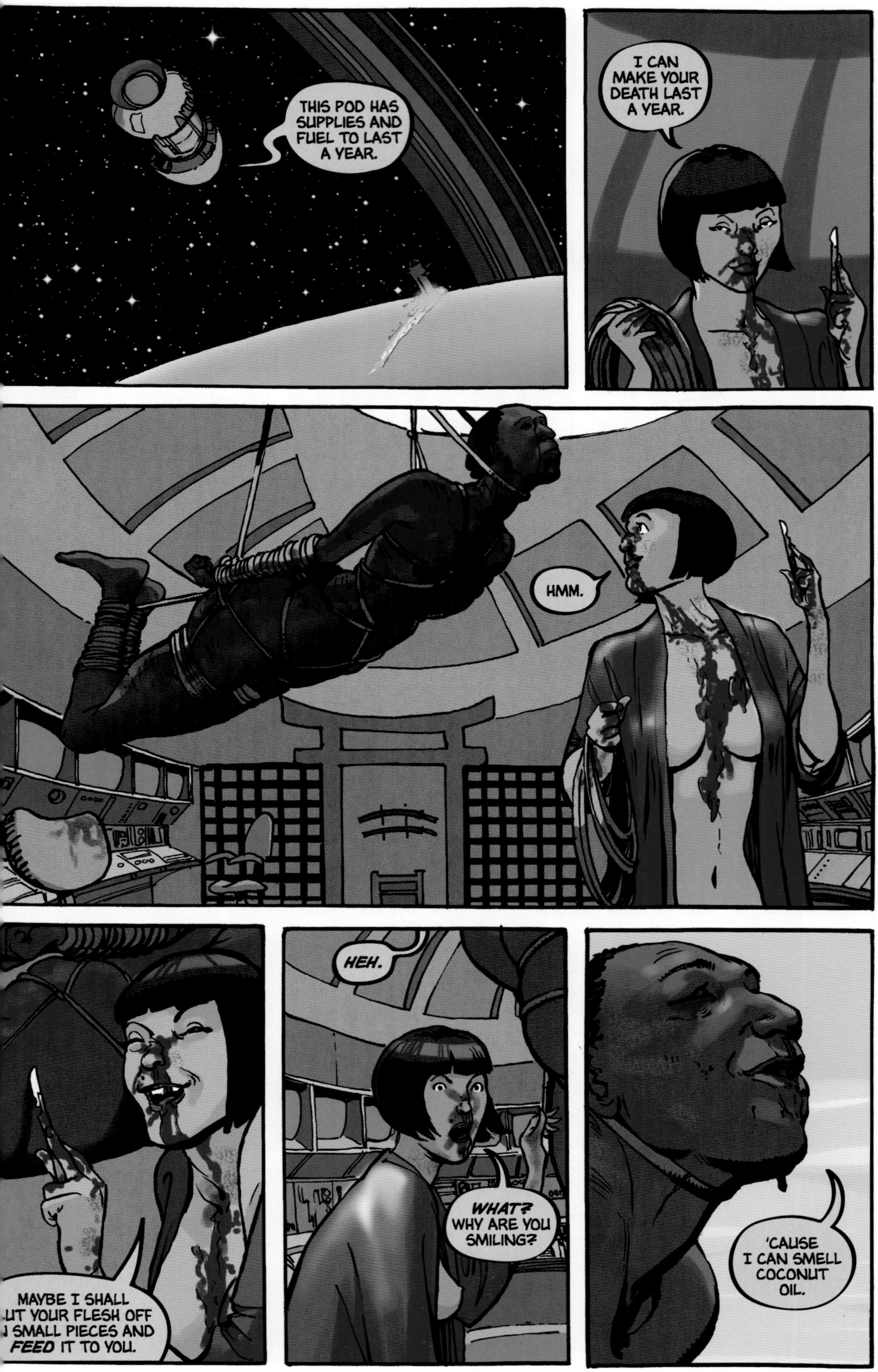
THIS POD HAS SUPPLIES AND FUEL TO LAST A YEAR.
I CAN MAKE YOUR DEATH LAST A YEAR.
HMM.
MAYBE I SHALL CUT YOUR FLESH OFF IN SMALL PIECES AND *FEED* IT TO YOU.
HEH.
WHAT? WHY ARE YOU SMILING?
'CAUSE I CAN SMELL COCONUT OIL.

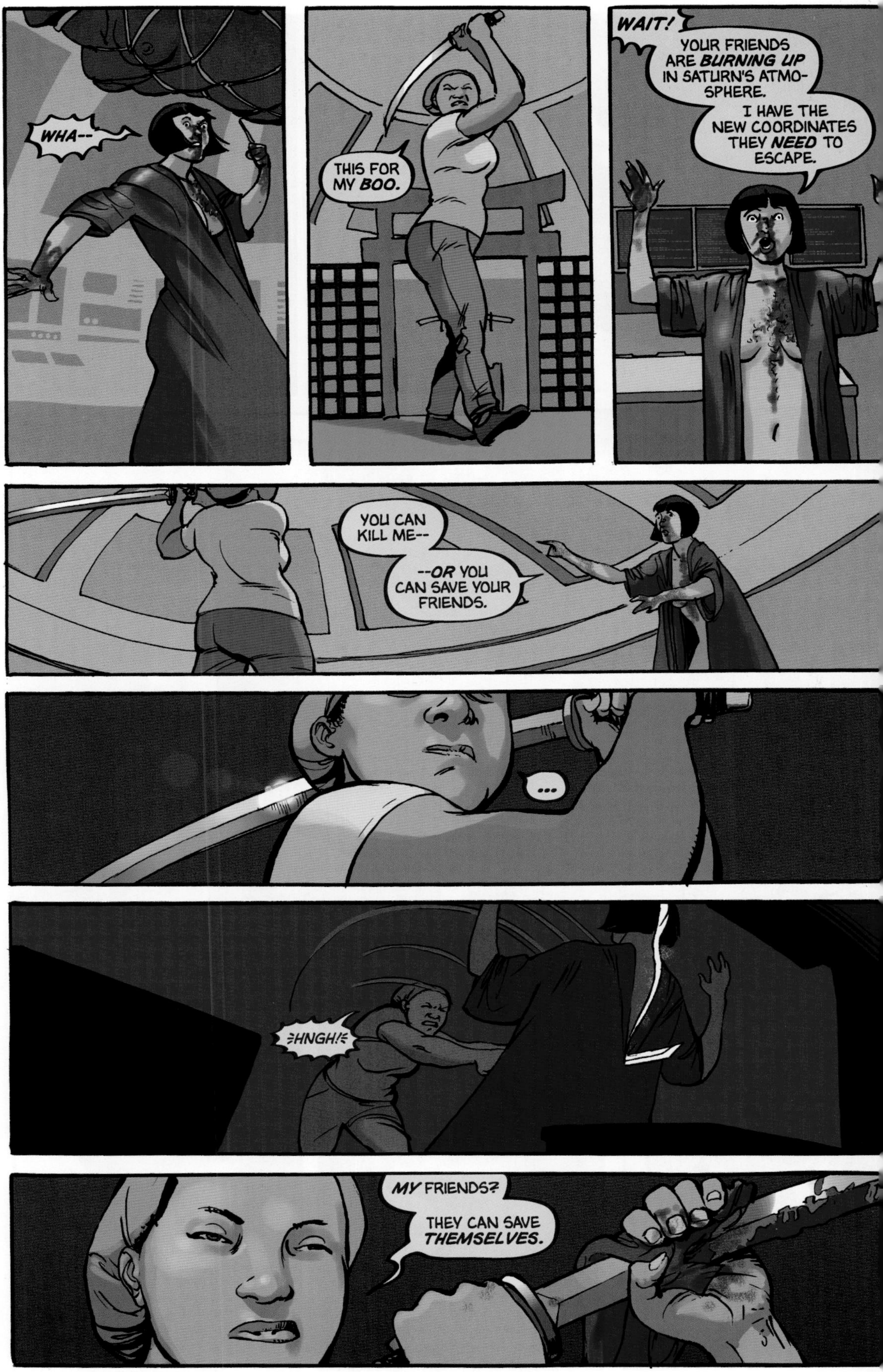
WHA--
THIS FOR MY BOO.
WAIT!
YOUR FRIENDS ARE BURNING UP IN SATURN'S ATMOSPHERE.
I HAVE THE NEW COORDINATES THEY NEED TO ESCAPE.
YOU CAN KILL ME--
--OR YOU CAN SAVE YOUR FRIENDS.
...
HNGH!
MY FRIENDS?
THEY CAN SAVE THEMSELVES.

BET IT'S "MU545HI." TRY THAT.

THERE'S GOTTA BE A *PANIC BUTTON* AROUND HERE SOMEWHERE.

UGH. THAT'S NO GOOD EITHER.

FUCK. I DUNNO... UH...

WE TRIED "SAMURAI," YEAH?

WHAT'S THIS?

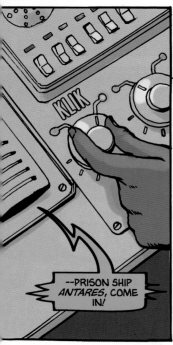

KLIK

--PRISON SHIP *ANTARES*, COME IN!

PRISON SHIP *ANTARES*--

!

OVER.

WHY HAS YOUR FLIGHT PLAN CHANGED AND THE ESCAPE POD BEEN EJECTED?

'CAUSE WE HAD US LITTLE *RIOT PARTY* AFTER YOUR CRAZY WARDEN STARTED KILLIN' US FOR KICKS!

SO NOW SHE'S TRYNA DESTROY THE EVIDENCE.

AND I DON' MEAN NO DISRESPECT, BUT...

YOU GOTTA *BE COOL* WITH US PRISONERS RUNNIN' THINGS NOW.

YOU PROBABLY TOO *WHITE* TO GO TO JAIL IF WE ALL DIE--

BUT I THINK YOU CAN KISS THAT CAREER *GOODBYE*.

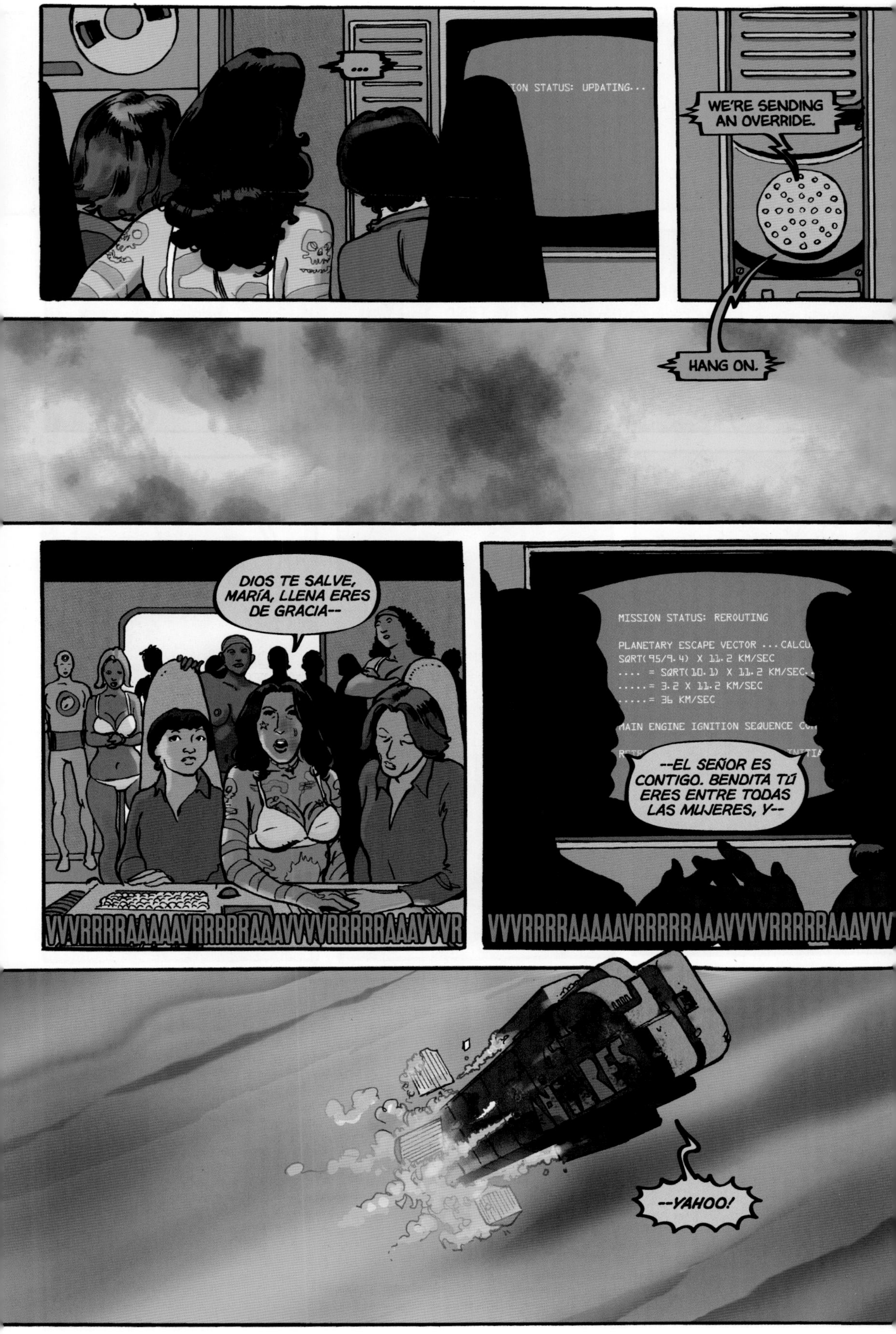
...
ION STATUS: UPDATING...
WE'RE SENDING AN OVERRIDE.
HANG ON.
DIOS TE SALVE, MARÍA, LLENA ERES DE GRACIA--
VVVRRRRAAAAAVRRRRRAAAVVVVRRRRRAAAVVVR
MISSION STATUS: REROUTING
PLANETARY ESCAPE VECTOR ... CALCU
SQRT(95/9.4) X 11.2 KM/SEC
.... = SQRT(10.1) X 11.2 KM/SEC
.....= 3.2 X 11.2 KM/SEC
.....= 36 KM/SEC
MAIN ENGINE IGNITION SEQUENCE CO
--EL SEÑOR ES CONTIGO. BENDITA TÚ ERES ENTRE TODAS LAS MUJERES, Y--
VVVRRRRAAAAAVRRRRRAAAVVVVRRRRRAAAVVV
--YAHOO!

BEHIND THE SCENES

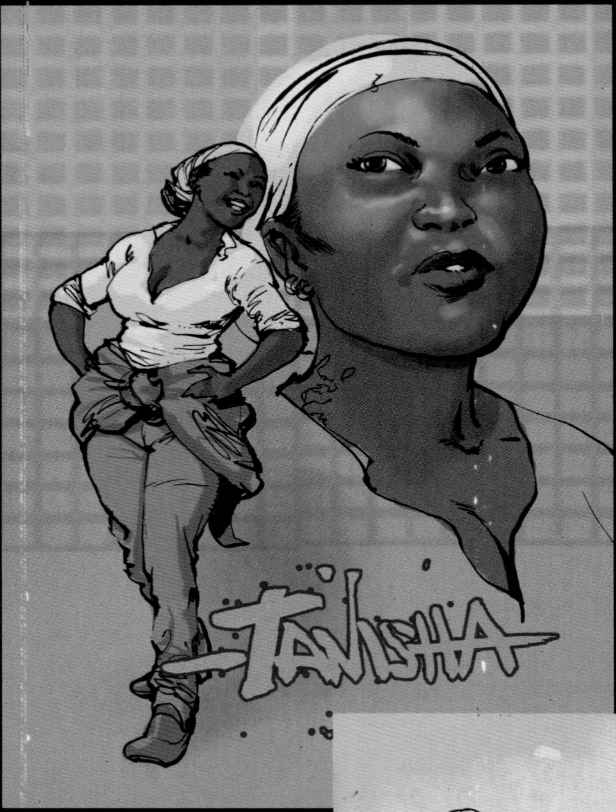
TANISHA

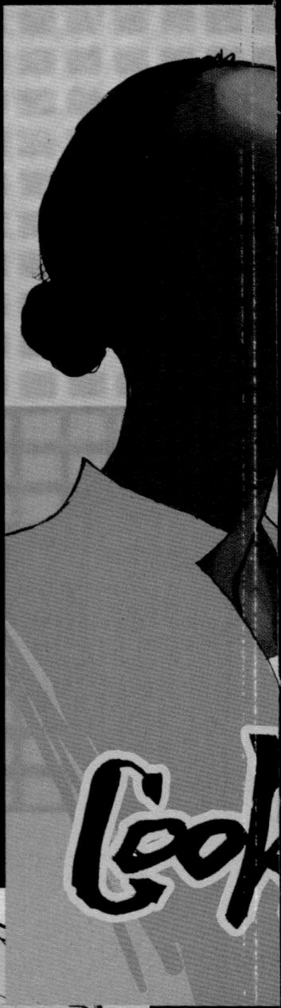

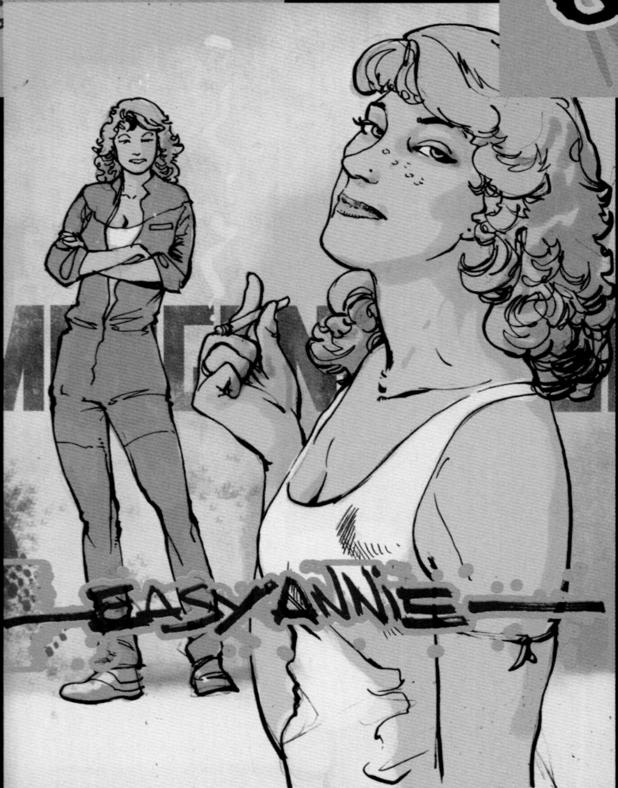
EASY ANNIE

CELL BLOCK E CHARACTER DESIGNS

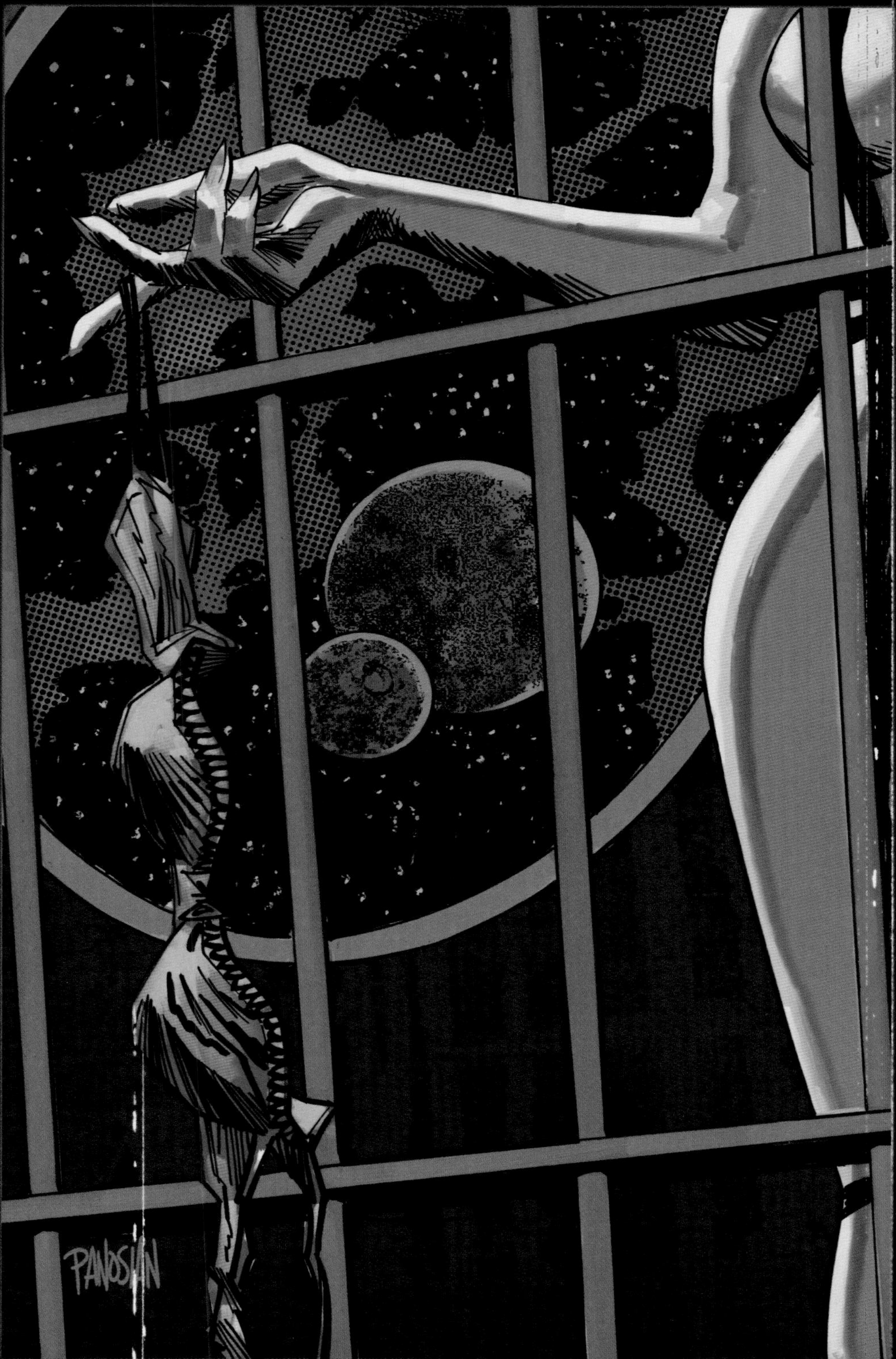
PANOSIAN

DAN PANOSIAN

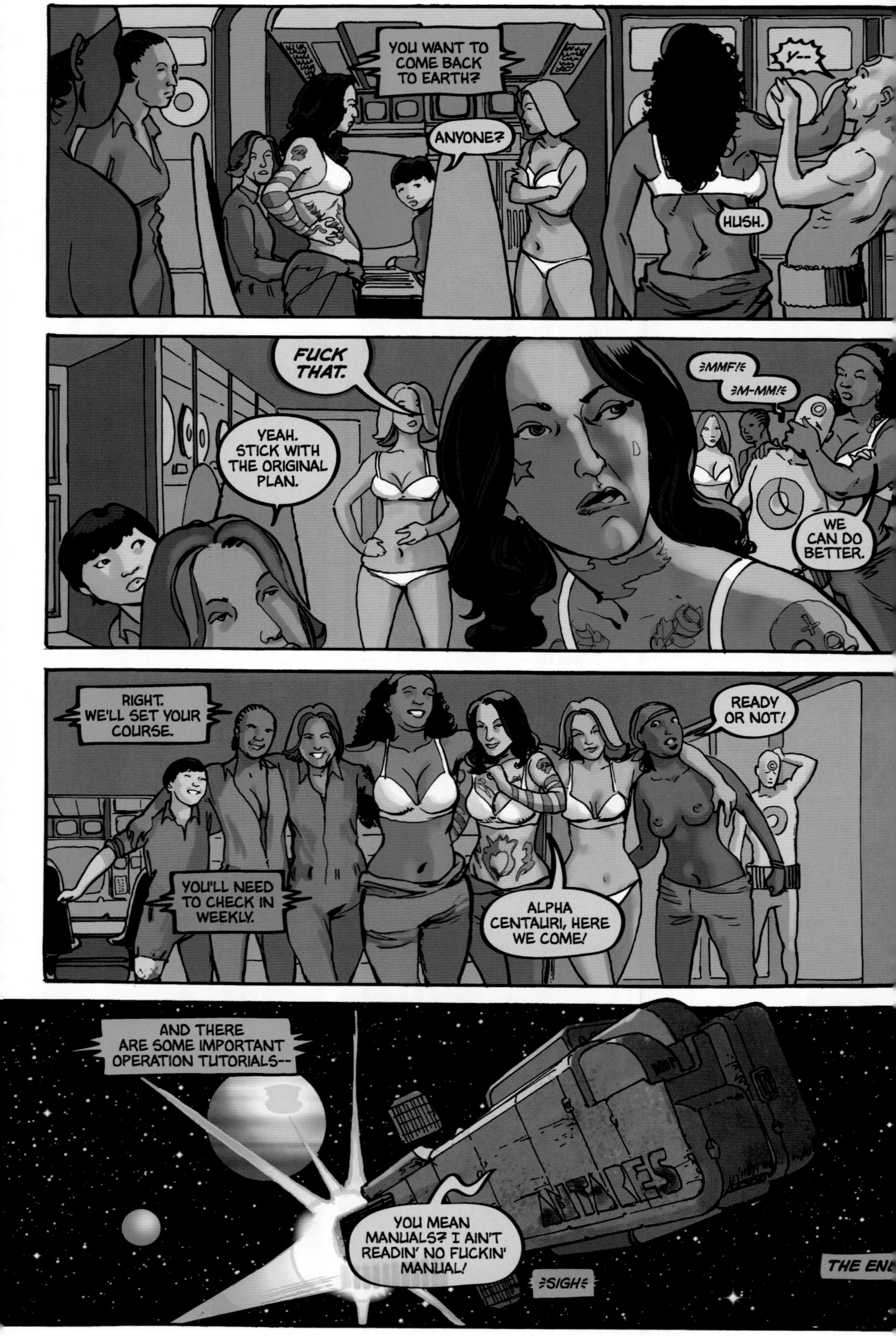
YOU WANT TO COME BACK TO EARTH?
ANYONE?
Y--
HUSH.
FUCK THAT.
YEAH. STICK WITH THE ORIGINAL PLAN.
MMF!
M-MM!
WE CAN DO BETTER.
RIGHT. WE'LL SET YOUR COURSE.
READY OR NOT!
YOU'LL NEED TO CHECK IN WEEKLY.
ALPHA CENTAURI, HERE WE COME!
AND THERE ARE SOME IMPORTANT OPERATION TUTORIALS--
ANTARES
YOU MEAN MANUALS? I AIN'T READIN' NO FUCKIN' MANUAL!
SIGH
THE END

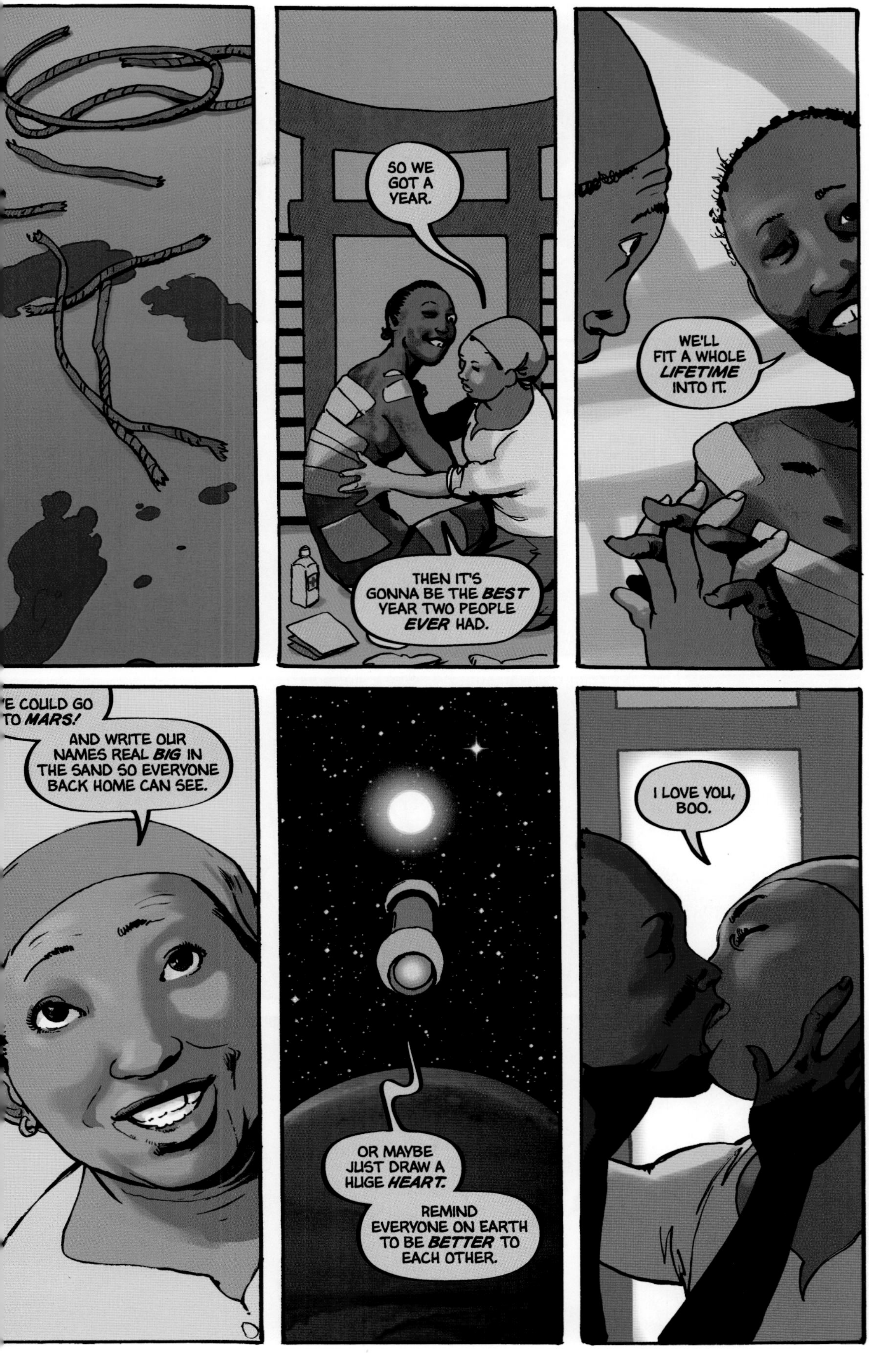
SO WE GOT A YEAR.
THEN IT'S GONNA BE THE *BEST* YEAR TWO PEOPLE *EVER* HAD.
WE'LL FIT A WHOLE *LIFETIME* INTO IT.
'E COULD GO TO *MARS!*
AND WRITE OUR NAMES REAL *BIG* IN THE SAND SO EVERYONE BACK HOME CAN SEE.
OR MAYBE JUST DRAW A HUGE *HEART.*
REMIND EVERYONE ON EARTH TO BE *BETTER* TO EACH OTHER.
I LOVE YOU, BOO.

END OF

FLIP BOOK FOR

NEXT FEATURE

REEL

ALSO BY ALEX DE CAMPI

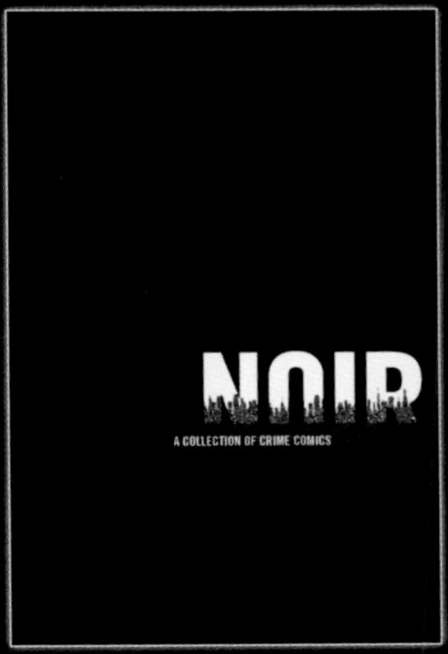
NOIR
A COLLECTION OF CRIME COMICS

NOIR: A COLLECTION OF CRIME COMICS
Brian Azzarello, Ed Brubaker, Sean Phillips, Jeff Lemire, Alex de Campi, David Lapham, Paul Grist, and others
978-1-59582-358-8
$12.99

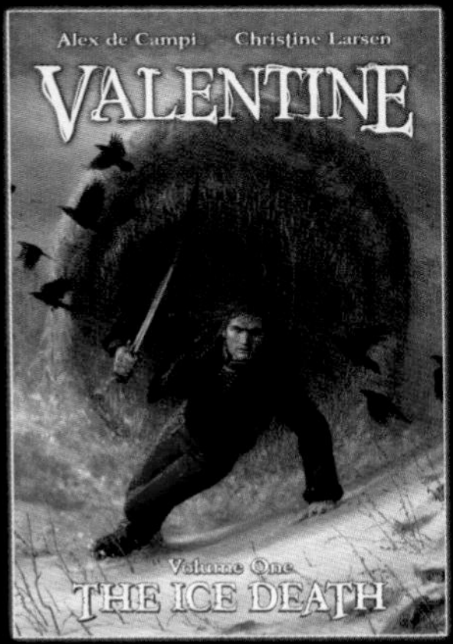
Alex de Campi
Christine Larsen
VALENTINE
Volume One
THE ICE DEATH

VALENTINE VOLUME 1: THE ICE DEATH
Alex de Campi and Christine Larsen
978-1-60706-624-8
$24.99

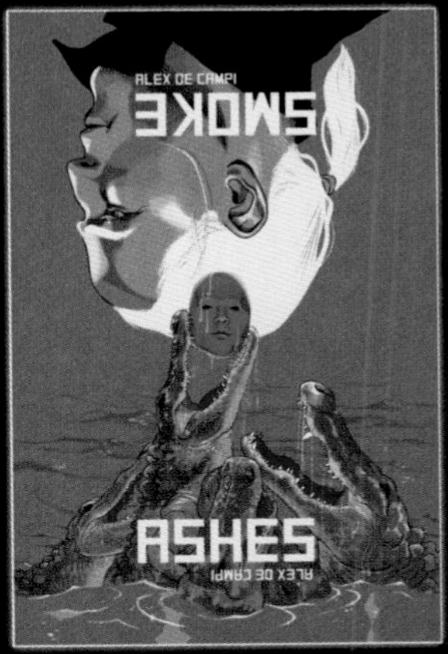
ALEX DE CAMPI
SMOKE
ASHES
ALEX DE CAMPI

SMOKE/ASHES
Alex de Campi, Igor Kordey, Carla Speed McNeil, Bill Sienkiewicz, Richard Pace, Colleen Doran, and Dan McDaid
978-1-61655-169-8
$29.99

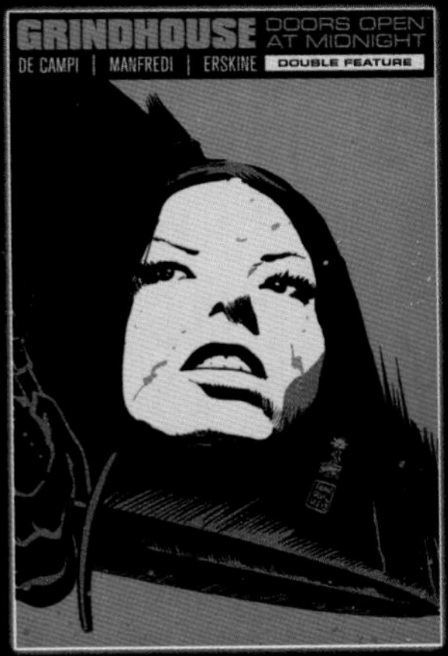
GRINDHOUSE
DOORS OPEN AT MIDNIGHT
DE CAMPI | MANFREDI | ERSKINE
DOUBLE FEATURE

GRINDHOUSE: DOORS OPEN AT MIDNIGHT VOLUME 2— BRIDE OF BLOOD & FLESH FEAST OF THE DEVIL DOLL
Alex de Campi, Federica Manfredi, and Gary Erskine
978-1-61655-378-4
$17.99
Coming November 2014

COMING SOON

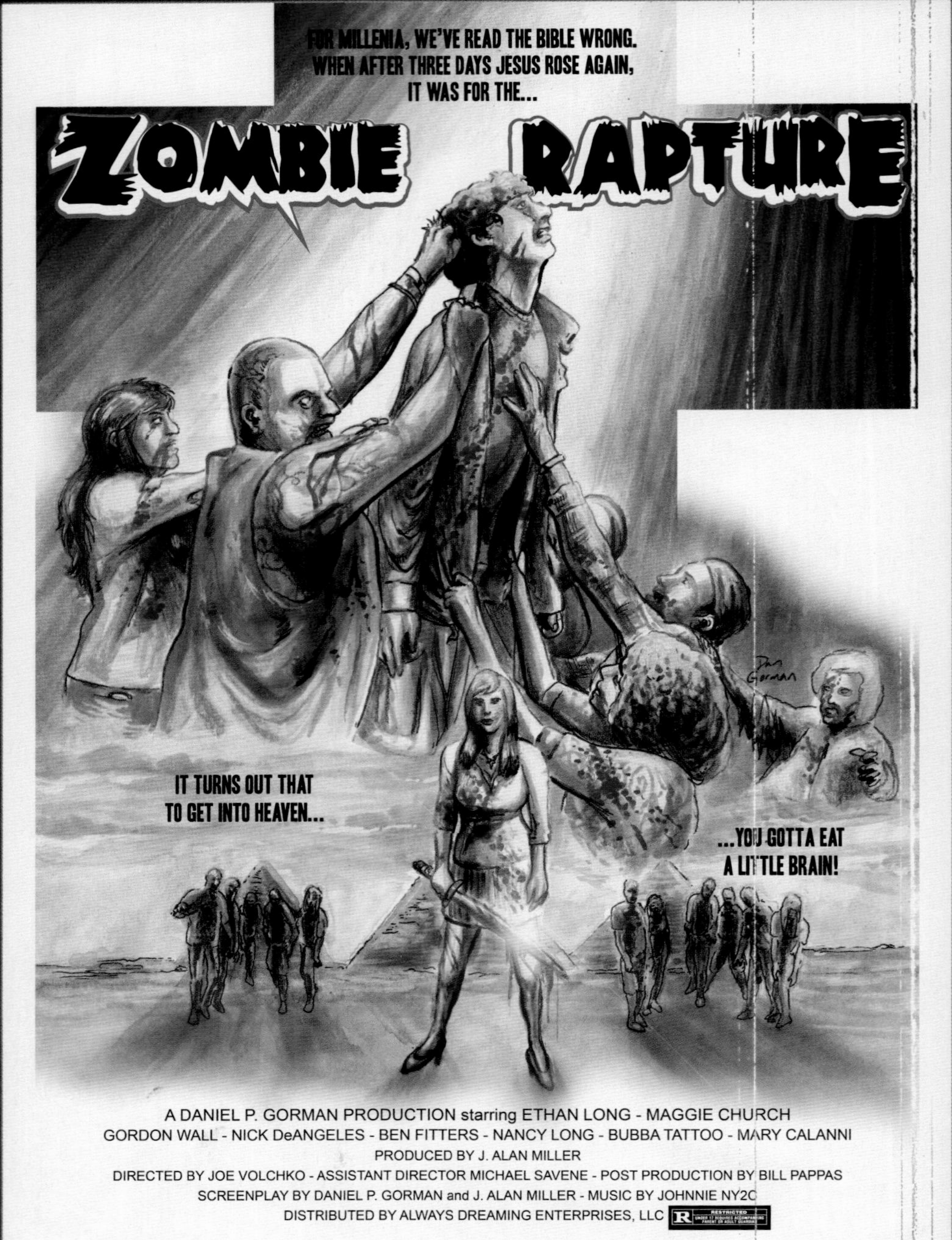
FOR MILLENIA, WE'VE READ THE BIBLE WRONG.
WHEN AFTER THREE DAYS JESUS ROSE AGAIN,
IT WAS FOR THE...
ZOMBIE RAPTURE
IT TURNS OUT THAT
TO GET INTO HEAVEN...
...YOU GOTTA EAT
A LITTLE BRAIN!
A DANIEL P. GORMAN PRODUCTION starring ETHAN LONG - MAGGIE CHURCH
GORDON WALL - NICK DeANGELES - BEN FITTERS - NANCY LONG - BUBBA TATTOO - MARY CALANNI
PRODUCED BY J. ALAN MILLER
DIRECTED BY JOE VOLCHKO - ASSISTANT DIRECTOR MICHAEL SAVENE - POST PRODUCTION BY BILL PAPPAS
SCREENPLAY BY DANIEL P. GORMAN and J. ALAN MILLER - MUSIC BY JOHNNIE NY2C
DISTRIBUTED BY ALWAYS DREAMING ENTERPRISES, LLC

DAN GORMAN

COMING SOON

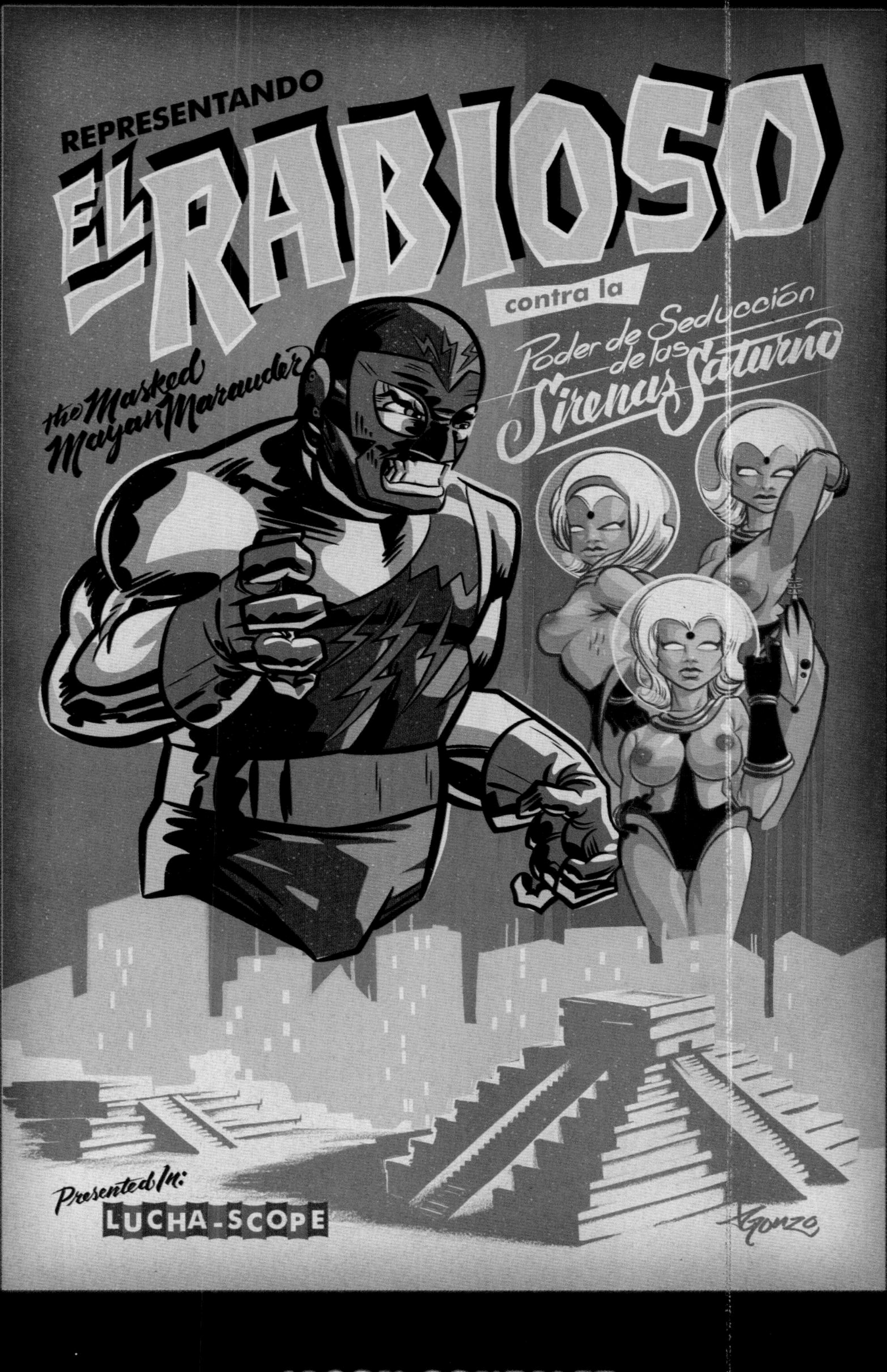
REPRESENTANDO
EL RABIOSO
contra la
Poder de Seducción de las Sirenas Saturno
the Masked Mayan Marauder
Presented In:
LUCHA-SCOPE
Gonzo

JASON GONZALEZ

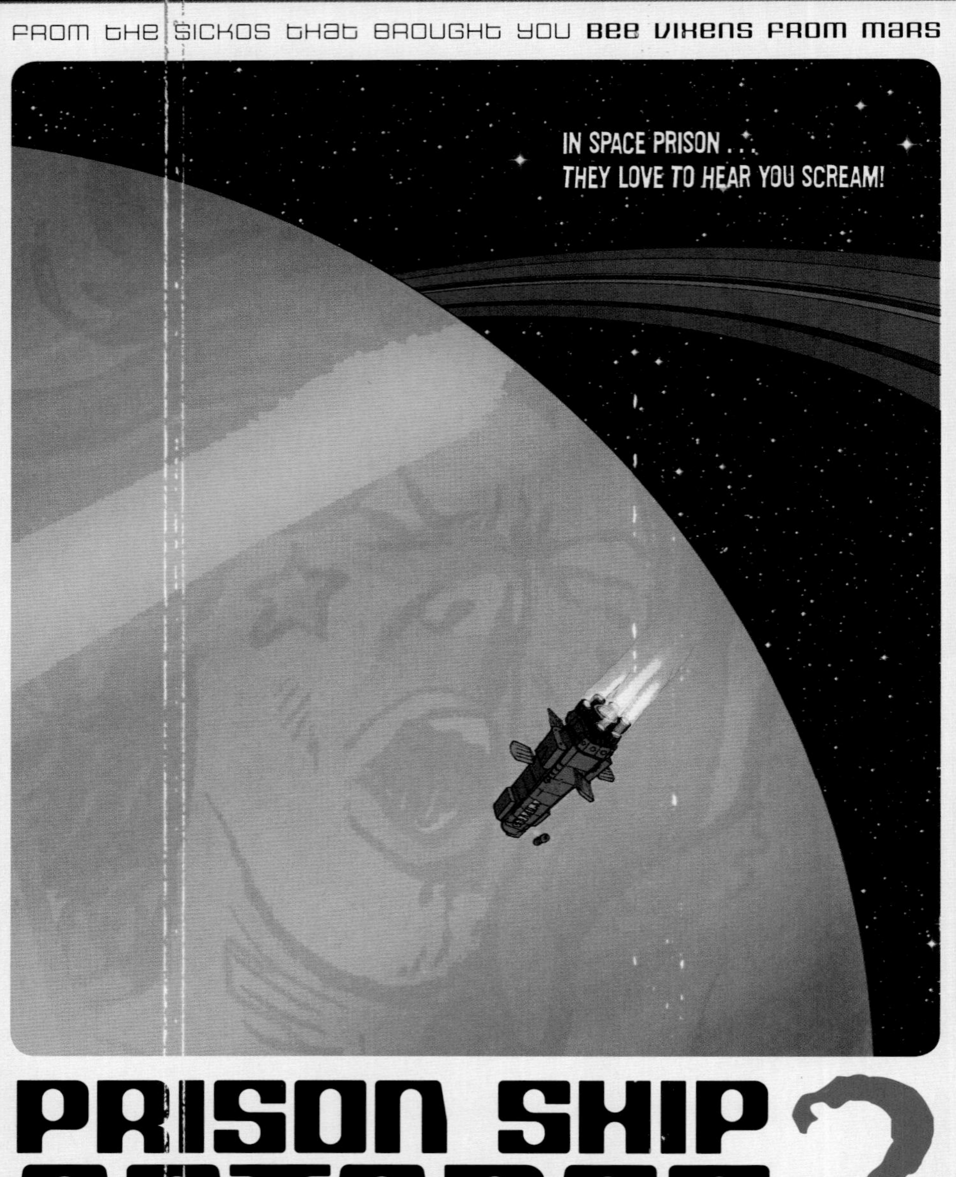
FROM THE SICKOS THAT BROUGHT YOU BEE VIXENS FROM MARS
IN SPACE PRISON . . .
THEY LOVE TO HEAR YOU SCREAM!
PRISON SHIP ANTARES 2
DARK HORSE COMICS PRESENTS AN ALEX DE CAMPI PRODUCTION "PRISON SHIP ANTARES 2"
THE OX EASY ANNIE SPANISH FLY COOKIE TANESHA SOLITARY THE "ABC" GUARDS AND THE MAD WARDEN
FILM EDITOR BRENDAN WRIGHT A.C.E. ASSISTANT EDITOR IAN TUCKER PRODUCTION DESIGNER JIMMY PRESLER CGI ARTIST RYAN JORGENSEN
PRODUCED BY MIKE RICHARDSON SCREENPLAY BY ALEX DE CAMPI DIRECTED BY CHRIS PETERSON
01•01•14

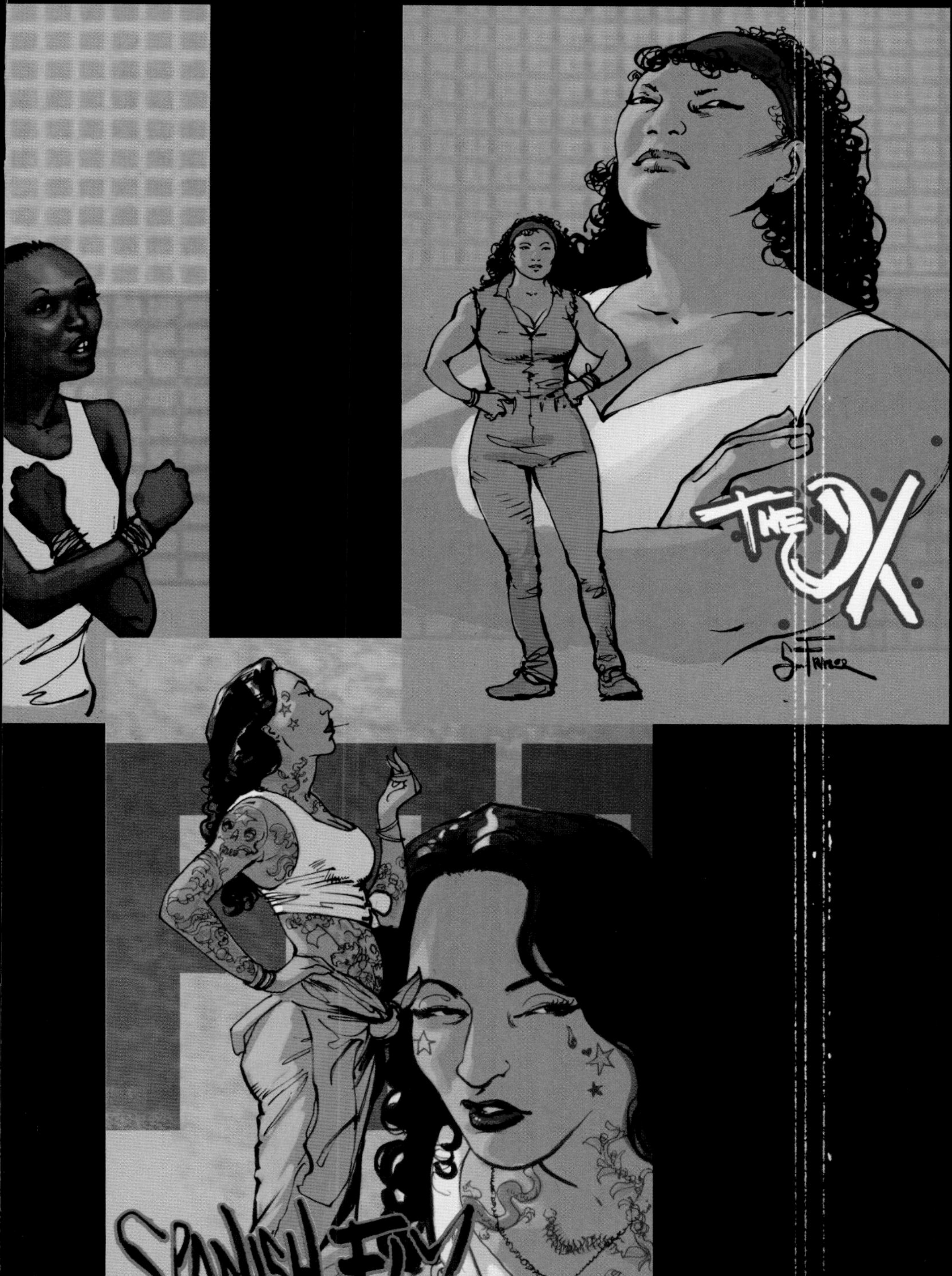
THE OX
SPANISH FLY

BY SIMON FRASER

END OF

FLIP BOOK FOR

REEL

NEXT FEATURE

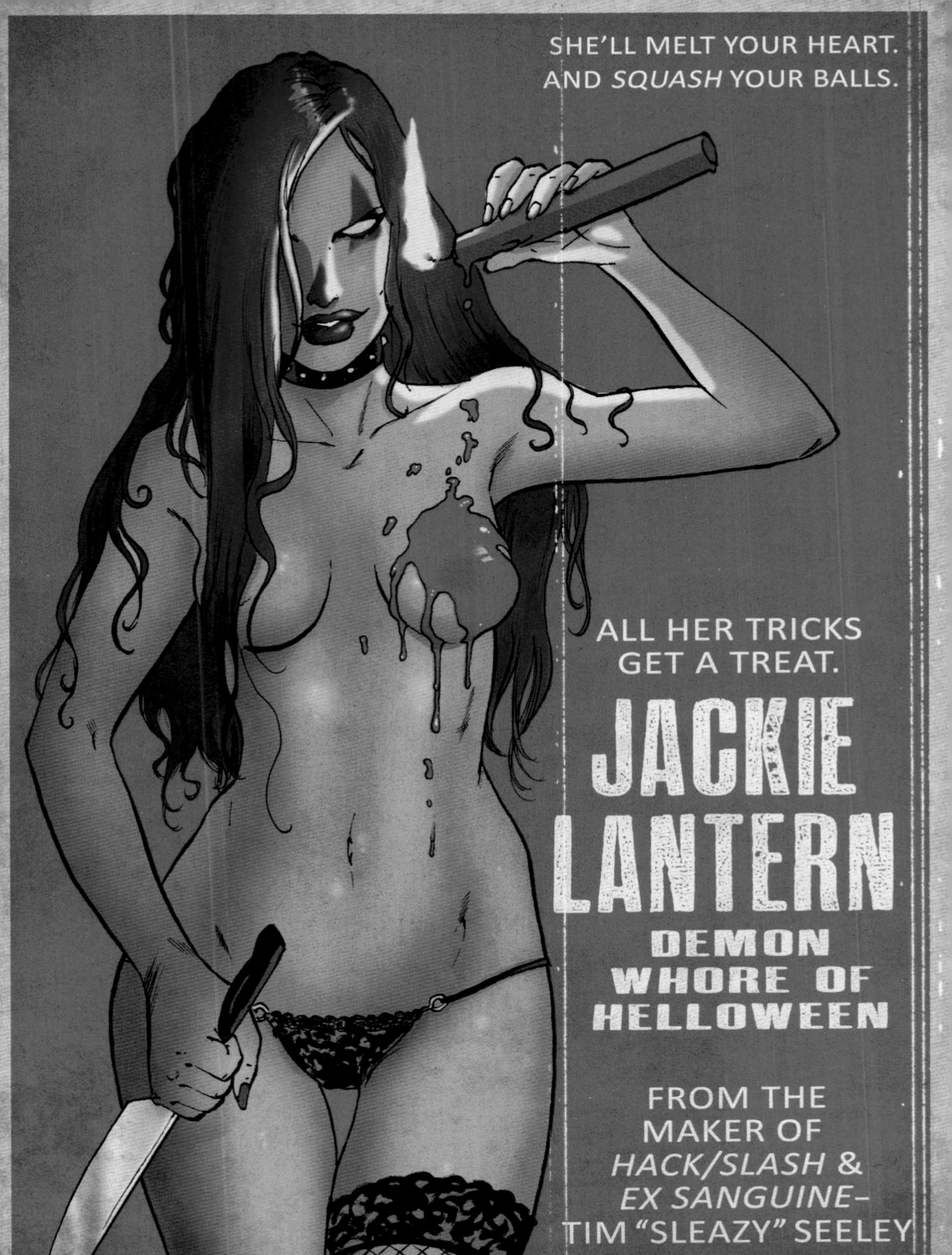
SHE'LL MELT YOUR HEART.
AND *SQUASH* YOUR BALLS.
ALL HER TRICKS
GET A TREAT.
JACKIE
LANTERN
DEMON
WHORE OF
HELLOWEEN
FROM THE
MAKER OF
HACK/SLASH &
EX SANGUINE–
TIM "SLEAZY" SEELEY

ALTERNATE TAKE

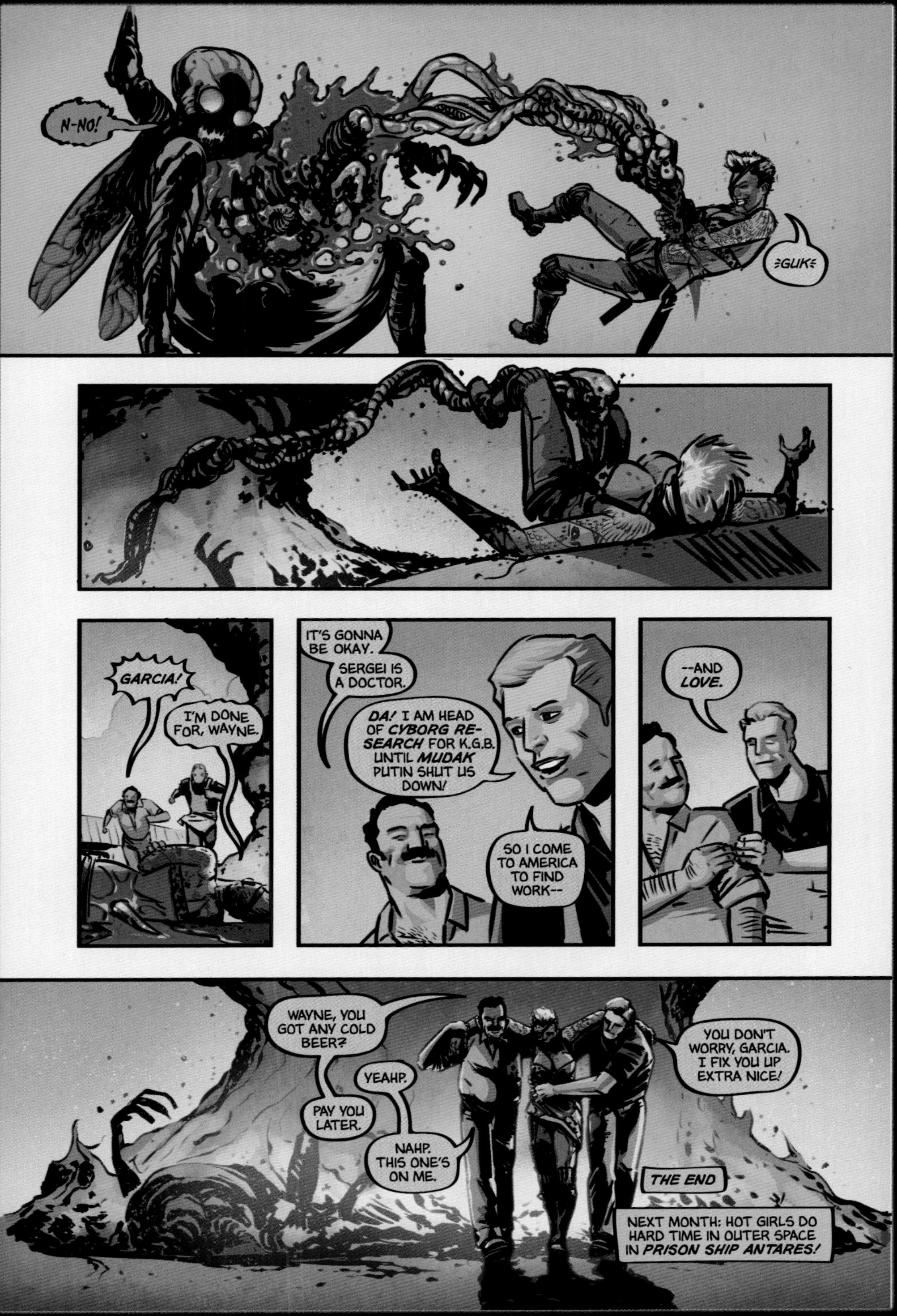
N-NO!
GUK
WHAM
GARCIA!
I'M DONE FOR, WAYNE.
IT'S GONNA BE OKAY.
SERGEI IS A DOCTOR.
DA! I AM HEAD OF CYBORG RESEARCH FOR K.G.B. UNTIL MUDAK PUTIN SHUT US DOWN!
SO I COME TO AMERICA TO FIND WORK--
--AND LOVE.
WAYNE, YOU GOT ANY COLD BEER?
YEAHP.
PAY YOU LATER.
NAHP. THIS ONE'S ON ME.
YOU DON'T WORRY, GARCIA. I FIX YOU UP EXTRA NICE!
THE END
NEXT MONTH: HOT GIRLS DO HARD TIME IN OUTER SPACE IN PRISON SHIP ANTARES!

This director's cut of *Bee Vixens from Mars* features an expanded final sequence, including a new double-page spread and a redrawn final page. This page is the original version of issue #2, page 24.

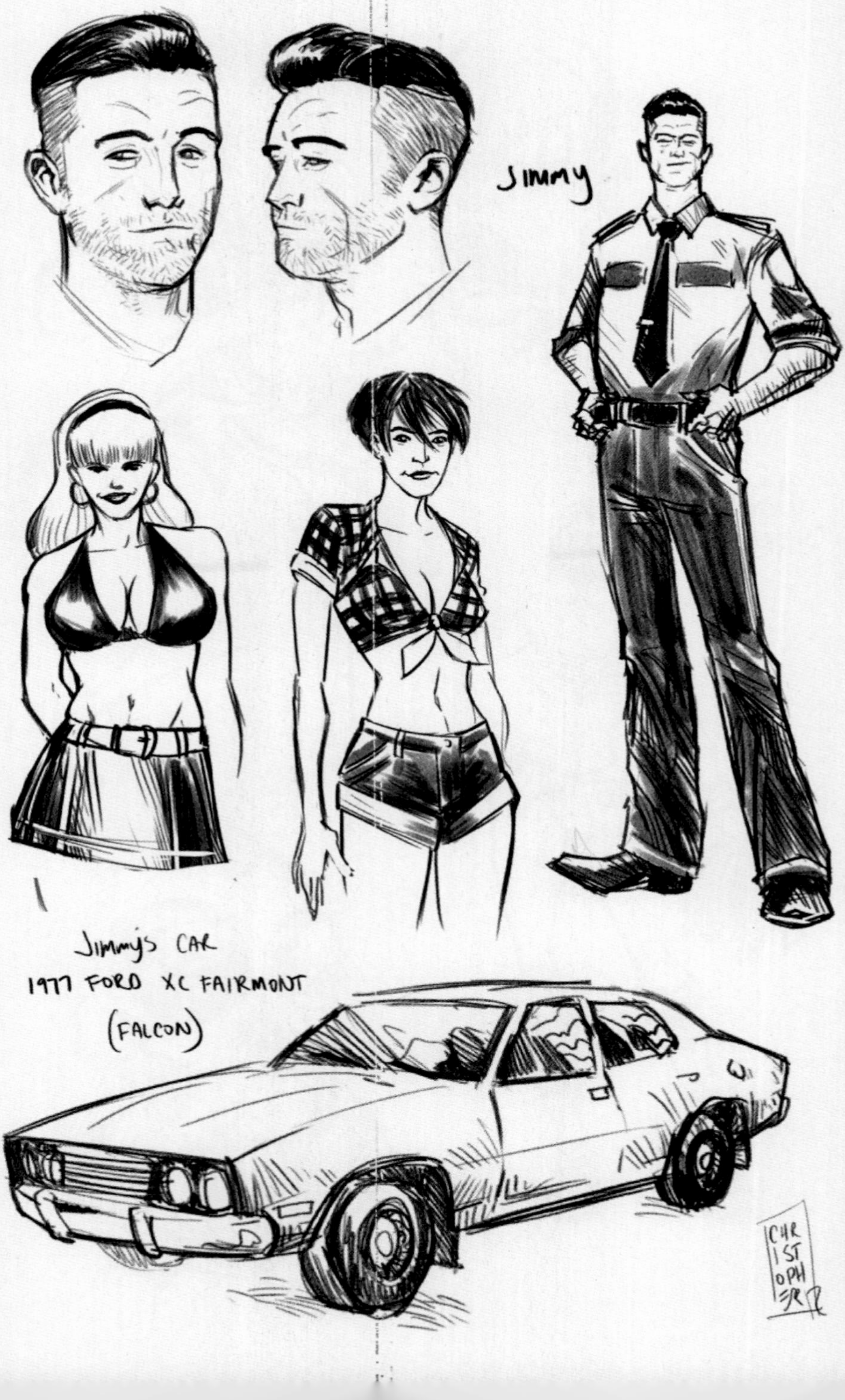
JIMMY
JIMMY'S CAR
1977 FORD XC FAIRMONT
(FALCON)
CHRISTOPHER

BEHIND THE SCENES

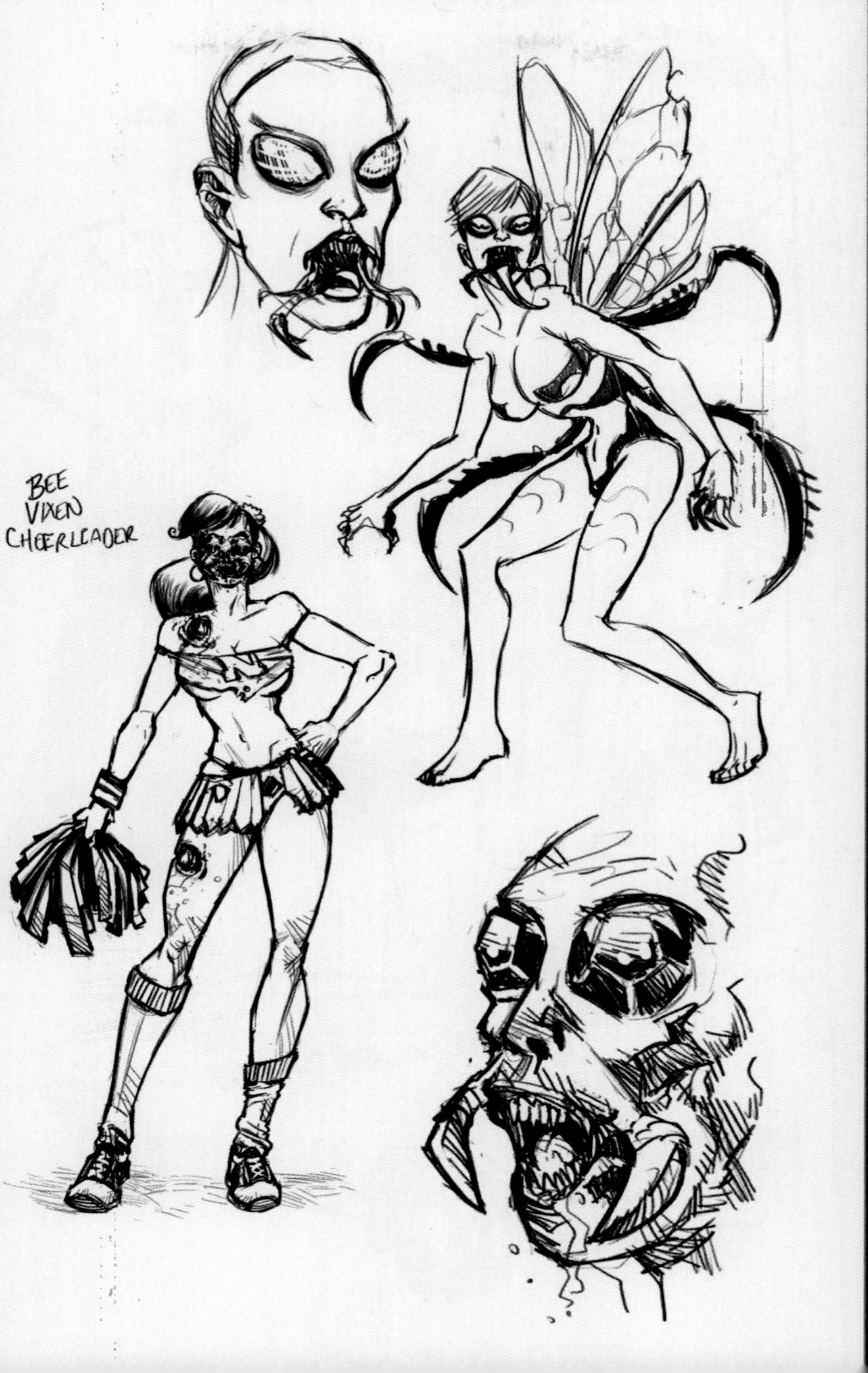

BEE
VIXEN
CHEERLEADER

BEHIND THE SCENES

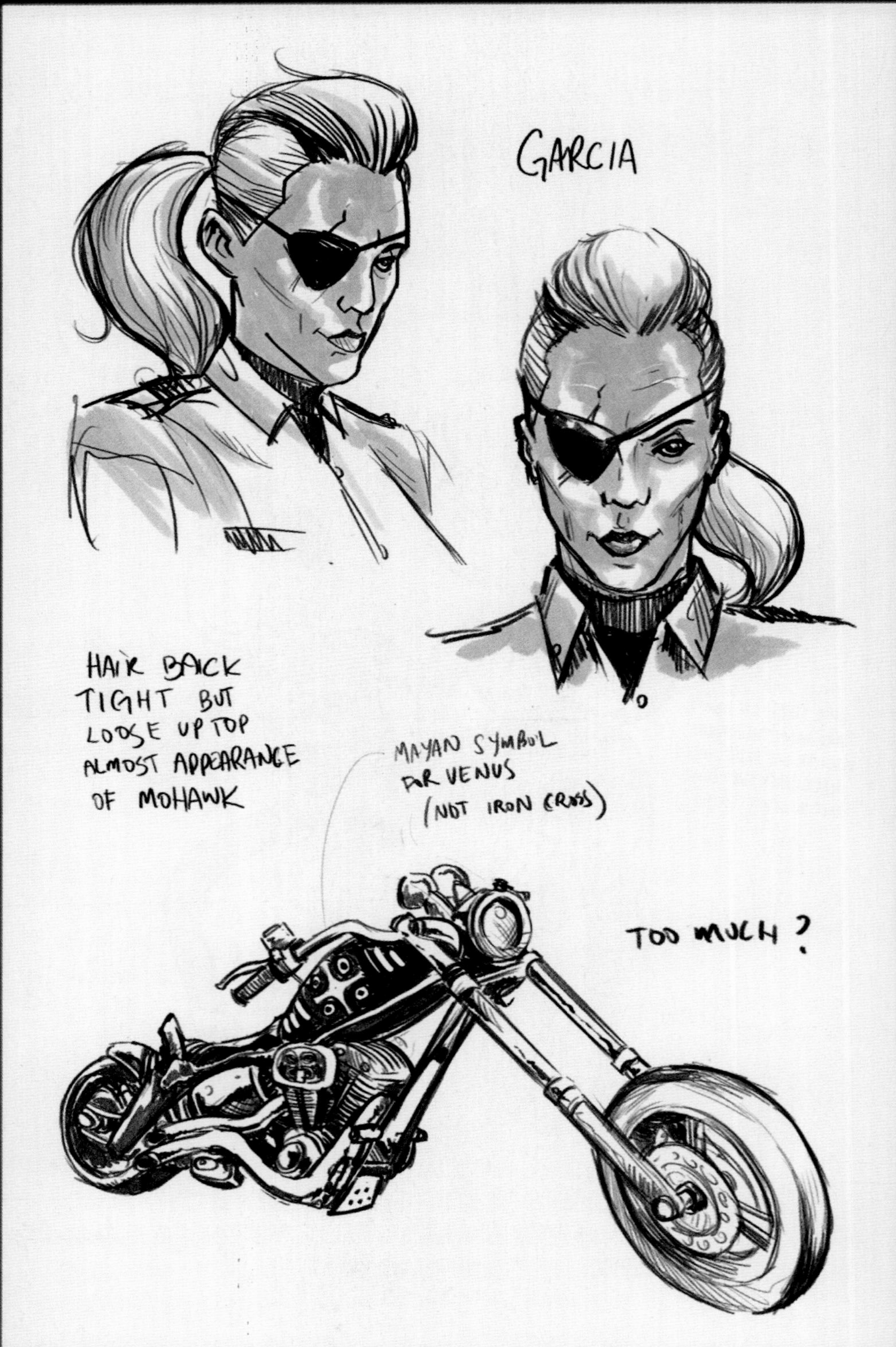
GARCIA
HAIR BACK TIGHT BUT LOOSE UP TOP ALMOST APPEARANCE OF MOHAWK
MAYAN SYMBOL FOR VENUS (NOT IRON CROSS)
TOO MUCH?

CHARACTER DESIGNS FROM MARS

FROM THE CREATOR OF **KAT & MOUSE** AND **AGENT BOO**

GRINDHOUSE TIME

WHEN GARCIA THE HUMAN
AND JIMMY THE SHERIFF
DISCOVER THE RED PLANET'S
MAGIC HONEY, THEY COME
FACE TO STINGER WITH . . .

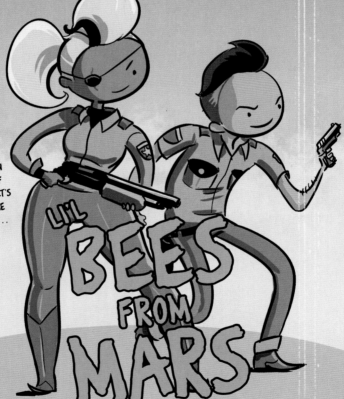

LI'L BEES FROM MARS

DARK HORSE COMICS PRESENTS AN ALEX DE CAMPI PRODUCTION "LI'L BEES FROM MARS"

GARCIA THE HUMAN   JIMMY THE SHERIFF   PAULINE THE BEE QUEEN   BUMBLEBEES   AND CONVENIENCE KINGS

FILM EDITOR BRENDAN WRIGHT A.C.E.   ASSISTANT EDITOR IAN TUCKER   PRODUCTION DESIGNER JIMMY PRESLER   CGI ARTIST RYAN JORGENSEN   DIRECTOR OF PHOTOGRAPHY NOLAN WOODARD A.S.C.

PRODUCED BY MIKE RICHARDSON   SCREENPLAY BY ALEX DE CAMPI   DIRECTED BY CHRIS PETERSON

11·06·13

CHRIS PETERSON

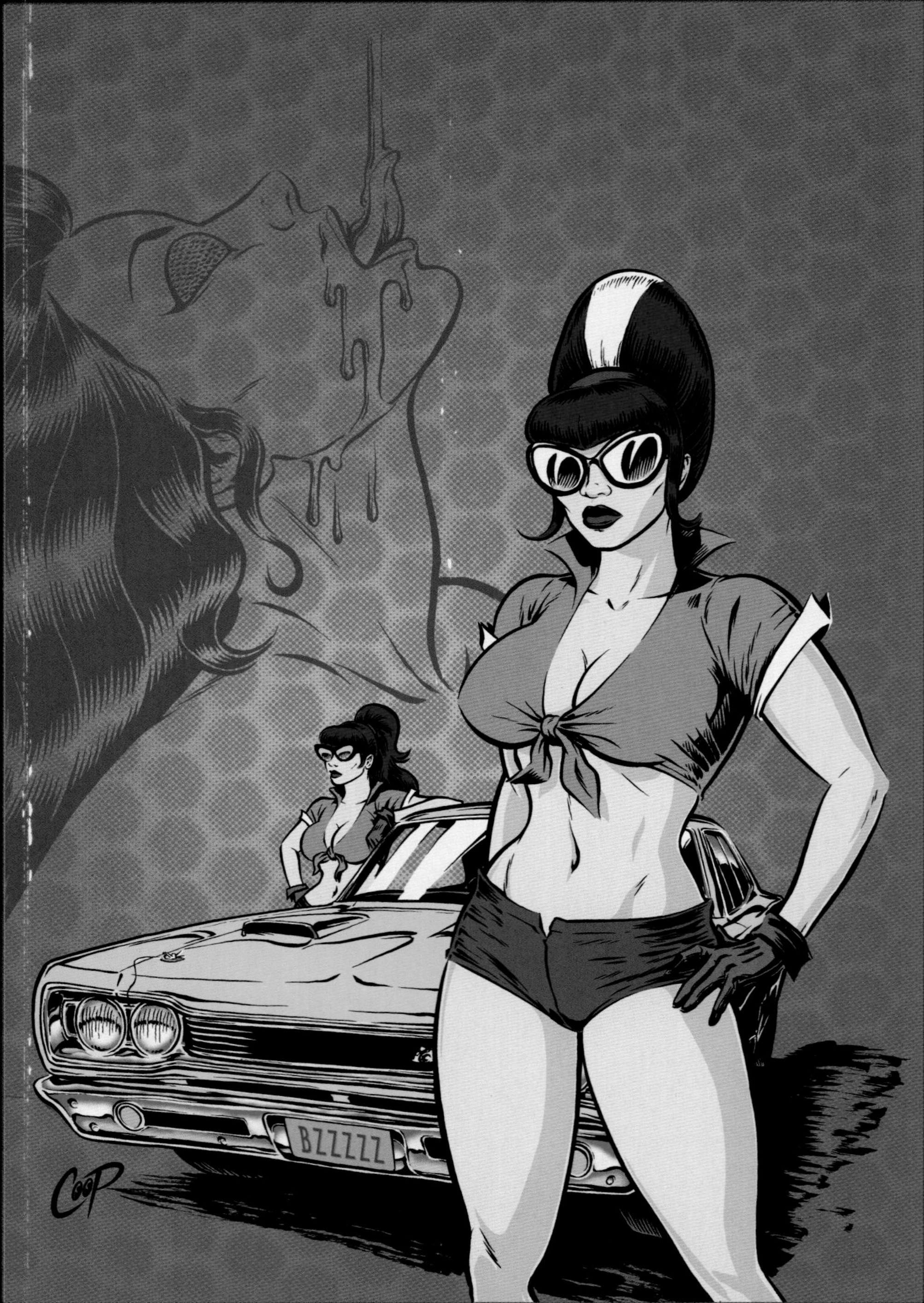
BZZZZZ
COOP

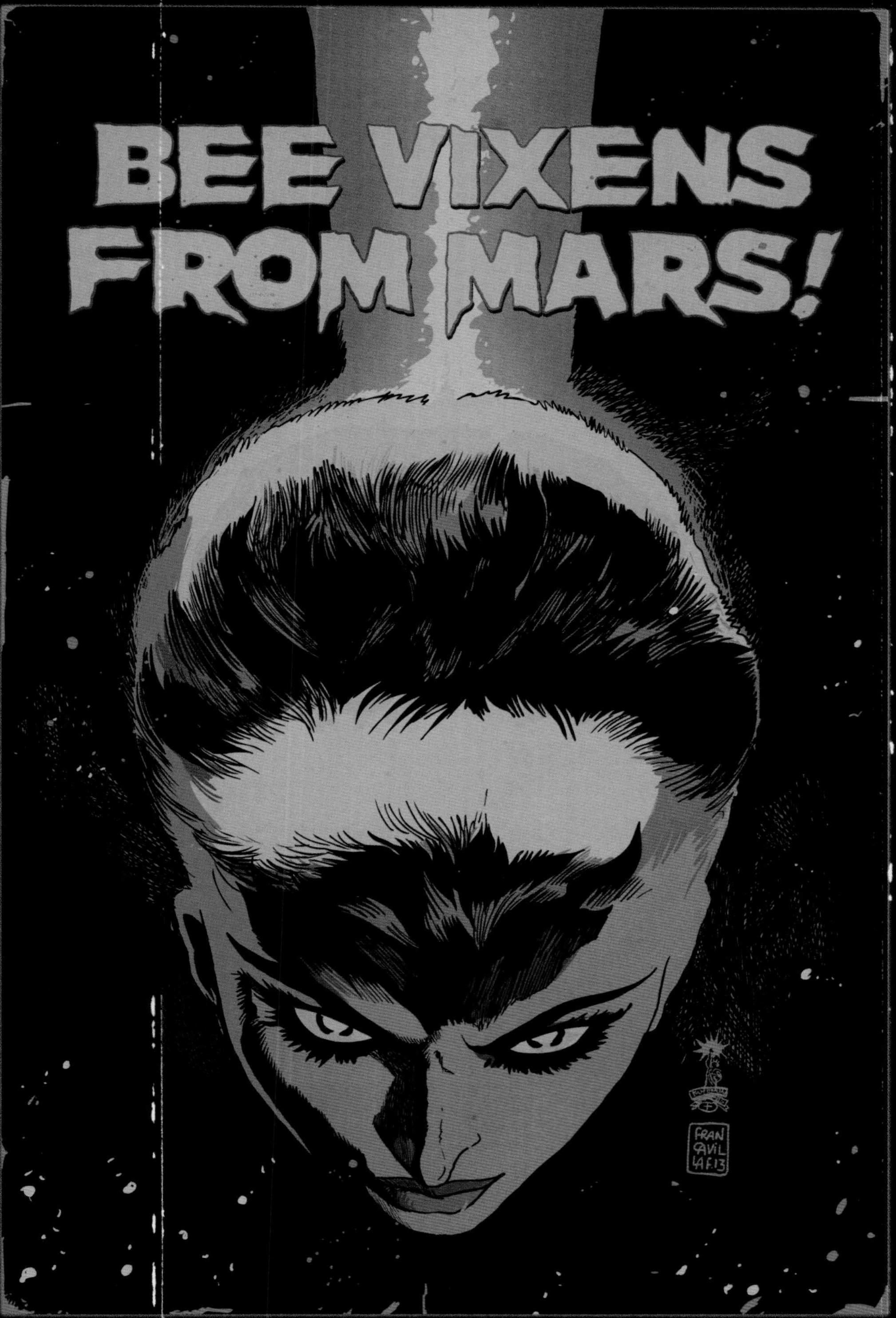
BEE VIXENS
FROM MARS!

FRANCESCO FRANCAVILLA

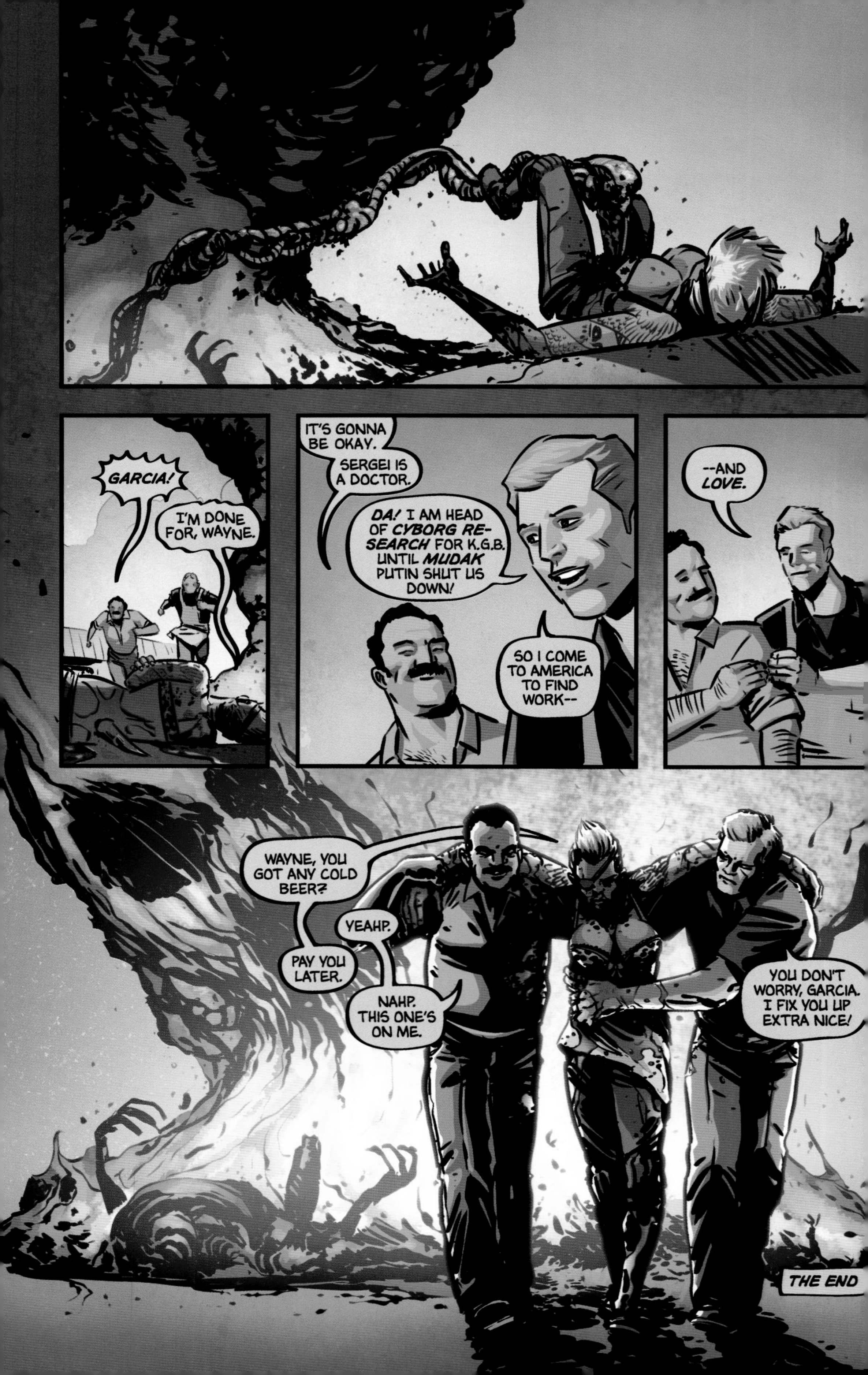
GARCIA!
I'M DONE FOR, WAYNE.
IT'S GONNA BE OKAY.
SERGEI IS A DOCTOR.
DA! I AM HEAD OF CYBORG RESEARCH FOR K.G.B. UNTIL MUDAK PUTIN SHUT US DOWN!
SO I COME TO AMERICA TO FIND WORK--
--AND LOVE.
WAYNE, YOU GOT ANY COLD BEER?
YEAHP.
PAY YOU LATER.
NAHP. THIS ONE'S ON ME.
YOU DON'T WORRY, GARCIA. I FIX YOU UP EXTRA NICE!
THE END

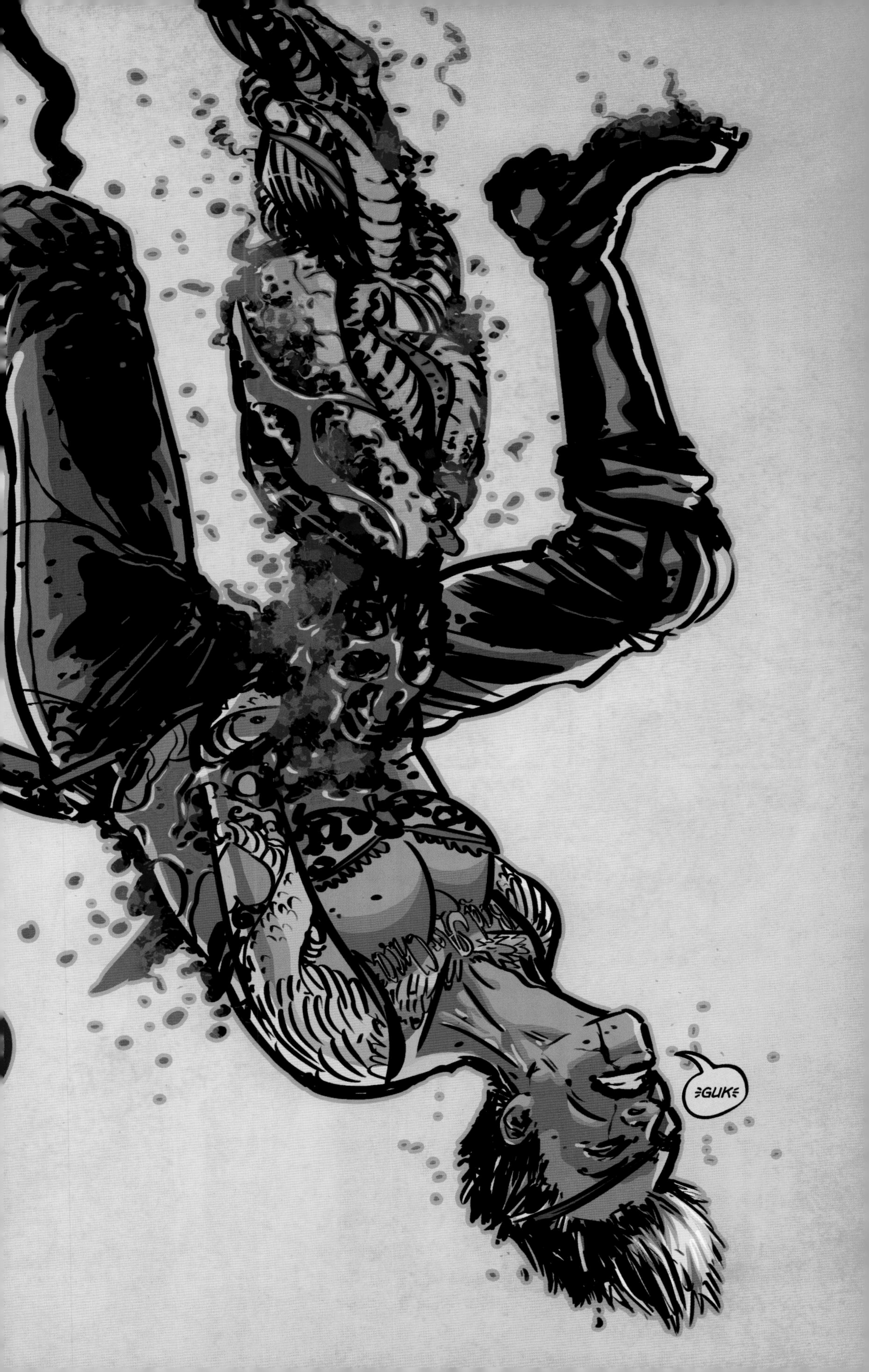
GUK